Teaching, Including, and Supporting College Students with Intellectual Disabilities

Teaching, Including, and Supporting College Students with Intellectual Disabilities provides higher education professionals and proponents of post-secondary education programs for students with intellectual disabilities (ID) with a comprehensive guide to developing new programs and inclusive practices for college students with ID.

Drawing on their own extensive experience with inclusive college programs, the authors outline lessons learned and offer helpful advice for developing, organizing, and implementing such programs. Covering topics from operating key program elements – such as career training and preparing for post-program success – to working with families and addressing safety issues, this book is both a practical resource and a springboard for generating innovative ideas to expand inclusive learning and living opportunities for individuals with ID.

This valuable resource provides a research-based overview of the key elements that any higher education professional or advocate should know when supporting students with and without disabilities.

Kelly R. Kelley is Associate Professor of Inclusive/Special Education at Western Carolina University, USA.

David L. Westling is the Adelaide Worth Daniels Distinguished Professor of Special Education at Western Carolina University, USA.

Teaching, Including, and Supporting College Students with Intellectual Disabilities

Kelly R. Kelley and David L. Westling

NEW YORK AND LONDON

First published 2019
by Routledge
52 Vanderbilt Avenue, New York, NY 10017

and by Routledge
2 Park Square, Milton Park, Abingdon, Oxon, OX14 4RN

Routledge is an imprint of the Taylor & Francis Group, an informa business

© 2019 Taylor & Francis

The right of Kelly R. Kelley and David L. Westling to be identified as authors of this work has been asserted by them in accordance with sections 77 and 78 of the Copyright, Designs and Patents Act 1988.

All rights reserved. No part of this book may be reprinted or reproduced or utilised in any form or by any electronic, mechanical, or other means, now known or hereafter invented, including photocopying and recording, or in any information storage or retrieval system, without permission in writing from the publishers.

Trademark notice: Product or corporate names may be trademarks or registered trademarks, and are used only for identification and explanation without intent to infringe.

Library of Congress Cataloging-in-Publication Data
A catalog record for this title has been requested

ISBN: 978-1-138-61807-7 (hbk)
ISBN: 978-1-138-61808-4 (pbk)
ISBN: 978-0-429-46137-8 (ebk)

Typeset in Sabon
by Swales & Willis Ltd, Exeter, Devon, UK

Contents

Acknowledgments vii
Preface viii

PART I
Preliminary Considerations 1

1 PSE Programs for Students with ID: Why, What, and How 3
2 Who Should Go to College? 19
3 Collaborating with University and Community Partners 33
4 Funding, Staffing, and Program Sustainability 48

PART II
Major Components 63

5 Recruitment and Admissions Procedures 65
6 Living on Campus 80
7 Course Participation 91
8 Career Planning and Job Training 105
9 Developing Campus Membership through Extracurricular Activities 118

PART III
Implementation and Coordination 131

10 Person-Centered Planning and Weekly Scheduling 133

11	Recruiting and Coordinating Student Volunteers as Natural Supports	148
12	Preparing for Post-Program Success	160

PART IV
Special Issues — 175

13	Providing a Safe Environment and Addressing Inappropriate Social Behaviors	177
14	Working Effectively with Parents and Families	187

Bibliography — 198
Index — 204

Acknowledgments

It truly takes a village to do what we do and this book was no exception. Over the years, we have had many wonderful colleagues and friends who helped make this vision possible. While it is hard to name them all, we wish to acknowledge some key individuals: The 36 inspiring trailblazers (UP students) and their families, who have made this journey possible over the years; our administrators at Western Carolina University, who have supported the innovative concepts and continued to sustain the UP Program; all our employers and faculty members, who have provided genuine lifelong learning opportunities for UP students and graduates. And also to our dedicated undergraduate students (natural supports), who have willingly sacrificed their time and continue to lead the way with higher expectations and opportunities for individuals with ID in their workplaces and communities. And finally, to our colleagues and friends, who have shared in the UP vision over the years and continued to stick with us in all the growth spurts and detours – especially Alison Morrison-Shetlar, Dale Brotherton, Susan Buchanan, Seb Prohn, Rebekah Norris, Gretchen Reece, Amy Rose, Mary Rompf, and the WCU Special Education faculty.

We would like to thank Ali Bovender, for kindly granting us permission to use her photograph for the cover image. We would also like to thank Ali Hale, the UP graduate featured in the cover image, for epitomizing the excitement of our graduates for their bright future.

And last but definitely not least, to our spouses and families for their unwavering support and sacrifices made to lend a hand or share their time. We are especially grateful to husband, David Kelley, who constantly gives 100% to share in this passion, from chaperoning trips, to moving program offices several times without complaint, and offering feedback on this book while never faltering to remind me what life is all about. And to Wendy Westling, for her support for this project and for many others for more than 40 years.

Preface

Western Carolina University's (WCUs) University Participant (UP) Program started as a pilot program in 2007 and continues to provide a robust inclusive, two-year, on-campus living and learning experience for college-aged persons with intellectual disability (ID). The UP Program is housed at WCU, a rural university located in Cullowhee, North Carolina. It has served as a model demonstration site for other programs in the U.S. and beyond.

The purpose of the program is to facilitate UP students' transition from secondary school to adult life with education, employment and independent living. UP students live in on-campus dormitories distributed throughout university residence halls under the same university policies that apply to all WCU students. On-campus life is fully integrated and inclusive. WCU undergraduate students provide paid and unpaid support to facilitate UP students living on campus, attending classes, engaging in social and recreational activities, becoming involved in student organizations, and developing friendships.

There are five learning areas emphasized throughout the college experience:

1) personal development
2) community participation
3) vocational preparation
4) social participation and learning
5) academic access.

As an approved Comprehensive Transition Postsecondary (CTP) Program, UP students work towards a UP Certificate of Accomplishment across these five learning areas and are awarded their certificate by WCU's Educational Outreach. Requirements for the certificate include completion of 1,800 hours within the five learning areas and achieving at least 80 percent goal mastery achievement within their Individualized Plan for College Participation (IPCP).

This book is based on what we have learned from the UP Program and the students who have enrolled in it. We invite readers to benefit from what we have experienced as we share our practices and lessons learned in the 12 years of the UP Program's life. Since this book is based on many of our firsthand encounters, all names referenced within this book have been replaced with pseudonyms. While any book is limited in what it can say, we are willing to share additional information and resources with other programs and families of young persons with ID interested in pursuing the college journey.

In writing and reflecting on our program practices we understand some may be unique to our circumstances and, in some instances, we have only briefly explained why we do what we do (or don't do). We recognize that some of what we discuss may not apply to all programs, and trust that in these cases programs will take what is useful and adapt what is necessary for their own use. Our hope is that this book challenges and serves as a resource to generate innovative ideas to better understand the nature of teaching, supporting, and including college-aged individuals with ID and other developmental disabilities.

Our hope is also that the book will provide practical applications and philosophical viewpoints centered around inclusive practices that have led to post-program success. To that end, the book is divided into four sections:

- Preliminary Considerations (why, what, how, who, and funding)
- Major Components (admissions, living on campus, course participation, career training, and campus membership through extracurricular activities)
- Implementation and Coordination (person-centered planning, recruiting and coordinating natural supports, and preparing for post-program success)
- Special Issues (safety and behavior issues, working with families).

The embedded figures and tables are included within each chapter as a quick guide for new development or expansions within PSE programs. We encourage multiple audiences to explore what we present in this book, especially public school personnel, university administrators, families, students with disabilities, college faculty, employers, job coaches, and college students taking courses to learn about individuals with disabilities. We believe that anyone who simply has a passion to further expand inclusive learning and living opportunities for individuals with ID across the lifespan will find this book relevant.

Part I
Preliminary Considerations

1 PSE Programs for Students with ID
Why, What, and How

Why College?

Let's begin with a simple but important question: Why should there be college programs for students with intellectual disabilities (ID)? The answer depends on your point of view.

For many young people, going to college has become an expectation. This is often true of individuals whose parents have gone to college, but it is also true for many others who become "first generation" college students. If you ask any college student why they decided to continue formal schooling after high school, you might get several different answers. For many it is related to pursuing a particular academic area, or having a career with long-term job stability. For others it offers a chance to mature, to become independent, and to begin a life away from home. Many will point to opportunities to meet new people, to explore personal interests, and to discover a path to the future. And for some, going to college allows them to achieve a desirable status. It means being able to say they graduated from college, or from a particular college or university. It is often a statement of personal achievement.

From the perspective of the student with ID, the importance of going to college is much like it is for any other young person: They want to get away from their parents, live on their own, make new friends, and pursue interesting post-secondary studies. They often have different academic interests like history, child development, or computer science. Others are looking for new adventures. Many know the kind of work they want, and they want to become better prepared for it. From their point of view, these are all legitimate reasons for them to attend college.

But a chance to go to college for a son or daughter with ID is also important from the parent perspective. Many parents realize that if they want their son or daughter to be as independent as possible, to exercise self-determination, and to experience life like other young people, they need a chance to break away, to live on their own, and to learn about life in the real world. When a son or daughter desires independence, when learning is a valued opportunity, and when they know their life goals, both the child and their parents are likely to see the importance of attending college.

But here we must emphasize the importance of the wishes and desires of the son or daughter. Sometimes students with ID are pushed toward college by their parents because of the wrong reason: some parents see college as a "next step," or a respite for themselves, or the "normal" thing to do. But in some cases the son or daughter doesn't have the interest, desire, or motivation to attend. And when this is the case, there is typically unhappiness, disappointment, lack of engagement, and failure in the student's (usually) brief college career.

Finally, colleges and universities themselves should see the value of programs for students with ID. They should know that today, formal learning beyond high school is an opportunity that should be afforded to everyone. Just as they have opened their doors to members of various minority groups, post-secondary institutions should do so for students with ID. As societal leaders in forming social values, institutions of higher education (IHEs) today have an opportunity – and we believe an obligation – to nurture the potential of individuals with ID as fully included citizens. Only a little more than half a century ago, these persons, solely because of their disability, would have had a life of confinement inside the brick walls of a foreboding, monolithic institution. Today, the chance to go to college allows them to be seen as individuals who have the rights and responsibilities of other citizens.

There is another good reason for colleges to offer programs for students with ID. Since we began the University Participant (UP) Program at Western Carolina University, we have greatly involved undergraduate students in the program. These students provide friendship and support for our students with ID, and their involvement plays a major function in allowing us to sustain the program. But we have come to see the value of the program to them, the students without disabilities, as well as to the students with disabilities. Somewhat unexpectedly, we have learned that a PSE program for students *with* ID can also be an important part of college for students *without* disabilities. We have seen students learn valuable life lessons by spending time with our students with ID. Some have decided on their college major and their life's interest because of these experiences; and in some cases, we have seen students decide to attend our university over another *because* of the program we have for students with ID. Clearly a PSE program can add value to a college or university beyond what it provides to students with ID. So for relatively little investment, not only can colleges and universities provide a meaningful education for college-age individuals with ID, they can also add a valuable component to the learning and living experience of many of their traditional students.

The Conceptual Framework of a PSE Program

Through our work in the UP Program, we have learned that in some ways there are important differences in college for students with ID and for traditional students. These differences emanate from facts and perceptions. The facts are that compared with adults without disabilities, adults with ID are less likely to make their own decisions, less likely to have a job, less likely to live independently, and less likely to have the same quality of life as those without disabilities. Additionally, the perceptions held by many are that persons with ID are less able to achieve these outcomes *because* of their disability, and are therefore relegated to a life of lowered expectations and a lower social status.

The fact is that a college student without a disability has much greater latitude than does one with ID. The student without a disability can make poor decisions, may be offensive to others, skip classes, party too much, and maybe even flunk out, and "the system" will often be forgiving. This same person may be able to continue in college, or enroll in another college, and might even graduate. They will most likely end up with a job and live somewhere of their own choosing.

On the other hand, if a college student with ID makes these same mistakes, their chance for remaining in college decreases, and positive adult outcomes are less likely to occur. People are likely to think that it was a mistake for this person to have attended college in the first place, and maybe, that college programs for students with ID are not worth having. So a college program for most students with ID should differ in at least some ways from a college program for more traditional students. Most notably, *a PSE program for students with ID should intentionally provide the structure, support, and learning opportunities that will be success-oriented and lead to greater independence as an adult.* The college experience should be designed to lead to as much independence as possible in the post-college world. It should help the student with ID become more self-determining, to make generally good decisions, to live as independently as possible, and to learn the hard and soft skills necessary to live and be employed in the community.

Because we think these outcomes are important, we have continuously stressed to our students, their parents, and various others that *the UP Program is an educational program. It is not a two-year vacation, a respite-care program, or a full-time activity center; it is a transition program designed to lead to success as an adult!* Although most colleges would say that these outcomes are desirable for *all* their graduates, rightly or wrongly, few traditional college programs are evaluated based on these outcomes. But within the UP model, we feel strongly that these outcomes should be the criteria on which we and other PSE programs for students with ID should be evaluated.

Think College, the recognized national leader in promoting PSE programs for individuals with ID, is housed in the Institute for Community Inclusion located at the University of Massachusetts Boston. As of this writing, the *Think College* (2018) database lists around 260 PSE programs for students with ID. Clearly a national trend is occurring that will likely continue to grow. As there are more than 4,700 two-year and four-year degree-granting institutions in the U.S., PSE programs for students with ID are only operating in about 5% of them, leaving the other 95% available for program development.

Grigal, Hart, and Weir (2012) provided a conceptual framework for a model PSE. The model includes eight key elements: academic access, career development, campus membership, self-determination, alignment with college systems and practices, coordination and collaboration, sustainability, and ongoing evaluation.

As is shown in Table 1.1, the UP conceptual model is similar but is expanded to show our key operational and instructional practices, the goals we hope for students to achieve while in the UP Program, and our post-UP Program goals. The diagram reflects our intended sequence of activity. That is, our key operations and instruction (i.e., inclusion, person-centered planning, self-determination, monitoring and evaluating individual progress, utilizing natural supports, and planning for transition) should lead to achievements in the program (i.e., personal development, social participation and learning, vocational success, academic participation and learning, and community participation), that should result in significant outcomes after the program has been completed (i.e., improved self-determination and decision-making skills, independent living with minimal support, community employment in a career of choice, and a desirable quality of life). The key instructional and operational practices are briefly explained below and then discussed in more detail in later chapters.

Instructional and Operational Practices

Not all colleges are the same and for many different reasons college programs for students with ID have different styles, features, and characteristics

Table 1.1 Conceptual Framework of the UP Program

UP Instructional and Operational Practices	UP Goals	Post-UP Goals
• Inclusion • Person-centered planning • Self-determination • Monitoring and evaluating individual progress • Using natural supports • Planning for transition	→ • Personal development • Social participation and learning • Academic participation and learning • Vocational success • Community participation	→ • Improved self-determination and decision-making skills • Independent living with minimal support • Community employment in a career of choice • Desirable quality of life

(Grigal, Hart, & Weir, 2014). This is not a bad thing. But from our perspective, the best programs are based on a set of valued instructional and operational practices. These are the underpinnings of the UP Program.

When we began to plan the UP Program, we started with a blank piece of paper and a question: What should the program look like? Our literature review turned up different models, but many were not what we wanted. We decided that if we were going to have a program, it should encompass the values that we have held and promoted during our careers. These values became the basis for the UP Program and are reflected in the operation of the program. Our key values included inclusion, person-centered planning, and self-determination. Along with these values, we realized that some additional practices would help us achieve better outcomes. These included monitoring and evaluating individual progress, utilizing natural supports, and planning for transition from the UP Program back into the community.

Inclusion

Philosophies about the most appropriate kinds of services for people with ID have evolved in the U.S. and Western societies over the past 200+ years. A widely held tenet today is that people with ID should be included as much as possible. We felt that if we were going to bring young adults with ID onto a college campus, it only made sense that they be fully included on the campus. Additionally, we felt that inclusion is one of the most effective learning opportunities for individuals with ID.

In the UP Program, students attend regular college classes with other college students, work on campus in jobs or unpaid internships, and live side-by-side with other college students in regular university residence halls. They also participate in a variety of activities and events in the same venues as other college students. We have found that over time, inclusion helps students gain independence and operate with more self-confidence in natural environments. They experience a life based on principles of normalization and therefore, we believe, enjoy a higher quality of life as compared with persons who are housed in, work in, or are taught in segregated settings. Additionally, students have the opportunity to learn a variety of "soft skills" from their peers that will be beneficial later when working on jobs or living in the community. They have the chance to develop independence, self-determination, and become responsible for their own behavior. These outcomes are facilitated by mentoring provided by same-age peers and the associated positive influences.

We have also found that having fully included students with ID is a benefit for students without disabilities. In a study we conducted a few years ago, 90% of the students who responded to our survey agreed or strongly agreed that "typical college students can benefit from attending a college that includes students with ID" and that "including students with ID in campus life is beneficial to other college students" (Westling, Kelley, Cain, & Prohn, 2013). Additionally, some respondents offered comments such as the following:

- *I feel as if it is important for us to include people with ID on a college campus because they deserve the right to an education just like the rest of us. Just because they have a disability does not mean they do not have dreams for their lives...*
- *I believe the UP Program is great for the typical college student and the students in the UP Program because we can learn from each other.*
- *I believe we all learn just at a different pace and no one deserves to be treated any differently. People with disabilities will not hinder the learning process of people without any disabilities in my opinion.*
- *I believe that students and people in general with ID are nothing but beneficial in other people's lives. Not only do they increase thankfulness for the little things in life, but they also allow people to gain understanding, knowledge, and acceptance of these individuals...*

Person-Centered Planning

Person-centered planning (PCP) is a process designed to "help plan a more satisfactory life" for people with ID (Westling, Fox, & Carter, 2014). As implied by the name, a PCP process focuses on the person with ID and includes that individual and others who are concerned about them. PCP is key to the UP model because we recognize the uniqueness of each of our students and the need for them to pursue individual interests and activities. Because they do not all learn the same thing, in the same way, in the same place, or at the same rate, we use PCP as a tool that allows us to individualize.

In the UP Program, we first use the PCP process to identify potential career choices, types of courses the student would like to take, work experiences, personal goals, how to reach those goals, barriers that might impede growth, and how to work around those barriers. We initially use the process when the UP student comes into the program to develop an *individual plan for college participation* (IPCP). The IPCP includes goals in our five key learning areas:

- personal development (e.g., communication skills, personal care skills, self-determination, etc.)
- social participation and learning (e.g., participating in university functions such as athletic events, belonging to university clubs or organizations)
- academic participation and learning (e.g., auditing three to four courses per semester)

- vocational success (e.g., learning specific job skills on- and off-campus), and
- community participation skills (e.g., using public transportation, budgeting, grocery shopping, etc.).

After the development of the initial IPCP, we continue to use the PCP process at individual monthly meetings with each UP student. During these meetings, the student leads the discussions. Those in the meeting who have something to say raise their hand and are called on by the UP student. The meetings will usually last at least an hour and often nearly two, and are adjourned by the student at the conclusion (see Chapter 10).

Self-Determination

Self-determination is another valued practice we have incorporated into the program. It has been defined as "acting as the primary causal agent in one's life and making choices and decisions regarding one's quality of life, free from undue external influence or interference" (Wehmeyer, 1992). An important part of the UP Program is to help students become more self-determined and to use sound judgment when making personal choices. To do this, we focus on helping UP students develop critical skills such as choice-making, decision-making, problem-solving, and goal-setting.

In the UP Program there are numerous opportunities for students to "act as the primary causal agent" in their own life. This begins when we ask each potential student during the application process why they want to go to college. In a few instances, we have seen parents who encourage their son or daughter to attend the program and promote their application, even though the young adult with ID has reservations. If we determine this to be the case, we encourage the family and the individual to wait for a year or so to consider if the UP Program is right for them. We want the student to make the choice.

Once an individual is accepted into the program, we begin using our PCP process to help the student determine career and academic interests, and to identify other personal development and social goals that should be pursued. Using the complete college catalog as our guide, we search for courses that may meet the student's career and personal needs and discuss them as viable options (see Chapter 7).

Moving beyond course selection, our weekly scheduling process, which includes planning for classes, work participation, and social and recreational activities, are directed by the student. Although we do include required activities that are critical to success – specifically attending classes and participating in work or internship duties – this leaves a great deal of time for the student to decide what they want to do, when, and with whom. There are a variety of opportunities on- and off-campus for achieving many of the goals that have been identified on the

IPCP, which means many opportunities for the student to become more self-determined. As a result, many have joined clubs, campus religious organizations, participated in Greek life, and engaged in countless social activities with non-disabled peers (see Chapters 9 and 10).

Monitoring and Evaluating Progress

Because we look at the UP Program as an educational program, we set, monitor, and evaluate individual goals for our students. Having individual goals and evaluating them are essential to achieving critical adult outcomes. So, we collect individual data, evaluate progress, and work with students to make changes where necessary if progress is insufficient.

Our progress monitoring takes different forms. As described above, if progress is insufficient, or if a change is needed in strategies to reach the goal, a discussion between the student, the UP staff, and other PCP meeting participants leads to a consensual decision. Through this process, we monitor performance in academic settings, in work settings, and in personal and social activities.

In addition to our evaluations at PCP meetings, we rely on feedback from course instructors, from supervisors in work and internship settings, and from the student volunteers who serve as paid employees. Evaluations of UP student performance are conducted twice a semester using online surveys completed by teachers and work supervisors. Student supports are asked to also use online surveys on a weekly basis to report on key personal skills like being on time for events or being suitably dressed for the weather or for a particular activity or event. Because we want to maintain a balanced and transparent approach, and because we need to also monitor the engagement of the supporting students, the UP students have an opportunity to evaluate those providing supports in the same way.

We also monitor the level of assistance or support required by each student on a weekly basis, and reduce support as much as possible in order to allow and encourage more independence. The reduction in support is shown in weekly schedules which are formed in collaboration with each student and which show in time segments the event or activity in which the student is to engage, and the person who will provide natural support during that time. As a student gains more self-confidence, more skills in self-determination, better campus navigation skills, and can demonstrate adequate safety skills, the need for supports can be reduced. Weekly schedules showing the number of hours of support that are required are monitored to show gains in independence over time. Some students ultimately gain total independence during the program, whereas others gain partial independence. The rates of gains by individuals can vary a great deal, but in general, all students show the ability for more independence (Prohn, Kelley, & Westling, 2018).

Some goals are of such importance that they are directly measured to show a student's progress. These are often in residential or work areas. For example, a student may need to reduce the time necessary to take a shower or to complete a particular part of their job. Or the student may need to improve cleaning up after preparing food in the commons area, or make sure that a critical part of a task is completed while on the job or working in an internship site. In cases like these, we may develop a self-monitoring system for the student so they can learn to monitor the behavior or skill that warrants improvement. Finally, on some rare occasions in which the student's behavior is a violation of the code of student conduct, we will develop a monitoring plan to be implemented along with a positive behavior intervention and support (PBIS) behavior intervention plan (BIP) (see Chapter 13).

Using Natural Supports

The concept of natural supports implies that persons without disabilities, who are already a part of the environment of the person with ID, can effectively support that person as opposed to employing a professional to provide the support. The practice was originally developed for use in community work settings (Nisbet & Hagner, 1988). In the UP Program we use students (mostly undergraduate, but some graduate students as well) as natural supports for the UP students with ID. Typically around 200 students volunteer each semester to serve as natural supports and they may support students from anywhere between 1 and 15 hours per week. Although the majority volunteer their time, when funding allows, we have paid nominal stipends to a few students within the existing volunteer pool (about 10%) so we could call on them if an unpaid support was not available.

Natural supports are present with UP students at all times if it is necessary for one to be present (that is, in those situations when a UP student hasn't developed sufficient independence, or lacks the skills necessary to successfully navigate or participate in an activity). Many times a person who has been in the role of a natural support morphs into a friend and will hang out with a student at unscheduled support times. These individuals will often accompany students to sporting events or to social events. Some students will have natural supports with them in their classes (usually taking the same class as the student) and some will support them as they do their homework. A natural support will also be assigned a room near students in a residence hall in order to provide support during the night or if emergencies arise.

We use natural supports for two reasons. First, it allows our students with disabilities to have a much more typical, active, and inclusive life on a college campus. The use of natural supports also provides students with mentors and role models to help them learn personal care and daily living skills, participate in various age-appropriate community activities, and learn through modeling how to interact with others in socially appropriate ways. Second, the use of natural supports makes the UP model much more economically feasible. If we were to tie a dollar figure to the volunteer time that is provided by natural supports, even based on minimum wage, it is well over $50,000 per year. Clearly the use of natural supports has both an instructional and learning benefit for the student, and a financial benefit for the program (see Chapters 4 and 11).

Planning for Transition

Achieving the post-program goals shown in Table 1.1 requires a concerted and collaborative effort from the outset. We have learned through experience that a student's parents are the most critical players when it comes to their son or daughter having a successful post-UP adult life. They know their offspring better than we do, they know their community better than we do, and they can have much more influence over the outcomes for their son or daughter than we can. We have known parents who have worked with us closely and agreed with our goals, and we have known others who, although not with malice, have limited the success their son or daughter could have enjoyed. In the former case, for example, a parent helped a son with Down syndrome find a job of his choice in his own community, live in his own apartment, and create a circle of support in his community. This young man now enjoys a very full life. In contrast, in another case, a young man with a mild ID, who showed much promise as a very able and successful UP student, ended up in a day program setting after completing the program because that was the placement his parents desired. Given the nature of an ID, it is not possible for any PSE program to achieve results not encouraged, supported, and sought by a student's parents. Therefore parental cooperation is essential.

Because we realized this early in our program, we now attempt to evaluate parents' attitudes toward potential outcomes for their son or daughter *before* they are admitted to the program. To do this we have developed a questionnaire for parents that must be submitted along with the application of the individual with ID to the program. This questionnaire asks about past approaches to inclusion and participation in family and community activities, and expectations for future living and working arrangements. If an individual is ultimately admitted to the UP Program, parents are required to sign a memorandum of understanding (see Chapter 14) that clearly specifies what *we* will do in the UP Program to achieve desirable outcomes, and what we expect *them* to do to also achieve these outcomes. Essentially, their job is to collaborate with us to reach the outcomes by supporting our efforts and also mapping and networking in their community to identify possible living and working options.

Once parents understand and agree with the key outcomes of the program, we use the PCP process to identify more specific outcomes for the student including type of employment and living arrangements they wish to pursue, and identify learning activities that can lead to these outcomes. These include courses the student will audit, the on- and off-campus work experiences, and other less formal activities. Through these experiences, the student has a chance to build a portfolio of experiences, accomplishments, and skills. If a community support agency or Vocational Rehabilitation is providing support to the student, we also collaborate with the agency so that all service providers are moving in the same direction.

In the second (and final) year of the program, our focus on post-UP outcomes intensifies. If possible we will place the student in a job in their community before the program ends. Sometimes, if a future job is not available, we will place the student in an unpaid internship to help them learn the specific skills for the job. Also in the second year, we will explore possible living arrangements. We will work with the family and their network as well as the student's on-campus network to explore possible roommates for post-UP life, and consider specific living situations (see Chapter 12). In all planning, we use PCP meetings to allow the student to make the final decision in determining living and working outcomes.

Strategies for Beginning a PSE Program

At this time, most colleges and universities in the U.S., around 95%, do not offer PSE programs for young adults with ID. Still, as more and more people learn about these programs and the significant impact they can have, the more they are likely to expand. For this to happen, it is important to understand key characteristics of colleges and universities, and how to work within the existing structures of these institutions to develop PSE programs.

From the outset, it is important to understand that colleges and universities take pride in their academic status and accomplishments, and rightly so. They tout their admission standards and the quality of their students, enjoy the rankings they achieve, publicize their standing in the academic world, and highlight the scholarly and artistic accomplishments of their faculty. They *do not* want to be seen as lax in their requirements for students, or in their expectations for student success. It is important to know this, because to propose that a college or university accept students who will not meet all of their existing expectations may require showing the institution how a PSE program for students with ID will not jeopardize their standing, but may, in fact, enhance it.

As we pursued developing the UP Program, we did so with an understanding of the realities of the university's self-perception, and developed our implementation strategy accordingly. The strategies and tactics that we used are discussed below.

Preliminary Considerations

Connect with Key Players

Buy-in and collaboration are essential to developing an inclusive PSE program. To begin, there must be a core group of faculty or administrators that supports the idea of a PSE program and fosters its development. Often this will include faculty members in special education or in a disabilities-related academic area. From this group there should emerge a general plan for the program, and the group as a whole should be willing to support the plan. Within the group, there should be one or more recognized champions who will steadfastly support the program. This will not be as important after the program has been successful, but at the outset, the future program will need a spokesperson who will explain it and defend it. Beyond this core group, the program developers should approach key persons on campus to enlist their support, answer their questions, and try to address any challenges or barriers they may raise.

When we began the UP Program, after gaining the support of the special education faculty, we contacted the following persons: The dean of our college (because the program was to be housed there), the dean of continuing education (because the certificate we planned to offer would come from here), the director of residential housing (because we planned for our students to live in residence halls), and a senior associate vice chancellor for academic affairs (because this individual had broad knowledge about the university and their support could open doors and remove barriers). Other key personnel that we eventually met with and "sold" on the program were the director of disability services, the director of the university physical plant, and the director of admissions. As the program continues today, all of these individuals remain as important allies.

Start Slow

In order to make the UP Program more tenable to those we approached, we proposed that we would start slow and would consider the program as a "pilot program." This meant that we would start with only one student and see how everything went during the first year. We felt that if we demonstrated that we were in a learning mode, that more people in the university community would be willing to give us a try. We did not place an administrator in a position of having to accept and support a permanent program that was unlike anything the university had ever experienced, because we knew this would be nearly impossible. We realized that the university *did not need* the UP Program in that it did not seem (at least at that time) to help the university move toward achieving its academic goals. Furthermore, we knew that if we became too overwhelming, that we would likely instigate fears and concerns and the program would be squelched before it could grow.

Stay Close to Established Policies and Practices

Most colleges and universities have well-established operational policies and procedures, and for several reasons, we wanted to operate within them instead of developing "special" practices. This meant that we would have an admissions process that would go through the admissions office using an application form very similar to the regular undergraduate application form. We found that our students could be admitted as "non-degree-seeking" students just as anyone else might be, so we did not have to create a new admission standard. It also meant that we would use existing courses and the course auditing guidelines that already existed. We did not have to make special arrangements for our students to be in credit courses, because there was already a policy that would allow them to audit courses and thus allow course accommodations.

In several other areas we were also able to operate within established policies. The Division of Continuing Education could award a "Certificate of Accomplishment" based on our performance criteria and our verification that the student had met these criteria. Students could get supports from the Office of Disability Services just like other students with disabilities because they had been admitted to the university. Students could be issued student "Cat Cards" that allowed them to pay for meals and gain entry into university events. And, notably, students were expected to follow the "code of student conduct" because they were living and learning on campus as were other students. In short, we tried to avoid any "special" changes in university policies or practices whenever possible.

Don't Threaten the Institution's Academic Status

Because we understood the values of institutions of higher education, we took steps not to infringe on these values. We did not ask that our students be given a waiver and admitted as a student who did not meet entry requirements, nor that they be given undeserved grades in courses or awarded degrees they did not earn. Instead, we found an entry status that would work for our program. We admitted only persons whose status in high school (as a student with ID) would preclude their admission to the university as an undergraduate student because we did not want to be viewed as a backdoor entry for persons who did not meet typical admission requirements.

In this same vein, we informed potential students that the courses they took could only be audited and could not count as credit toward a degree, and that the program resulted in a certificate as opposed to a degree. All of this was done so that the university did not view the UP Program as "watering down" admission requirements, academic standards, or degree requirements. This was not done to demean the value of the students' learning experiences, but to negotiate a successful program to be included within an institution that valued scholarship, and on the surface, could be at odds with what we were proposing. Of course we realize that there are some students with ID and developmental disabilities who could be admitted and matriculate satisfactorily at the university, and of course we would support the normal admission process and enrollment for these students. But given that they had adequate potential for success in the traditional college way, they would not be eligible for admission to the UP Program.

Don't Expect a Free Ride

We also knew better than to ask the university to let us have the program for nothing. For the most part, colleges and universities are more like a business than a charity: They don't give much away (except for the scholarships they have available, none of which our students qualified for). So from the outset we presented our students as students who would pay their own way. They had to pay the same tuition and fees as all other students. Although this presented an expense to parents and families, it allowed us to point out to whomever asked that the UP Program was not something the university was giving to the students, but something they were paying for, just like everybody else. This helped us diffuse the argument made by some that UP students were taking something away from other students.

Publicize Success and Share the Credit

As President Truman once said, "It is amazing what you can accomplish if you do not care who gets the credit." We found that the more success we had with the UP Program, and the more we credited the institution, the faculty, the students, and the entire university community, the more we were embraced by the university. Whenever we made presentations about the UP Program, especially to community groups, or when we were contacted by the media about the program, we always gave credit to the support we received from the university administration and to our colleagues on campus who were so helpful in the development and implementation of the program. By doing this, more and more, we extended ownership of the program to the university community and let the key players get positive attention for allowing us to maintain the program. And we were not being facetious. In fact, we were receiving a great deal of support and we really thought it would be helpful to the program if we acknowledged that support.

Be Careful

One university administrator, who is one of our greatest supporters, has constantly reminded us, "You are one accident away from being kicked off campus." While this sounds harsh, it is true. Although the program brings many benefits, a college or university *does not need* a program like the UP Program to be successful. Even though the institution may recognize the benefits of the program, and may even be very supportive, it will not have a program if it is viewed as a liability, not if it can avoid it.

There are several situations that could result in a legal action being taken against a college or university as the result of a PSE program for students with ID: a student could get injured, could injure someone else, could go missing, could be involved in a crime, could be the victim of a crime, etc. When you take an individual who may not yet have developed sound and mature judgment and place him or her into such an open and free environment as a college campus, unfortunate events can occur. Of course this is true both for students with ID and for typical college students. But for better or worse, the college or university needs the latter group, it does not need the former group, nor is it required to have it.

Final Thoughts

There is a tremendous gap between the current number of PSE programs for students with ID and the number that will be developed over the coming years, and this is something that we are very excited about. In this chapter we have tried to lay out two important sets of principles that we think should be the basis for developing programs or improving current programs.

First is the need to establish a conceptual model on which the program should be based. From our experience with our own program and with other programs, we know that there is a great deal of variation that exists among programs. For some, the only desirable practice and outcome is to get individuals with ID into some kind of program on campus. There is little thought about how their lives should be lived once on campus, how to help them attain important skills, how to include them, or what life should be like after they finish the program. In some cases, the program is the end goal in and of itself. We disagree with this approach. We maintain that a program must be guided by sound values and that these values should be the foundation for both the practices and outcomes of the program. Without such values, many will ask about why there is really a need for the program and the likelihood of success will be diminished.

Second, developing a PSE program for students with ID requires an understanding of the culture of higher education and adequate political astuteness to navigate within that culture. We feel that it is essential for the program to develop internally. Even if the initial impetus to develop a program comes from external forces, like parents, it is important to get key buy-in from important persons who are inside the system and who will be in agreement about the value of the program and the need to support it. With this, strategic actions can be used to weave a valuable and viable PSE program into the fabric of the college or university.

References

Grigal, M., Hart, D., & Weir, C. (2012). *Think College standards, quality indicators, and benchmarks for inclusive higher education*. Boston, MA: University of Massachusetts Boston, Institute for Community Inclusion.

Grigal, M., Hart, D., & Weir, C. (2014). Postsecondary education for students with intellectual disabilities. In M. Agran, F. Brown, C. Hughes, C. Quirk, & D. Ryndak (eds.), *Equity and full inclusion for individuals with severe disabilities: a vision for the future* (pp. 275–298). Baltimore, MD: Brookes.

Nisbet, J. & Hagner, D. (1988). Natural supports in the workplace: A reexamination of supported employment. *Journal of the Association of the Severely Handicapped, 13*, 260–267.

Prohn, S. M., Kelley, K. R., & Westling, D. L. (2018). Students with intellectual disability going to college: What are the outcomes? A pilot study. *Journal of Vocational Rehabilitation, 48*, 127–132. doi: 10.3233/JVR-170920.

Think College (2018). *College search*. Retrieved from: www.thinkcollege.net/?Itemid=127

Wehmeyer, M. L. (1992). Self-determination and the education of students with mental retardation. *Education and Training in Mental Retardation, 27*, 302–314.

Westling, D. L., Fox, L., & Carter, E. W. (2014). *Teaching students with severe disabilities* (5th ed.). Columbus, Ohio: Pearson.

Westling, D. L., Kelley, K. R., Cain, B., & Prohn, S. (2013). College students' attitudes about an inclusive postsecondary education program for individuals with an intellectual disability. *Education and Training in Autism and Developmental Disabilities, 48*, 306–319.

2 Who Should Go to College?

The Emergence of College Programs for Students with ID

According to the U.S. Department of Education's National Center for Educational Statistics (2017), in the fall of 2017, more than 20 million students were planning to attend a college or university, an increase of more than 5 million since 2000. Further, as the number of young people attending college has increased, so has the diversity of college students. Today, most college students are young women, and the number of students from minority backgrounds is constantly increasing. Clearly, going to college today is not just for an elite group of students.

The reason for the increase in college students is that many people today view college as an essential, basic component of education. In essence, today, going to college for at least two years is like completing high school in the 20th century: It is a life necessity. In fact, in 2015 President Obama proposed that two-year colleges should be tuition-free. Since then, although there has been no federal legislation, several states now offer two years of tuition-free college to their citizens (Lobosco, 2017).

As going to college becomes more common for the general population, it makes sense that more and more individuals with an intellectual and/or developmental disability (IDD) also wish to attend college, and it also makes sense that more and more colleges are offering programs for these students. Before 2000, there were only a handful of college programs for students with ID, but today there are close to 300 such programs, with most states in the U.S. having at least one program.[1]

The increase in college programs for students with ID was facilitated by the Higher Education Opportunity Act (HEOA) of 2008 (PL 110-315). This act provided initial funding for a five-year period (2010–2015) for 27 model-demonstration projects (either individual programs or consortia). These programs were implemented in 23 states. Forty-two institutions of higher education (IHEs) participated in the initial round of funding, affecting about 6,000 young adults with ID. The programs were referred to as "TPSIDs" (transition and postsecondary education programs for students with intellectual disabilities) and they were supported by a grant-funded coordinating center, *Think College* (Grigal, Hart, & Weir, 2013). In 2015, grants were awarded for 25 second cohorts to new or returning TPSIDs to continue expansion and enhancement of high-quality inclusive educational experiences (Grigal, Hart, Papay, Domin, & Smith, 2017). *Think College* is considered a leading center of information about the movement in the United States today for college students with ID. Its website (https://thinkcollege.net), offers an abundance of information about current programs as well as writing and research about these programs.

Characteristics of PSE Programs for Students with ID

In 2014/15, the TPSID model demonstration programs included students who had been classified in high school as students with intellectual disability (ID), autism, other health impairments, and developmental delays. In the TPSID programs, the majority of students, 89%, had an ID and/or autism. Further, 57% of TPSID students were male, 43% female; 73% were white, 15% African American, and 11% Hispanic; and more than 90% were between the ages of 18 and 25 (Grigal, Hart, Smith, Domin, & Weir, 2017).

Perhaps the most important outcome of the HEOA and the TPSID projects was the creation of an expectation that inclusive college programs could be developed for individuals with ID, that existing funding mechanisms (such as Pell Grants and work study opportunities) could support these students, and that like other college students, going to college would lead to better career outcomes for young adults with ID. Today, PSE is considered an important transition goal for many high school students with ID and other developmental disabilities, and data are showing that PSE for students with ID is resulting in better outcomes such as community living and community employment (Moore & Schelling, 2015; Ross, Marcell, Williams, & Carlson, 2013).

As with colleges in general, PSE programs for students with ID vary considerably. Table 2.1 shows some of the variations that exist across programs.

Although PSE programs for students with ID are designed for students who meet the traditional definition of persons with ID (deficits in measured intelligence and adaptive behavior requiring some amount of support), as noted in the TPSID data, other students with disabilities such as autism spectrum disorders (ASD) or traumatic brain injury (TBI) may also be admitted to some programs. Even though the specific disability criteria may vary from program to program, in general, students who are admissible to PSE programs will have a confirmed ID (based on a recent IQ score) even if they also have a secondary disability such as ASD. Most importantly, students in PSE programs will not meet the regular undergraduate admission requirements of a college or university, otherwise they would be required to apply using normal admission procedures and evaluated based on traditional criteria.

Table 2.1 Key Characteristics of PSE Programs for Students with Intellectual Disabilities

---

Four-year traditional college and university programs: These programs are located on traditional four-year college or university campuses. They may or may not include residential provisions for students with ID.

Two-year community college programs: Many programs are located on two-year college campuses. Like other students who attend these colleges, students with ID are often attending only during class times and return home when not attending classes.

Residential services: Some four-year colleges and universities, though relatively few, offer on-campus or off-campus residential living opportunities. Residential programs may be fully integrated so that students with ID are living with other college students, or they may have separate residences.

Dual enrollment: Some PSE programs on college campuses serve dually enrolled students. These students are still attending high school and are served under IDEA, but some or all of their academic work occurs on a college campus.

Two- to four-year programs: PSE programs usually last between two years (the majority of programs) and four years.

College curricula: The coursework for students with ID in some PSE programs is drawn from courses available to all college students. Students with ID often audit these courses, though sometimes they may take them for credit. Accommodations will be allowed to help make the course more accessible.

Special curricula: Some PSE programs will have special curricula for students with ID, or will have individual special courses available to support these students.

Vocational and career preparation: Many PSE programs include a vocational training component that requires students with ID to work on part-time jobs or internships while they are in the program. Students are supervised and supported to learn specific job skills and related social skills.

Personal and social development: In some PSE programs students with ID will have individual goals or objectives that include improving specific personal and social skills. These may include academic skills, daily living skills, community participation skills, social skills, etc.

Program fees: Students with ID will typically be charged the same fees as other college students. Additionally, PSE programs often charge additional fees to cover program costs. Fees can range from a few thousand dollars to over $50,000 per year.

Sources: Grigal et al., 2015; Thoma et al., 2011.

What Kinds of Students with ID Will be Successful in College?

Traditional students are usually accepted into college through a competitive process that considers their past academic performance (based on grades), their potential to be successful in college (based on SAT or ACT or similar standardized test scores), and their general fit with the college to which they are applying (based on key experiences usually shared in application essays). The requirements and procedures for admitting students with ID to a PSE program vary from one program to another, but are different from traditional admission procedures because PSE programs cannot use traditional admission criteria. In some programs, large numbers of students are admitted with fairly loose criteria, but in others, like Western Carolina's University Participant (UP) Program, admission may be more competitive because of fewer available slots.[2] Although we present a set of recommended admission procedures in Chapter 5, here we discuss important characteristics and experiences that we believe will make individuals with ID more viable applicants for many PSE programs, improve their participation in the programs, and lead to post-program success.

Varied and Inclusive Life Experiences

Adolescents and young adults with ID who have had a wide variety of life experiences with family, friends, and classmates are more likely to be successful in college than those who have been sheltered and secluded. The best experiences for applicants will have been inclusive, involving individuals without disabilities, and occurring in various home, school, and community environments. The most qualified applicants with ID will have been involved in integrated organizations, activities, and events such as scouting, faith-based congregations, clubs, and teams. Additionally, from an early age they will have had chores and responsibilities at home, and engaged with friends, neighbors, and relatives out of the home. Social participation like going to others' birthday parties, spending the night at a friend's house, going to camp, attending meetings and events, and working in a part-time job, are all generally good indicators of the potential for success in a PSE program.

Individuals who have had such experiences have demonstrated their interest in the kind of meaningful engagements and interactions that will be expected in a PSE program. In college, they will be expected to attend classes, work at jobs or internships, participate in social events, and may live in residence halls with other college students without disabilities. And they will do these things *without close adult supervision*. Doing these things will feel more natural and will come easier to young persons who have been exposed to similar conditions and activities throughout life. Such individuals are likely to have demonstrated they are able to function without the continual presence of their parents or another adult, and therefore will be able to function more maturely and independently.

High Expectation for Success

In order for students with ID to successfully enter and participate in a PSE program, it is important that they expect to be successful in the program and afterward – they should be "success-strivers." If this expectation is present, engaging in activities to achieve success will be a daily goal. The most successful college students believe that they will be successful and pursue their studies and other activities based on this notion. Whether the student has an ID or is a traditional college student, they should be fortified by the notion that if they are willing to work hard, they will be successful in college and beyond.

Early literature on persons with ID noted that they were often considered *failure-avoiders* instead of *success-strivers*, and that they were more likely to have an *external locus of control* than an *internal locus of control* (MacMillan, 1977; Westling, 1986). This meant that they felt like others had more influence over their lives than they did themselves, and that if they tried to do something on their own, they would be more likely to fail than to succeed.

Today we put a great deal of emphasis on persons with ID achieving self-determination because we believe all people should have a say in their lives. But if individuals do not think they can be successful, they will not be inclined to exercise self-determination and instead will exhibit *outerdirectedness*. That is, instead of trying to complete a task or solve a problem, they will look to others (often parents) to do so.

Being a failure-avoider results in not attempting to learn new skills and engage in new activities. This phenomenon is supported by observations that show many persons with ID are more likely to respond in ways to avoid failing at a task or activity, rather than to make an effort that might lead to success, but might also result in failure. It was noted that failure at a specific task often resulted in subsequent avoidance of the task, and further, that there was also a generalized expectation for failure. Subsequently, however, it was theorized that the reason many persons with ID acted to avoid failure rather than pursue success was because of the many experiences they had with failure, rather than any inherent condition associated with their ID. In other words, having an ID does not necessarily mean that a person will be primarily motivated by avoiding failure, but the individual may tend to do so if failure is a regular part of life.

The implication of this is clear. If persons with ID are to have an expectation for success instead of a fear of failure, it is important that they experience events that allow them to have a high probability of success. Parents and teachers must be sure, therefore, that as children and adolescents, persons with ID learn to be successful and, if they fail, have sufficient support and sufficient opportunities to improve their performance and ultimately to be as successful as they can.

Sufficient Personal Skills and Appropriate Social Behavior

Although we expect that students in PSE programs will learn a great deal while they are in the program, we also expect that they will come into the program with a fairly well-developed set of personal skills. These skills should allow them to care for themselves (although some support may still be required), communicate adequately (although various communication skills may still need to be developed), and interact with others in a socially acceptable fashion. We don't necessarily need to see a particular level of adaptive behavior, and total independence is not necessary or expected, but we do expect that students should be as independent as possible in terms of personal care and demonstrate an adequate range of social behavior.

Daily living skills, or those skills that allow an individual to take care of themselves (such as personal hygiene skills, dressing skills, and keeping one's living space in an orderly way) are ultimately important for living independently, or as independently as possible. Since these skills are important for living in the community, it is important that they be adequately demonstrated in college. To the extent that students possess skills when they arrive, they are ahead of the game. Of course we expect that being in college will be a great learning opportunity, especially if they are living in on-campus residence halls, but by demonstrating a high degree of daily living skill level, we can see that a student has the ability and the interest to learn additional skills in this area. Our job then becomes one of filling in the gaps that exists to help equal the living and learning playing field for everyone.

Communication is another area that is relevant to being successful in a PSE program. It is widely known that individuals with ID often have difficulty with speech and/or language usage. Limits in one or more of these human abilities can affect communication, and communication can affect how well someone does in a PSE program. But the point is not that the student should have perfect articulation, voice, or fluency; or that they have a well-developed vocabulary or grammatical structure. What is important, though, is that the student makes an effort to communicate, is willing to communicate, and understands the importance of communication. Students who are completely non-verbal may be successful in a PSE program if they are willing to use the communication ability that they have, even if it requires the use of an assistive technology device. On the other hand, a student may have perfect diction, but will not request assistance when it is necessary, will not participate in class, or will not respond when asked a question or given a direction. If such issues exist with regard to communication, it will be difficult for the student to be successfully engaged in the day-to-day activities of a PSE program.

And finally, the issue of social behavior is often considered by PSE programs. A college campus is like other communities: There is an expectation for socially appropriate behavior and many college campuses, like Western Carolina, have a student code of conduct. Anyone who violates this code is subject to disciplinary action or being dismissed from the university. Having an ID does not exclude a student from being subject to the rules and regulations stated in the code of conduct.

When most students arrive on a college campus, they behave like they just left high school . . . which is somewhat expected. For many, it is the first time they are living without adult oversight in their day-to-day lives. Subsequently, they often are seeking new ways to have fun and to test the boundaries of their newly found freedom. This is perfectly normal behavior. But the reality is, ultimately there *are* boundaries – whether they are explicit or implicit – and they need to be respected.

The question is not whether or not applicants with ID exhibit totally correct etiquette or well-established forms of social behavior. The question is whether their behavior is so out of bounds that the probability for behavior change seems low, or seems like it will take too long. For example, if an applicant to a PSE program clings to their mother or father throughout a visit to the campus and they never demonstrate any interest in expanding social connections, most likely we will wonder if they will be more socially engaged in the future if accepted to the program. Or, if an applicant is constantly unresponsive to a support student's prompts, we might wonder if the applicant will be amenable to such forms of support in the future. In contrast, when we look for individuals whom we think will be successful in our PSE program, we look for the following characteristics: Has an ability to build rapport and warmth, has a concern for others, can self-monitor their own behavior and has personal management skills and self-directions, is as self-reliant as possible, shows initiative and motivation, is enthusiastic about being in the program and attending college, is adequately alert, and is respectful of others.

Self-Determination, Self-Management, and Self-Responsibility

As we discussed earlier, too often individuals with ID acquire an unhealthy reliance on others. Fortunately, we see many students who are able to overcome this characteristic when they enter our PSE program, and often, to the surprise of their parents, learn to speak for themselves and address their own interests. One such student was a young woman whose parents informed us when she was admitted of her great interest in working in the childcare area, which was subsequently agreed to by the student. However, after several semesters the student informed us that she had lost interest in working with children and wanted instead to work in the hospitality field. Her parents were shocked when they heard this, but we strongly reinforced her decision and gave her more coursework and job experience working in hotels and motels. In another case, the parents expected their son to return to live with them at their home after going to college – "for just a little while" – but he told them he wanted to stay in the area of the college and get his own apartment with a roommate. Again, there was shock, but ultimately the young man moved into his own apartment. While such personal evolutions are common for all college students, generally they are more difficult for students with ID who have been subjected to protection and direction throughout their lives.

Self-determination has been a targeted outcome for individuals with ID for about 30 years. It was defined by Michael Wehmeyer (1992) as "acting as the primary causal agent in one's life and making choices and decisions regarding one's quality of life, free from undue external influence or interference." Later Wehmeyer (1996) said that certain critical experiences were "component elements of self-determined behavior." These included: choice-making; decision-making; problem-solving; goal-setting and attainment; self-observation, evaluation and reinforcement; exercising internal locus of control; having positive attributions of efficacy and outcome expectations; having self-awareness and having self-knowledge. Furthermore, he stated that strengths in these areas would allow an individual to exhibit four essential characteristics necessary for self-determination:

- *autonomy*: acting according to one's own preferences, interests, and abilities, independently and free from undue external influences
- *self-regulation*: deciding what strategies and tactics to use in particular situations, in setting goals for oneself and working to achieve these goals, in problem-solving, and in monitoring one's own performance in these tasks
- *psychological empowerment*: a belief that one has control over important circumstances, that is, an internal locus of control, and a belief that one has the skills to achieve the desired outcomes and that by applying these skills the desired outcome will occur, and
- *self-realization*: the individual has a reasonably accurate knowledge of themselves, their strengths, and their limitations, and acts in a way that capitalizes on this knowledge.

We seek students for our PSE program who exhibit at least some degree of self-determination, and then we try to reinforce this ability when they are in the program. During the admissions process, we try to determine if the applicant really wants to go to college, if they are really interested in our program, or if the application is more the desire of the parents. An individual who is pushed by their parents to attend college will often not be successful, especially if they do not ultimately find the value of the college experience. Many students who truly want to be a part of the UP Program evidence a level of enthusiasm that cannot be coached or faked. They know what they want to study, what they want to do when they graduate, and are willing to work hard to be successful. These are applicants who will most likely be admitted to the program.

Self-management and personal responsibility are related characteristics that we also value, and when we see students with such abilities, we usually think they will be successful in the program. Simple actions can be telling. Students who sign in at open house events, carry their own belongings, who clear their own tray after a meal, who keep their personal space orderly, who remember to take their own medication, or who know how much dessert to allow themselves are showing that they can monitor their own behavior, that they know what they should do, and that they do these things with little prompting. These are signs of maturity that are not necessarily related to intellectual development, but to a life of learning to be personally active and responsible. This, we think, is a critical factor for success in college and beyond.

What Kinds of Families Are Important for Success in College by Students with ID?

As might be inferred from the previous sections, we view the role of parents and families in supporting their son or daughter as being critical for students with ID in ultimately being successful both during and after college. This can't be surprising. We have noted that many life experiences and personal characteristics are essential for a student with ID to be ready for college, and clearly families and parents must encourage, promote, and facilitate these. What may be surprising to some is that this role of parents must continue while the student is in college to better assure a successful outcome. We have learned through experience that this support is so critical, that we (1) evaluate the potential of parents as support partners as much as we evaluate the applicant as a potential college student, and (2) require a written agreement that parents will continue to provide certain kinds of support. If we have an indication that parents are not in agreement with us on desired post-program outcomes, or if we perceive they are not willing to provide the material, mental, and emotional support that is necessary during the program, we are not likely to admit the student. Some have expressed disagreement with this practice, but we know that without parent cooperation and parent support, that during the program and after graduation, the UP student is likely not to be successful. That's how important parents and families are to success. Some of the forms of cooperation and support we expect from parents are discussed below.

Parental Expectations

As with the students themselves, parents must hold high expectations for their son or daughter. Studies have clearly shown that the involvement and support of parents are the most significant factors for a person with ID to have a successful adult life (Kelley & Prohn, 2018; Papay & Bambara, 2016; Test et al., 2009). Therefore, during our first meeting with parents of applicants, usually during our open house, we explain clearly what *our* expectations are so parents and family members can determine if they align with *their own expectations*. Briefly, we expect parents to agree on the following post-program outcomes:

Community living. Most adults with ID have the ability to live independently or with some support in their own home, and we expect that after completing a PSE program they should do so. The home may be a house, an apartment, a modular home, or some other structure they consider to be their home. This does not include any form of congregate living like a group home or an "intermediate care facility." And it does not include the parents' home or a sibling's home. The home should be chosen by the individual with ID, or at least its characteristics and features should be clearly expressed. Additionally, who, if anyone, lives in the home with the person with ID must be selected by that person, or at least agreed to by them.

Quite often, when we first present this desired outcome to parents, many of them look at each other in disbelief because they have never expected their son or daughter to have their own home. But we have evidence that our graduates can achieve this goal, and after enjoying independence in college, it is something that nearly all want. To have an expectation for anything less would be disheartening and unnecessary. Therefore, this is an important expectation for us, and it is important for parents to share this expectation if their son or daughter is going to achieve it.

Community employment. We also expect that a PSE graduate will be employed in the community, having at least a part-time job (or more than one) that pays at or above minimum wage, and this must also be a parental expectation. This clearly excludes working in a sheltered workshop earning a fraction of minimum wage, or being placed in an adult activity center. Outcomes such as these would suggest expectations that are far below that which can be accomplished and certainly do not require participation in a PSE program.

There is clearly evidence that persons with ID can work in the community even if some degree of support is required (as in supported employment), or if a unique job must be designed or developed for them (as in customized employment). For some individuals, self-employment may be considered an option. A recent graduate of the UP Program, with the support of his family, is now working to develop a website to promote and sell his own brand of BBQ sauce using the culinary and marketing skills he developed in the UP Program. So being an entrepreneur can also be considered a successful outcome. Most PSE programs prepare students for working in regular jobs, in career areas of their choice. So this same expectation by parents and applicants may be an important consideration.

A high quality of life (QOL). Most college graduates not only earn more in their lifetime, but are happier and healthier, so reports Jamie Merisotis in the *Huffpost* (2016). Parents should expect that after college their son or daughter should be able to enjoy life, living as independently as possible, having a variety of choices, and exercising self-determination.

This means that as we plan for living and working in the community, we must also consider what QOL aspects of life also require planning. To be happy living in the community, beyond simply having a home and a job, means having some friends and social acquaintances, having a source of transportation, having a choice of leisure and recreational activities, and sometimes engaging in civic participation. For most individuals with ID these are all possible, as research has clearly demonstrated (Brown, Shiraga, & Kessler, 2006; Ross et al., 2013).

Parental Support

Beyond having very positive expectations, parents must show a willingness to continue to provide support to their son or daughter. But there are different ways to provide support and parents should know the ways that will be helpful and the ways that will impede learning and development.

When students come into the UP Program, we expect parents will have demonstrated strong support for their son or daughter throughout life, and will continue to do so even while in the program. This expectation is so critical, that in the UP Program, we require parents to sign a memo of understanding (MOU) indicating that their support and cooperation in various ways will be provided.

But what kind of support should be provided? As we have discussed previously, individuals with ID sometimes avoid failure by looking to parents to provide direction. This outerdirectedness will not lead to self-determination and, more likely, will lead to a life of more dependence and less independence. On the other hand, if sufficient support is not provided, failure may occur and the individual may ultimately become a failure-avoider and not take risks necessary for learning. The key, then, is to provide the *minimal amount of necessary and effective support* that will increase the likelihood of success, while *decreasing support as success increases.*

While support might initially be rather direct and intrusive, during subsequent opportunities, the support may be faded to the least amount necessary. Ultimately, the young learner should be able to engage independently in the task, or as independently as they possibly can. This principle can be applied to specific tasks such as getting dressed or brushing teeth, or to routines such as cleaning one's bedroom or clearing the table after dinner. This process of providing more-to-less support delivers an important message to the learner. It says, *I want you to be successful and I'll help you to get there, but sooner or later you will be able to do this on your own.* In the UP Program, we understand the need for support and provide it as much as necessary. But we also understand the need to fade support and we do this as much as we can, as soon as we can, and as often as we can.

The process of fading or reducing support is applicable both to specific tasks and to the accumulation of activities across time. In other words, as the individual grows and becomes more mature, support in general can and should be faded. As independence increases, support should decrease. Unfortunately, this can be more difficult for parents. They have often become so accustomed to providing support, protection, and shelter, that learning to back off giving directions and corrections is difficult. But it is critical that they learn to do so if their child, as an adult, is going to be as mature and independent as possible. For this reason, individuals with ID who have had the right kind of parent support, and who continue to have the right kind, are more likely to do well in a PSE program.

Final Thoughts

The opportunity for young adults to attend a typical college or university represents a significant addition to their educational opportunities, and one that can be greatly beneficial to their adult life. Unlike public school attendance, college attendance is not an entitlement, it is not required or mandated under any state or federal law (just as it is not for any college student). Additionally, having a PSE program for students with ID is not necessarily a required component of a college or university. So while PSE programs present an educational opportunity for many, they also raise an important question that is central to this chapter: Which persons with ID should attend college?

Different PSE programs have different admission policies and practices. Unlike traditional admission procedures, when students with ID are considered for PSE programs, there are no uniform assessment instruments that are used by all colleges and universities as there are for students without disabilities. There is no SAT or ACT-like test that can be used to evaluate college readiness, and high school evaluations for students with ID do not always provide valid information that predicts performance in a PSE program. So most programs are left to determine their own admission policies. In Chapter 5, we discuss in detail the procedures we use in the UP Program. We feel we have been successful (and fair) with these procedures and can recommend their use to other programs.

Our purpose in this chapter, however, has been to discuss individual and family characteristics that we believe make an individual with ID ready to be successful in a PSE program. What we feel is most important is that when entering a PSE program, the individual with ID should have a personal vision for their life, be committed to learning the skills and developing the characteristics that will let the vision be realized, and be committed to engaging with others who also have visions and aspirations for the future in a vibrant community of learners.

Because we believe that past behavior and activity generally predicts future behavior and activity, we examine the kind of life the individual has had before applying for college. We look to determine if their life, regardless of the degree of ID, has been relatively robust and active, or sedentary, reclusive, and protected. Students with the former lifestyle are much more likely to be successful, mature learners than those with the latter lifestyle.

But the lifestyle of an applicant is strongly influenced by the commitment of the parents and families, and so is the future success of the student in a PSE program . . . and beyond. So when considering viable applicants for a PSE program, we must also consider how well the family will support the student, and whether they will move in the same direction to reach program and post-program goals. Experience is a great teacher, and it has taught us that without the family's commitment, our efforts in providing a high-quality education may be for naught.

The outcomes that most PSE programs desire for their graduates, those that we have previously discussed, are commonly supported by both professionals and advocates for persons with ID. We know that if we want these outcomes to occur, we must provide as much preparation for them as we can. And if we do, and if the student is ready to learn, and if the families are committed to the same outcomes, success is likely to occur.

Notes

1 The *Think College* search engine allows interested students and their families to search throughout the U.S. for colleges based on various features.
2 Because it is fully inclusive, the WCU UP Program only allows eight students with ID at one time.

References

Brown, L., Shiraga, B., & Kessler, K. (2006). The quest for ordinary lives: The integrated post-school vocational functioning of 50 workers with significant disabilities. *Research and Practice for Persons with Severe Disabilities*, 31, 93–121.

Grigal, M., Hart, D., Papay, C., Domin, D., & Smith, F. (2017). *Year one program data summary (2015–2016) from the TPSID model demonstration projects*. Boston, MA: University of Massachusetts Boston, Institute for Community Inclusion.

Grigal, M., Hart, D., Smith, F. A., Domin, D., Sulewski, J., & Weir, C. (2015). *Think College National Coordinating Center: Annual report on the transition and postsecondary programs for students with intellectual disabilities (2013–2014)*. Boston, MA: University of Massachusetts Boston, Institute for Community Inclusion.

Grigal, M., Hart, D., Smith, F. A., Domin, D., & Weir, C. (2017). *Think College National Coordinating Center: Annual report on the transition and postsecondary programs for students with intellectual disabilities (2014–2015)*. Boston, MA: University of Massachusetts Boston, Institute for Community Inclusion.

Grigal, M., Hart, D., & Weir, C. (2013). Postsecondary education for people with intellectual disability: Current issues and critical challenges. *Inclusion*, 1, 50–63. doi: 10.1352/2326-6988-1.1.050.

Kelley, K. R., & Prohn, S. M. (2018). Postsecondary and employment expectations of families and students with intellectual disability. *Journal of Inclusive Postsecondary Education*. Advanced online publication at https://kihd.gmu.edu/jipe/jipe-articles

Lobosco, K. (2017). Tuition-free college is getting bigger. Here's where it's offered. *CNN Money*. Retrieved from http://money.cnn.com/2017/05/16/pf/college/states-tuition-free-college/index.html

MacMillan, D. L. (1977). *Mental retardation in school and society*. Boston: Little, Brown & Company

Merisotis, J. (2016). Want to be happier and healthier? Then go to college. *Huffpost*. Retrieved from https://www.huffingtonpost.com/jamie-merisotis/want-to-be-happier-and-he_b_8288354.html

Moore, E. J., & Schelling, A. (2015). Postsecondary inclusion for individuals with an intellectual disability and its effects on employment. *Journal of Intellectual Disabilities, 19*, 130–148. doi: 10.1177/1744629514564448.

National Center for Educational Statistics (2017). *Fast facts: back to school statistics*. Retrieved from https://nces.ed.gov/fastfacts/display.asp?id=372

Papay, C. K., & Bambara, L. M. (2016), Best practices in transition to adult life for youth with intellectual disabilities. *Career Development and Transition for Exceptional Individuals, 37*, 136–148. doi: 10.1177/2165143413486693.

Ross, J., Marcell, J., Williams, P., & Carlson, D. (2013). Postsecondary education employment and independent living outcomes of persons with autism and intellectual disability. *Journal of Postsecondary Education and Disability, 26*, 337–351.

Test, D. W., Fowler, C. H., Richter, S. M., Mazzotti, V., White, J., Walker, A. R., . . . & Kortering, L. (2009). Evidence-based practices in secondary transition. *Career Development for Exceptional Individuals, 32*, 115–128. doi: 10.1177/0885728809336859.

Thoma, C. A., Lakin, K. C., Carlson, D., Domzal, C., Austin, K., & Boyd, K. (2011). Participation in postsecondary education for students with intellectual disabilities: A review of the literature 2001–2010. *Journal of Postsecondary Education and Disability 24*, 175–191.

Wehmeyer, M. L. (1992). Self-determination and the education of students with mental retardation. *Education and Training in Mental Retardation, 27*, 302–314.

Wehmeyer, M. L. (1996). Self-determination as an educational outcome: Why is it important to children, youth, and adults with disabilities. In D. J. Sands & M. L. Wehmeyer (eds.), *Self-determination across the life span: independence and choice for people with disabilities* (pp. 17–36). Baltimore, MD: Paul H. Brookes.

Westling, D. L. (1986). *Introduction to mental retardation*. Englewood Cliffs, NJ: Prentice-Hall, Inc.

3 Collaborating with University and Community Partners

Two important facts were pointed out in the first two chapters. In Chapter 1, we noted that about 95% of all colleges and universities *do not* offer postsecondary education (PSE) programs for students with intellectual disabilities (ID), and are not obliged to do so. Therefore, in order for these opportunities to develop and expand, colleges must recognize the importance of the programs and services they can provide. We then suggested some approaches that could be helpful in developing PSE programs for students with ID in colleges and universities.

In Chapter 2, when discussing the best candidates with ID to attend college programs, we discussed the importance of families and the necessity for collaborating with them in order for students with ID to be successful. We argued that the involvement and commitment of families is as important to the success of the individual as is the commitment of the student.

In this chapter, we will explain key higher education personnel relevant to developing and operating PSE programs, and their roles within a university. Again we will stress the importance of collaborating and engaging meaningfully with these individuals and their offices. We will also discuss important community agencies that are external to the college or university and how they can benefit PSE programs and students in them.

For transition to be effective, it is necessary for individuals and their agencies to bring their separate roles and resources together so the student with ID can achieve success within the program and after it is completed. University personnel must engage in their respective roles, and different community agencies should operate using a person-centered approach while the student is in the PSE program, and continue providing support after the PSE program as long as the individual is eligible for the agency's services. The PSE administrator, or a designated coordinator within the PSE program, should have the responsibility of organizing and involving representatives of the university and external community agencies in each student's PSE program.

Key Partners Inside the Institution

A typical university has central office administrators including a president or chancellor; a provost; vice-presidents or vice-chancellors; and directors along with their administrative support staff.[1] Each has a specific area of responsibility to maintain the functioning of the university: They oversee all of the institution's academic programs, deciding which to develop, continue or eliminate; manage the institution's finances and budget, deciding where and how to spend money; admit students and monitor their academic performance; facilitate student affairs in academic and non-academic activities; keep student records, including grades and transcripts; manage contracts and grants between the university and other agencies; manage the physical plant and the grounds; and solicit funds from donors. Running a university is not too different than running a town or small city.

Over the years, as we have operated our PSE program, we have made important contacts and connections with the individuals in central administration who have held various positions. Those who have been most significant to the operation of our program are discussed below. We think it is necessary for anyone developing or improving a PSE program for students with ID to establish positive relations with these individuals.

Chancellor (or president) and provost (or vice-president for academic affairs). These are the two individuals at the top of the administrative structure on a college or university campus. The chancellor or president is over all aspects of the institution, from academics to the physical structure, and is also the chief fundraiser on campus, a role that may require quite a bit of time. The provost (or vice-president for academic affairs) is directly under the chancellor or president and is in charge of all of the academic programs. They are the administrator over the deans and directors of the different colleges, centers, and institutes on campus.

It is necessary that these individuals formally approve of the PSE program, because without their approval, a PSE program cannot operate or even be on campus. Ideally they should be PSE program champions, but if not, they must at least approve of the program's presence on campus. Their backing, even though it may be passive, tacit, and without as much visibility, is essential. Usually they will not initiate a PSE program, and, in fact, initially they may not understand the purpose of the program or realize its value. But if they do not at least allow the program on campus, it will not develop, much less flourish. On the other hand, if a chancellor or provost supports a PSE program, they can do a great deal for it. Their support will send a message to the rest of the campus about the value of the program. Other key players on campus will know of their support and it will often open doors that might otherwise stay closed. Ultimately, they may also help with the funding and longevity of the program.

Director of admissions. This individual and their staff manage the university's application and admissions process, and are responsible for selecting students who will attend the university. The number of students enrolled in a college or university is often a key metric of the institution, and the director of admissions will have targets to achieve, including the number of applicants, the actual number of students enrolled, and the key quality indicators of these students (such as SAT scores and high school GPAs).

As we discussed in Chapter 2, students with ID cannot be admitted to a PSE program using the same criteria as used for other students (the admissions process we have used in the UP Program is discussed in Chapter 5). Nevertheless, PSE students must be formally admitted to the university, so collaboration with the director of admissions is necessary, even though their role in who is actually admitted may be more or less pro forma.

As a PSE program is being planned and developed, it is important that an admissions process be developed, such as the one we describe in Chapter 5, and the director of admissions must be engaged as a collaborator in the process. Once established, the role of this individual may be relatively minimal, but at least when a program is being developed, they must "sign on" to the arrangement. Whatever admissions process is ultimately developed, the director of admissions must agree to it, and usually will want it to align with, or be incorporated into, the existing admissions process.

Director of residential programs. Although there are still not too many, some PSE programs provide on-campus residencies for students with ID (or have this as an option), and we expect this to increase as programs continue to develop or expand. If a residential component is part of a PSE program, collaboration and agreements should be sought with the person who oversees these services on campus. This key partner can be critical in developing and operating a PSE program. Ultimately, while they may not be able to veto a program, controlling the residential component – whether embracing it, inhibiting it, or limiting it to a segregated location – will significantly affect the nature and quality of the program.

In our estimation, having students with ID live on campus in an inclusive residence hall, as we do in the UP Program, is an important part of their learning experience. Chapter 6 provides procedures for operating a fully inclusive residential program. Preliminarily, it is important for program developers to anticipate the issues that residential living personnel will raise. Most all of these will be about safety and liability. For example: Will students with ID living on campus be a danger to themselves or others? Will they be safe? Will they need extra supervision and, if so, who will provide it and pay for it? Will there be any special accommodations or provisions necessary for them? Having understandings and agreements with the person in charge of residential programs will be important if this option will be available to students with ID.

Director of disability support services (sometimes called accessibility resources). Because of Section 504 of the Rehabilitation Act of 1973 and the Americans with Disabilities Act (ADA), all colleges and universities receiving any amount of federal funding for any reason are required to provide access to individuals with disabilities to all institutional programs and activities. This means they must provide support and "reasonable accommodations" for persons with disabilities who self-identify (Association on Higher Education and Disability, 2018). Typically, under the direction of disability service professionals, all colleges or universities will provide support for students with learning disabilities, visual or hearing disabilities, and physical disabilities. But if the college or university has a PSE program, they must also provide support for students with ID in the program. In Chapter 6 and 7 we discuss some of the support that may be provided by the office of disability support services that will be helpful in campus residence halls and college classes.

The director of disability support services can be a significant ally for the development and operation of a PSE program, therefore it is a good idea for the PSE staff to know who this person is and what services they may provide. It is also important to know the limitations of their services. For example, they cannot require college instructors to modify the content of their courses for students with ID, or even to change their teaching style. However, they can help students with gaining access to the material through the provision of resources and different kinds of supports. Although not intended to support only students with ID or to operate PSE programs, they will often be helpful to the students with ID and the PSE program.

Director of financial aid. Some PSE programs are designated as "comprehensive transition and postsecondary programs" (or CTPs), a status created by the Higher Education Opportunity Act (HEOA) of 2008 to allow college students with ID to receive financial support. A college or university must apply to the U.S. Department of Education to become a CTP, a process that can be assisted by *Think College* (2018). When a PSE becomes a CTP, students in the program are eligible for Pell Grants, Federal Supplemental Educational Opportunity Grants, and Federal Work-Study programs.

If the PSE program is a CTP, all of the above sources of financial aid will be managed by the financial aid office. More importantly, it is necessary that this office, not the PSE program, submit the application to become a CTP. Of course input from the PSE staff about the nature of the program will be necessary, so it's important that a working relationship be established.

Although being a CTP and providing financial aid to students with ID will be a relatively small role for a financial aid office, it may be an extremely important one for students in a PSE program. We have found that many parents of students with ID did not begin to plan for college until their child was older. Therefore, financial aid is often important for them.

Deans. Universities are divided into separate colleges, such as Arts and Sciences, Engineering, Business, Education, Health and Human Services, etc. Like the university as a whole, each of these colleges has its own administrative personnel. The academic leader and administrator of a college is the dean. A dean is usually a tenured, senior faculty member who has elected to pursue an administrative role. They will answer to the provost or the vice-president for academic affairs, and be responsible for all academic and operational aspects of the college, usually including the college's budget. The dean must make or support a number of important decisions, such as how the college should be configured into different academic departments, what majors the college will offer, what courses will be taught at what time, who will be employed as faculty within the college, and how the college's allocated budget will be spent.

Deans can interface with PSE programs in different ways. They may convey the importance of the PSE program to their department heads and faculty members and encourage their involvement in it; highlight its purpose and function at faculty meetings; and encourage faculty members to support students with ID in their courses. In some cases, a dean may provide material support for the PSE program. For example, the college may be the administrative home of the program, may provide it with office space, resources, and materials; and may even provide funding for the program.

Department heads, chairs, and directors. Departments, schools, institutes, and centers may operate with their own administrator within a college, with the administrator answering to the dean. The most common of these is the academic department, such as English, Social Work, or Special Education, each with its own department head or chair. This individual will usually be a senior, tenured faculty member and will be the administrator over the faculty members within the department.

A department head or chair may serve for a fixed period of time, or may hold the position indefinitely, and will either be appointed by the dean (usually a head), or elected by the faculty (usually a chair). They will often control a departmental budget and make decisions about course scheduling, teaching assignments, and sometimes conduct faculty evaluations and determine faculty salaries. Sometimes departments will be clustered together into a school, and instead of each department having its own head or chair, the school will have a director who will answer to the dean. Sometimes colleges will also have institutes or centers that will have unique roles and they will also have their own director or administrator. Often these are entities that operate with external funding sources.

The department head or chair is the administrator closest to the faculty and the person most aware of and responsible for faculty activities. For this reason, department heads or chairs can be very influential in the success of a PSE program. They may know which faculty and courses might be best for students with ID, communicate directly and often with faculty members about the PSE program, and may collaborate with the PSE program in seeking external funding through contracts and grants. This may be important because, depending on the governance of the university, a PSE program may not be able to apply for external funding without an alliance with an academic program. Also, like a college, a department can offer financial and material support for a PSE program, such as providing a course release for a faculty member to work with the PSE program.

Faculty members. In most PSE programs, like the WCU UP program, students with ID enroll in college courses along with other college students. Often they are auditing courses, but in some cases will take the course for credit. In addition to these courses, they may take courses or lessons developed by the PSE program to meet their unique learning needs. In order to take regular college courses, and to be able to participate in them in a meaningful way, the course instructor, a faculty member in the college in which the course is offered, should agree to have the student in class and encourage their participation. If this is to be done well, the faculty member will have to develop some unique arrangements that they might not otherwise do for traditional students. We discuss these arrangements in Chapter 7, but the main point here is that it is important for the PSE staff to build and maintain positive relations with faculty members in order to facilitate the inclusion of students with ID in their courses. As relationships are built, it's helpful to know that research has shown that faculty members are generally accepting of students with ID as long as the students are not disruptive in class (Gibbons, Cihak, Mynatt, & Wilhoit, 2015).

Obviously, whether or not an individual faculty member is supportive of PSE programs and students with ID going to college will affect a student's success in a course offered by the faculty member. At WCU, over 95% of the faculty members we have approached to accept a UP student into one of their classes have done so. At this point in time, we have had nearly 160 faculty members on our campus accept UP students. We feel that this degree of success with faculty members is due to the following factors:

- Most importantly, we understand and respect the interest a faculty member has in their subject matter, and we encourage them to find ways to share critical course content with students with ID. We ourselves are faculty members (and have had students with ID in our courses), and we understand that the instructor is usually teaching a course about a subject they care about.
- We have adopted a policy of not "forcing" a faculty member to take a student with ID if they do not wish to do so. We think to do so would result in an ongoing battle and ultimately damage the program. As noted above, we have been very successful with this approach. Nevertheless, if a faculty member pushed back against us, we would not engage in an administrative or legal confrontation to have a student enrolled in the course. We think this could result in damage to the program.
- We communicate with the faculty member before the student enrolls, and we explain what will be required. We also listen to any concerns the faculty member has and address them as candidly

as possible. As the PSE program continues, issues and concerns among faculty are likely to diminish. But at the beginning, there may be a need in some cases for providing support for the faculty member.
- There must be clear requirements for the student with ID in the course, even though the student may not be expected to complete all usual course requirements. Requirements can be negotiated with the course instructor so they, the student with ID, and the PSE staff all have a clear expectation of the individualized course requirements. The intention of taking a course is so that the student will achieve as much knowledge as possible in the course, and the instructor needs to have a clear understanding of how this translates into course requirements.
- The involvement of a sizeable portion of the faculty, if not all faculty, is essential for the success of an inclusive PSE. Therefore, once a year we celebrate the faculty who have taught students in the UP Program (as well as employers who have hired them) by offering a luncheon and recognizing their contribution and giving an award to the "UP Faculty Member of the Year."

Support staff. Anyone who has worked in a college or university in any capacity understands the critical roles played by staff members. These individuals are responsible for providing administrative assistance at all levels, and for the day-to-day operation of all non-academic activities. They are like the musculoskeletal system of the body: They support the key organs and the life functioning of the institution.

Students in a PSE program and the PSE staff will interact with support staff in numerous ways and will benefit from the knowledge they have of their units or departments, and the administrators and faculty within them. Support staff may provide information about a wide variety of topics such as when a course might be offered, how to enroll in a course, when a faculty member has office hours, or when a particular facility opens or closes. Any encounter with a support staff person can be helpful, so good relations should always be maintained.

One of the main ways we have interacted with support staff is as employers for our UP students. As we discuss in Chapter 8, all of our students must be employed for at least ten hours per week every semester while they are on campus, or if not employed, they must be engaged in an internship. We support students in finding jobs in the local community and on campus, and our contacts for on-campus jobs are usually support staff. Their roles range from administrative assistant to the provost, to groundskeepers, to daycare providers. Knowing who are in these roles, having an idea about their responsibilities, and maintaining good relations with them helps to open doors and keep them open for various kinds of supports to our students.

Students. Going to college allows many learning opportunities, only some of which occur in a college classroom. As we discuss in Chapter 11, it is essential to the operation of a PSE program that a significant group of college students without disabilities provide support for the program and to the students in it. We explain how to recruit and manage these natural supports in Chapter 11, but here we point out the obvious: Students with ID and the PSE staff need to fit in well with the institution's student body.

Much of the interaction between students with and without disabilities will be a structured part of the PSE program, but much of it will not. We have conducted research that has shown that most students on campus are supportive of students with ID attending college, and the better they know them, the more supportive they are (Westling, Kelley, Cain, & Prohn, 2013). Other studies have reported similar findings (Gibbons et al., 2015; May, 2012). This is important for a couple of reasons. Most importantly it means that most universities need not reject the idea of a PSE program because of concerns about acceptance by other students. Second, it means that true and full inclusion of students with ID can be arranged and promoted. Whether structured or unstructured, this can provide an infinite number of learning opportunities for both students with and without disabilities. The settings in which personal interactions can occur include virtually all the settings on campus. Students in the UP Program routinely interact with other students in residence halls, classes, the university center, the recreational center, athletic events, sororities and fraternities, various student clubs, faith-based organizations, wilderness activities, and in the local community. Their constant interaction with other students improves their social behavior, their communication skills, their worldly knowledge, and mostly, their confidence to be included as a member of society.

Other key campus partners. As we said earlier, a university or college is much like a small town or city, so there are many potential partners we have not discussed. It is important to remember that students with ID in a PSE program are valid members of the student body. Therefore, they will have access to the same programs and services as other students. Some that are commonly present on campus and worth noting, knowing about, and interacting with are listed in Table 3.1.

Key Partners in the Community

It is important to remember that a PSE program is foremost a transition program. It is intended to serve as a springboard for launching individuals with ID from adolescence into community living during adulthood. The implication is that a PSE program cannot act without collaborating with community agencies, organizations, individuals, and businesses that will contribute to the transition process. Businesses can offer jobs in career areas that are of interest to PSE students and program graduates, and several community agencies have the responsibility, the resources, and the expertise to facilitate an inclusive life in the community. Therefore, the

Table 3.1 Other Key Campus Partners and Their Roles

Campus Partner or Department	Role or Potential Contribution(s)
Center for service learning	Assists with service learning activities and finding students to serve as natural supports/mentors
Code of community ethics administrators and staff	Informative about behavioral or ethical issues, such as the student code of conduct
Development or university foundations office	Understands fundraising and development to help a PSE program seek additional funding
Dining hall staff	Provides dietary modifications for eating disorders or food allergies. Can also provide some adapted eating utensils or modifications
Educational outreach/continuing education	Provides helpful resources for certifications and continuing education. Can also provide assistance with summer camps or offering continuing education units (CEUs)
Emergency services and public safety officers	Provides safety seminars and responds to emergencies
Facilities management	Improves physical accessibility and physical plant assistance
Health and human services academic departments	Provides speech, occupational or physical therapy diagnostic assessments and interventions
Health services/counseling staff	Provides health screenings, emergency medical services, and/or behavioral counseling
Legal services, grants and contracts	Knows and understands protocols for legal external contracts or grants with particular funding or liability issues
Office of public relations	Promotes program awareness, activities, successes, and upcoming events to media outlets in a systematic manner
Tutoring, career, and student success centers	Provides extra tutoring and support for academic and career success

PSE staff must develop and nurture relationships with various individuals and organizations outside of the university or college. The key community partners are described below.

Local businesses. It is necessary to establish partnerships with businesses so they can serve as employment sites while students are *in* the PSE program, and also *after* the program. As we discuss in Chapter 8, community employment should be one of the important outcomes of PSE programs, and this outcome will be more likely if students have had successful work experience while in the program. Therefore, we consider work experience to be an essential component of a PSE program. This means that when students are in the program, PSE staff must identify local businesses (as well as on-campus operations) that might serve as sites for part-time employment (or unpaid internships in some cases, as we discuss in Chapter 8).

We have found that most businesses are receptive to this idea of employing college students or graduates with ID if they have an employment need, and if the student is supported and supervised to the extent necessary. This is a responsibility that must be taken on by the PSE program. Developing a pool of local businesses and nurturing their commitment to supporting PSE students through job offerings should be an important goal for a PSE program.

Likewise, it is important to identify businesses in the student's post-program community so that as graduation approaches, communications with those businesses can take place and employment options determined. Ultimately the student must approach the business and apply for employment, but the program has a role in seeing that this occurs.

Vocational Rehabilitation. Vocational Rehabilitation (VR) is a state-level agency authorized by Congress that operates under the auspices of the Rehabilitation Services Administration (RSA), which regulates it and provides it with funding. The purpose of VR is to assist individuals with disabilities by funding services, such as education and training, that will help them find and keep jobs, preferably in a career of their choice. VR has funded some students in PSE programs, or in some cases, the programs themselves.

Every state has a VR division and a VR director, and every state has essentially the same charge as all other states. However, there is variation among states with regard to how VR operates and the different services they will fund for individuals with ID. Additionally, there may be variation *within* states between local VR offices, with counselors in some offices providing support for some services, but others in the same state not supporting these services.

Many students with ID will be eligible for VR services, and many will already have a VR counselor when they enter the PSE program. Others may come into the PSE program without VR funded services, but may be eligible for them. In the former case, a PSE staff member will need to establish contact with the VR counselor and invite them to become a participating member of the student's college experience. In the latter case, a PSE staff member should contact the local VR office to determine if a new student may be eligible for VR services.

It will be beneficial to both PSE students and the PSE program if VR will provide funding for all or part of a student's PSE program, or fund a portion of the entire program. Although relationships with VR state and local offices may be difficult to navigate, if a student is eligible for funding, it will clearly be a benefit to the student and the program. Therefore, VR should be considered an essential partner for most PSE programs.

Benefits counselors. Because of their disability, students with ID may receive public benefits, including one or more of the following based on their eligibility: Social Security, Supplemental Security Income (SSI), Social Security Disability Insurance (SSDI), and Medicaid and/or Medicare. They may also be eligible for state benefits, which of course vary from state to state. These public benefits are intended to prevent individuals from becoming destitute because of their disability, and in this regard, they are helpful. But they carry with them several disadvantages. Mainly they may serve as a disincentive for a regular life that includes working, earning a living wage, living where and with whom one wishes, saving money, owning personal property like a car, and so on (Nord & Nye-Lengerman, 2015). Many families will be concerned that if their son or daughter is employed, they will lose these benefits.

Because of this concern, PSE programs should develop an association with benefits counselors who can provide accurate information to their students and the students' families. Benefits counselors can provide information about what is allowable in terms of income, savings, and ownership; and how a person may retain key benefits while still pursuing typical life outcomes. One source of benefits counseling is the Work Incentives Planning and Assistance Program (WIPA) provided by the Social Security Administration (North Carolina Council on Developmental Disabilities, 2016). This program has benefits counselors in regional areas of a state who can provide information about the benefits of employment and dispel the myths about working. The services are free, but there are a limited number of counselors.

Public transportation. Being able to find and use public transportation is an essential need for individuals with ID to live in the community. Therefore, developing knowledge of the public transportation system available to students while they are in the PSE program and after they complete the program will be important. This may include campus transit, public buses, door-to-door transit, taxis, and app-based rides. Students should learn to use these systems while enrolled in the PSE program, and should plan to use similar systems when living in their post-program community. This implies that the PSE staff should be familiar with systems in both locations that a student will need to use. Important information that should be acquired by the PSE staff include routes, schedules, fees and how to pay, stops, and accessibility. This information is usually available online or by calling the transportation agency.

LME/MCOs and community service agencies. Many persons with ID will be eligible for different kinds of services supported by funding through Home and Community Based Services (HCBS) Medicaid waivers. Funding is for services such as providing assistance in the person's home, or various services in the community, and may include services while participating in a PSE program. In many states, these funds are distributed by the state and managed by local management entities/managed care organizations (LME/MCOs). An LME/MCO has the responsibility of determining a person's eligibility for different types of support, and how many weekly hours of support or funding is available to the person. However, this funding is not an entitlement, and states typically have long waiting lists for persons with disabilities and their families seeking the Medicaid waiver support.

The LME/MCO does not directly provide services. Instead, the person with ID and their family may select and employ an eligible community service agency, or a community rehabilitation provider, to provide the service. This agency is then paid by the LME/MCO to provide the service for the eligible individual. This arrangement separates the funding from the service and allows more self-determination.

For several reasons, PSE programs should become familiar with the LME/MCOs and the community service agencies in their area, especially those providing services to any of their students. Students with ID may bring services with them into the PSE program, and these services may improve the chances of the student participating in and being successful in the PSE program. In some cases, PSE personnel may communicate with the LME/MCO (along with the student and the family) to seek approval for certain services while the student is in the program. In our own UP Program, one community service agency, with funding from our local LME/MCO, employed and trained some of our undergraduate students to provide direct services to UP students on campus. This arrangement was helpful as it allowed the UP Program to save funds it would have had to otherwise spend to support the students.

As students with ID are completing the PSE program, and moving into a post-program community, potential funding from an LME/MCO and services from one or more community agencies should be explored. Although the student and their family must make contact and apply for funding and services, the PSE program should be aware of the potential for funding and services in order to help prepare for community life after the PSE program.

Other community partners. In addition to the above, other partnerships may also be beneficial to the PSE program and the students with ID and their families. These partnerships may be initially established while students are in the program, and continue after the conclusion of the program.

- **Family support networks** are informal connections between the families of individuals with ID. Through these networks, past and present PSE students' family members may provide information, suggestions, ideas, and mentoring to each other.
- **Other colleges and schools** may be useful allies for PSE programs. Interactions with other PSEs can provide useful insights about funding, organization, research, and other mutual interests.
- **Advocacy organizations** should also be allies for both PSE programs and programs' students and their families. These organizations may be active at the local, state, and national level. Some that we have interacted with have included our state Developmental Disabilities Council, our state Postsecondary Education Alliance, our state University Center of Excellence in Developmental Disabilities (UCEDD), the Arc, Disability Rights, and TASH.

Principles for Building Successful Collaborative Partnerships

From the beginning of Western Carolina University's UP Program, we have tried to build collaborative relationships at every opportunity, both within and outside of the university. We firmly believe that the more we collaborate with other key individuals, organizations, and agencies, the more our program and its students will benefit. Collaboration has allowed us to bring a better educational program and support services to our students, has led to more sources of support, and has given us greater visibility in our community and beyond. All of this has resulted in a more stable program with a greater promise of longevity. As we have developed and nourished partnerships, we have abided by the following principles:

- **Transparency:** We have an open door and open window policy, and are always available for ongoing communication. Anyone and everyone can see our program, our operational procedures, and our values at work.
- **Trust and integrity:** We communicate honestly, say what we mean and mean what we say. We want people to like us, but more, we want people to believe and trust us.
- **Dependability:** We want to have a seat at the table with many different people and their agencies, ready to develop new opportunities and partnerships. We have learned that there will be some concern, even urgency, with having students with ID on a college campus and we want everyone to know that we are readily accessible.
- **Openness:** We know we have brought a new social and educational enterprise to a traditional university setting, and there will be no quick end to the discussions and questions about doing this. We accept the need to explain what we do and why, to resolve conflicts, and to make changes if there are valid reasons to do so.

- **Efficiency:** A college campus is always busy. Administrators, faculty, staff, and students are always moving quickly and working overtime. So we try to avoid increasing their workload, and avoid creating "special" or new systems when we can use those that already exist. Increasing the workload of another individual or office without providing additional financial resources is never popular.
- **Celebration:** We take time to celebrate successes together, and we are always eager to give credit to those who support us, so we can celebrate the diversity and inclusion we bring to campus.
- **Proactiveness:** By their nature, PSE programs carry associated risks. Therefore, it is important for programs to know about these risks, own them, and try to manage them.
- **Accept feedback and criticism:** No one has everything figured out; everyone can improve. So we ask for feedback and address the issues we need to address.
- **Think OUTSIDE the box:** Staying inside the box never created a successful, inclusive PSE program . . . or much else, for that matter. We try to always stay open to a different way of thinking and doing things, and never look at the need for change as a sign of failure or an inadequate program.

Final Thoughts

It seems we are at a point in history when the purpose and nature of higher education is changing. Up until the last half of the 20th century, higher education was only available for a relatively elite group of people. Mostly it was an opportunity that was passed down from one generation to the next. It was how society developed its doctors, lawyers, professors, and ministers, and it was mostly an endeavor for white males, and for the well-heeled and well-to-do. This began to change after World War II when the GI Bill (or the Servicemen's Readjustment Act) was passed in 1944. Because of the available funding, this law allowed regular citizens who were now military veterans to afford a college education. As we moved forward into later generations, many of the children of these veterans saw college as an expectation, and so the ranks of colleges and universities continued to swell. Then, the civil rights era of the 1950s, 1960s, and 1970s led to more minority individuals having access to college. And currently, as we pointed out at the beginning of this chapter, women and minorities are now matriculating at a greater rate than ever before, even outpacing traditional students from yesteryear. And more than ever before, college is being seen as a necessary educational undertaking for a successful life.

We think going to college is also an important part of the total educational experience for young adults with ID. Like other college students, they are at a point in their lives where they have acquired their most mature level of intelligence, and are ready to move forward into adulthood. They usually have ideas about what they want in life and are looking for a path to achieve their dreams and wishes. College offers that path.

But there is no doubt that being a college student with ID pushes the boundaries of who should attend college more than has ever occurred before. It is not an outlandish concept, but it is still one that will strike some people as at least unusual. For this reason, it is important that many partnerships be formed and nourished. More partners mean better understanding, more success, greater stability, and more longevity. Our experience has been that there will be a few barriers and roadblocks, but that over time, these will diminish. Interestingly, this has been found to be the case in most PSE programs (Plotner & Marshall, 2015).

Note

1 Position titles may vary across institutions.

References

Association on Higher Education and Disability (2018). *Access and accommodations*. Retrieved from https://www.ahead.org/professional-resources/accommodations

Gibbons, M. M., Cihak, D. F., Mynatt, B., & Wilhoit, B. E. (2015). Faculty and student attitudes toward postsecondary education for students with intellectual disabilities and autism. *Journal of Postsecondary Education and Disability*, 28, 149–162.

May, C. (2012). An investigation of attitude change in inclusive college classes including young adults with an intellectual disability. *Journal of Policy and Practice in Intellectual Disabilities*, 9, 240–246.

Nord, D., & Nye-Lengerman, K. (2015). The negative effects of public benefits on individual employment: A multilevel analysis of work hours. *Intellectual and Developmental Disabilities*, 53, 308–318. doi: 10.1352/1934-9556-53.4.308.

North Carolina Council on Developmental Disabilities (2016). *Disability benefits counseling first!* Retrieved from https://www.nccdd.org/disability-benefits-counseling.html

Plotner, A. J., & Marshall, K. J. (2015). Postsecondary education programs for students with an intellectual disability: Facilitators and barriers to implementation. *Intellectual and Developmental Disabilities*, 53, 58–69.

Think College (2018). *Requirements of comprehensive transition programs*. Retrieved from https://thinkcollege.net/think-college-learn/comprehensive-transition-programs/requirements-comprehensive-transition-programs

Westling, D. L., Kelley, K. R., Cain, B., & Prohn, S. (2013). College students' attitudes about an inclusive postsecondary education program for individuals with an intellectual disability. *Education and Training in Autism and Developmental Disabilities*, 48, 306–319.

4 Funding, Staffing, and Program Sustainability

While all PSE programs may operate differently, funding and staffing are essential elements for any program. Notwithstanding the rare event of receiving a significant endowment, there are several challenges associated with achieving adequate financial standing. First, in most states, there is no line item funding for PSE programs within the budgets of colleges or universities. Unlike the English or Chemistry Department, most institutions do not have traditional commitments to PSE programs, so usually there is not a set amount in budgets earmarked for these programs. This does not mean the institution could not seek such funding, but generally top–down funding is rare.

Second, the enrollment of students with ID in a PSE program is often limited. For example in the UP Program, we only enroll eight students at a given time. This means that when funding is sought, either internally or externally, the funding source will inevitably ask why there are relatively few students. So even if an institution were to fund a program based on the number of students served, funding would likely be very limited. And finally, given the limited staff that we and most programs have, investing in the time and effort to seek funding, for example through writing grants and working with the university's development office, is usually not sufficient to achieve a significant financial goal.

As we have faced these challenges, we have operated on a few key principles that affect our finances. First, our primary goal has been to avoid placing an extraordinary financial burden on our families and students. Most families of students with ID are not wealthy, and many have not included college savings within their budgets. Second, however, we have recognized that no student can attend the university or our PSE program without paying, and therefore normal tuition and fees can be charged. We also have recognized the need, and believe it is fair, to charge for costs related to the individualized planning and support required for students with ID. Third, we have attempted to constantly demonstrate the value of our PSE program, not only in terms of how it impacts individuals, but how it can be leveraged to help us pursue external funding related to its existence. This has allowed us to argue that the program has fundamental financial value to the university. Finally, and most importantly, we have realized that at least for the present, adequate funding for our PSE program must come from multiple sources, a process often referred to as "braided funding." Even though there are financial challenges, we have found some strategies that have led to relative financial stability and allowed us to achieve an adequate staffing arrangement. This chapter proposes the utility of these strategies to maintain PSE programs. We begin by reviewing a brief history of our own funding.

A Brief History of UP Program Funding

Western Carolina University's (WCU's) University Participant (UP) Program has become an integral part of the WCU campus since the program began in 2007. Annually, the two-year program directly affects eight students with ID who are living on campus and enrolled in classes, and indirectly affects another 200+ undergraduate students, most of whom provide natural support to the UP students as unpaid volunteers in service learning courses. Within this group, a relatively small subset of approximately 20 undergraduates are paid hourly or through stipends to perform more extensive duties in the program.

Since its initiation, the UP program has operated with funding from different sources. After the program began in 2007 with zero funding for one student, it was vitalized with external funding over a five-year period (2010–2015), and is currently maintained primarily with internal funding provided by the university. Table 4.1 provides a list of the external funding grants received by the program.

When the first student began in what was referred to as a "pilot program," there were zero dollars allocated to support the program. Subsequently, as shown in Table 4.1, external grants and gifts were received, with the largest coming from the U.S. Department of Education as a $2.5 million grant for the period of 2010 to 2015. We received this funding to "expand and enhance" the UP Program as a model-demonstration project. During this time, the program was operated entirely through this source of external funding.

Subsequent to grant funding, support for the UP Program has been provided by WCU and our College of Education and Allied Professions (CEAP) to cover three recurring components of the program: (1) a 0.75 full-time equivalency (FTE) faculty position who serves as program co-director and coordinator; (2) a 1.0 FTE employee who serves both as an administrative assistant and employment support specialist; and (3) a small amount of operational funding (approximately $55,000) used primarily to support the paid natural supports, printing, telephone, travel, and any other operational needs. Additionally, the program benefits from the assignment of up to three graduate assistants (10–20 hours per week) and typically one undergraduate-level intern from a variety of campus

Table 4.1 Funding for the WCU UP Program: 2007–2018

2007–2010: No significant funding.

2010–2013: Funding through the Walmart Foundation in partnership with the Arc of Haywood County ($100,000 per year for three years).

2010–2015: TPSID grant from the U.S. Department of Education, Office of Postsecondary Education ($2,500,000 for five years, 25% match).

2011–2013: Small gifts and donations from private donors used for student scholarships ($19,500).

2015–2018: Recurring university funds for course release for faculty, staffing, and program operations (approximately $180,000 per year).

---

programs (i.e., Psychology, Communication Sciences and Disorders, Social Work, Higher Education Student Affairs).

As implied previously, since the program began, UP students have paid tuition and fees at the same rate as all other traditional undergraduate students, including tuition for the courses which they audit, and fees for on-campus housing, meal plans, and student activities. Initially, much of this cost was reimbursed to students through a partnership with Vocational Rehabilitation (VR) and also through some community foundation scholarships. More recently, families have been responsible for more costs as VR has curtailed its support.[1] Unfortunately, at this time, there is no financial mechanism for these funds to come directly to the UP Program.

The total cost to attend the UP program for one year is between $17,000 and $21,000, depending on the cost of tuition for a different number of credit hours taken, required student activity fees, residence hall cost, and the meal plan selected. Out-of-state students pay up to $12,000–$14,000 more per year. The cost also includes a UP student support fee of $2,500 per semester to cover individualized support and program operational costs.

According to Martinez and Queener (2010), some PSE programs for students with ID charge in the neighborhood of $30,000 to $50,000 per year *beyond* the standard institutional cost of attendance. Based on this information and on our own investigations into other programs, we have concluded that our costs are quite reasonable and might be considered a "fair cost" by institutions wishing to begin a program, or consumers pursuing a program. Although many parents did not plan or save for their children with ID to attend college, many are willing to explore various ways to pay for this experience but parents must realize that there is a great deal of variability in costs, as is true for all college expenses.

Options for Budgets and Staffing

As with personal finances, we tend to make things work with what we have. This has also been the case with UP Program operation. As discussed above, we have had rather robust budgets from grant funds, but have also learned to operate on reduced budgets. When asked the question of what it takes to operate a PSE program, our answer is usually, "How much do you have?"

For a PSE program similar in size and nature to the UP Program, that is, a program of about eight students with ID, who are fully included and living on campus, and with a substantial volunteer pool of around 200 undergraduate students per semester, a budget of between $200,000 and $400,000 per year is probably required.

A Minimum Budget vs. a Dream Budget

In Table 4.2, an approximation of the current UP Program budget is shown, which is close to $200,000. This rather minimum budget provides for essential positions and expenses that we cannot do without if we are to operate the program as is described throughout this book. What is not shown in the figure is the "sweat equity" required for the program to operate, including a great deal of voluntary work by students, uncompensated work by faculty and staff, and volunteer work by current and former parents, former students, and friends of the UP Program. Within our program, we have used creative planning and collaborative partnerships for operating the program, have been conservative in the use of funds, and have often found ways to do things with very little or no cost.

If we were able to have all the funds we would like to operate our program, we would have a staffing pattern and corresponding budget such as is shown in Table 4.3, which is our "dream budget." Here we show the personnel positions and other expenses that might be funded with a

Table 4.2 Minimum Budget for Program Operation and Staffing

- **Program Director and Coordinator ($60,000).** 75% release time to serve as program administrator and manage day-to-day operations. Assumes the individual has a current faculty or staff position requiring a master's or doctoral degree.
- **Administrative Support Associate/Employment Specialist ($55,000):** Manages budget, office organization, and payroll of part-time employees; facilitates employment details and training on job sites, requires an associate or bachelor's degree.
- **Paid Natural Supports ($60,000):** Undergraduate students who work 10–15 hours per week.
- **Suitemates or residential support stipends ($14,000):** Four suitemates per semester.
- **Academic in-class supports ($5,000):** Helps with class accommodations, projects, and homework.
- **Other expenses ($6,000):** Emergency cell phone ($800), travel ($3,000), scheduling software ($1,000), postage, printing, advertisements ($1,200).

Note: Figures include estimated salaries and benefits.

52 Preliminary Considerations

Table 4.3 Dream Budget for Staffing and Program Operation

- **Program Director ($10,000):** 25% course release time per semester to focus on fiscal management and research.
- **Program Coordinator ($60,000):** Manages day-to-day operations, requires at least a master's degree.
- **Administrative Support Associate ($40,000):** Manages budget, office organization, customer service, and payroll of part-time employees, requires an associate's degree.
- **Career Development Coordinator ($45,000):** Manages all employment details and training on job sites, requires an associate's or bachelor's degree.
- **Faculty Liaison/Researcher ($53,000):** Manages academic aspects of the program, coordination of assignments with faculty and academic supports; manages research and accommodation needs in correlation with disability services personnel, requires at least a master's degree.
- **Graduate Assistant ($10,000):** To help with scheduling, university connections, research and dissemination efforts. One GA at 20 hours per week, or two GAs at 10 hours per week.
- **Suitemates or residential support stipends ($14,000):** Four suitemates per semester.
- **Academic in-class supports ($5,000):** Helps with class accommodations, projects, and homework.
- **Paid Natural Supports ($59,300):** Undergraduate students who work 10–15 hours per week.
- **Community Facilitator ($45,000):** Supports post-program community employment and living for at least one year after the program. Requires at least an associate's degree.
- **Marketing/Videographer/Social Media/Outreach ($50,000):** Responsible for highlighting success stories for public relations and recruitment. Requires a bachelor's degree.
- **Other expenses ($8,700):** Staff cell phone and office phones ($1,500), travel to conferences and meetings ($5,000), scheduling software and educational subscriptions ($1,000), postage, printing, advertisements ($1,200).

Note: Figures include estimated salaries and benefits.

budget in the neighborhood of around $400,000 per year. This is a little more than about twice our current budget (as shown in Table 4.2), but it is based on the kinds of needs we have wished for and worked for over the years. And, if we were asked to start a program from the ground up, this would be the figure we would request.

Essential Positions

Program director and coordinator. Table 4.2 includes positions that are essential to operating a PSE program. At the very least, we have found there has to be an individual who serves as both the chief executive officer (CEO) and the chief operating officer (COO) of the program, and this position must be full-time or nearly full-time. This person serves as the "hub" for the team and must have a broad view of the organization and activities of the program. While CEO/COO must be "hands-on" to complete many of the program's activities, they must also be able to delegate tasks to others. In the UP Program, this individual, the senior author, is a tenured faculty member who is allowed to contribute 75% of their time to the program.

Administrative support associate/employment specialist. On the right hand of the director/coordinator, wearing two hats, is the administrative support associate/employment specialist, the only full-time person completely devoted to UP Program duties. As shown in Table 4.2, this individual manages all the business issues of the program and also works directly with the UP students as they oversee the employment training component of the program. As shown in the "dream budget" in Table 4.3, this person's duties could be divided into two separate positions. This would probably be necessary for a program that was at the beginning stages.

Paid student supports. Although it is possible to have unpaid students provide much support, in some cases, the nature of the support and the degree of commitment make paying a small group of students a wise investment. Therefore, as shown in Table 4.2, we employ a small percentage of paid natural supports per year to provide 10–15 hours of support per week. These individuals assume significant roles in the program, often serving at times and in ways for which other undergraduate students are unavailable or unable to do. They are often responsible for more sensitive tasks such as job coaching, homework support, and sometimes personal hygiene or residential care needs. They are paid an hourly wage slightly above minimum wage.

Another need in the budget is for suitemates or residential support students. These individuals are also undergraduate students who are housed in the residence halls near the UP students and are responsible for being present throughout the night in case a UP student requires support. Typically we have three to four suitemates per semester depending on the level of support needs with incoming UP students. Finally, as the budget in Table 4.2 shows, we spend a small amount of funds to employ undergraduate students as in-class supports to assist students with the academic component of the program.

We hire undergraduate students using a variety of funding sources. Some are paid through funds provided to the program by the university, as is noted in Table 4.2. Others are paid using work study funds because they qualify for these funds and our program is authorized to employ them. As discussed below, other students are hired with Medicaid waiver funds and are technically employees of a community service provider, but are providing direct support to our PSE students.

Unpaid student supports. One essential position we have relied greatly on is our unpaid student supports. Obviously, we cannot include these students in our budget, so we recruit them using different approaches. We have found that students in special education, recreational therapy, communication sciences and disorders, psychology, or social work fields eagerly jump into our program for the hands-on experience it provides.

After students start supporting the students in the UP Program, sometimes as a required activity, they often remain for several semesters and tell their friends about their experiences. This word-of-mouth support helps build our pool of natural supports and increases overall community awareness about our program (see Chapter 11).

Supplemental Positions

Beyond the above "essential positions," there are a few other individuals we have sought out to provide important services to the program but have not included them in our minimum budget. When funding is available, we have offered these individuals small contracts or stipends. When it is not, we have asked them to volunteer, or have asked someone else to provide support for them.

Parent mentor. Over the past several years we have contracted with a former UP student's parent to serve as a parent mentor. This individual has successfully transitioned her son from the UP program back into the community, and is very familiar with the challenges of being a parent while a student is in the UP Program and afterward, and how to deal with them.

The parent mentor attends open house events, coordinates and facilitates parent meetings, sends parents information and resources that can help them help their son or daughter be successful, and is available for individual consultation and discussions with parents. Having a parent provide such services is not only a way to reduce the burden on PSE staff, but also provides a perspective that cannot be offered by professionals. This position is a good investment for supporting parents and families and can help create high expectations for the students with ID before, during, and after the program.

Graduate assistants (GAs). GAs are funded by grant funds and/or by different academic departments. When we have had grant funds, we have been able to employ GAs to provide different, specific services within our program. We have also benefitted from GAs coming from other academic departments that have dedicated one or more GAs to support our program. We have used GAs from related academic fields to help with program operations, outreach, orientation camps, research, and data collection. This is often a win-win arrangement for all involved: The PSE program benefits from the service, the GA benefits from the experience, and the academic department contributes to the PSE program.

Faculty liaison/researcher. This position was originally funded by the TPSID grant, but more recently the duties have been managed by the project director/coordinator. The role of a faculty liaison is to work with faculty, in-class supports, and students with ID in order to make sure the academic component of the program is functioning as well as possible. A person in this position should be familiar with principles of Universal Design for Learning (UDL) and be able to assist faculty members to make their course more accessible to students with ID. The research part of this position allows a PSE program to collaborate with other universities on activities such as program development, data collection, outreach, and recruitment efforts to continue to promote policy changes at local, state, and federal levels.

Identifying Effective PSE Program Personnel

As noted above, there are several important roles and responsibilities necessary for successfully operating a PSE program. It is important to realize that some roles can be more sensitive than others, and this should be taken into consideration in the hiring process.

We have found that many PSE positions require well-developed interpersonal skills, problem-solving abilities, self-sufficiency, and the potential to build positive relationships among key campus and community stakeholders. PSE personnel will often be required to interact with university administrators and faculty, employers, family members, community service providers, undergraduate and graduate students, and, of course, students with ID. Sometimes, employee roles may change within a program requiring increased personal flexibility. The roles given to PSE personnel can also change based on team members' strengths and weaknesses.

We have learned that job descriptions can be written, interviews can occur, hiring decisions can be made, and then at some point, unique strengths of an individual will be realized. In such cases, we have not been afraid to shift some roles around to improve our work as a team. Ultimately, no matter what title or position someone has, the students and program should continually remain at the forefront of any decisions made about personnel.

Creating Partnerships and Using Braided Funding

Over the years, we have found several ways to expand or maximize financial partnerships to benefit the program and/or the students and their families. These arrangements are discussed in the following sections. Because our financial resources must be drawn from different funding buckets, we refer to this as "braided funding." Many PSE programs today use this arrangement successfully. As this is done, however, it is often important to keep in mind the source of different funds and how the funds may and may not be used.

Funding through Internal Partnerships

Approval as a comprehensive transition postsecondary (CTP) program. The reauthorization of the Higher Education Opportunity Act (2008) allowed us and other PSE programs to become an approved *comprehensive transition postsecondary (CTP)* program, a status which all PSE programs for students with ID may pursue. Having the CTP status means that students with ID, even though they are not degree-seeking students, are eligible to receive a Pell Grant, Federal Supplemental Educational Opportunity Grants, and Federal Work-Study support.

At this time, the Federal Student Aid office located in the U.S. Department of Education (USDOE) has approved 93 programs as eligible CTPs. To be a CTP, PSE programs must meet certain eligibility requirements including the following: (1) they must be offered by a college or career school approved by the USDOE, (2) designed to support students with ID as they prepare for gainful employment, (3) be a program that provides academic advising and a structured curricula, and (4) require students with ID to participate for at least half of their academic and internship courses with their non-disabled peers (see https://studentaid.ed.gov/sa/eligibility/intellectual-disabilities).

Many of our students have benefitted from Pell Grant support and have been employed as work-study students.

Development office. Nowadays, virtually all colleges and universities have offices of development (or advancement) responsible for pursuing scholarships, endowments, or other financial gifts. This office can be a helpful partner to a PSE program for soliciting and accommodating donors interested in supporting progressive programs for individuals with ID. Funding can often be used either for program operations or for student scholarships.

Because many traditional scholarships require degree-seeking students, this requirement can be an unintended obstacle that limits the number of scholarships available for students with ID. Therefore, partnering with this office can allow for a specific focus on fundraising events or activities to help provide supplemental scholarship support to students in PSE programs. Further, as families and other friends of our program have expressed interest in helping with current or future program needs, or supporting students with scholarships, we have found that by having a designated account through this office, we can offer them an avenue to exercise their financial generosity.

When soliciting funds, the more transparent a program can be related to its needs and how funds will be used, the better. For this reason, we have tried to clearly communicate to potential donors suggested levels of giving and how funds will be used. Table 4.4 displays how contributions of various amounts could be applied to program and student costs.

Contracts and grants office. Another potential source of funding is federal, state, and foundation grants. It is often helpful to work with a college's or university's contracts and grants office to seek funding opportunities, prepare applications, and manage successfully funded projects. Like the development offices, the contracts and grants office

Table 4.4 Suggested Levels of Giving and Associated Program Costs

---

$100,000: Provides program operating costs for one year.
$50,000: Employs a faculty liaison/researcher or employment personnel for one year.
$20,000: Provides full support (including tuition and fees) for one UP student for one year.
$10,000: Supports one graduate assistant to provide program support for one year.
$5,000: Supports one undergraduate student to serve as a program scheduler for one year.
$1,000: Supports one live-in suitemate for a UP student for one year.
Suggested levels of giving for endowment support (payable over multiple years)
$1,000,000: Provides $50,000 per year.
$500,000: Provides $25,000 per year.
$100,000: Provides $5,000 per year.
$50,000: Provides $2,500 per year.
$25,000: Provides $1,250 per year.

---

can be helpful in locating and applying for funds. A significant difference, however, is that most contracts or grants are not gifts, but require specific activities be conducted for the acquired funding, such as training personnel or producing materials. As contracts or grants are sought, programs should keep in mind the need for the funded project to be able to pay for itself, as well as bring some benefit to the program. Income is good, but some income isn't enough to cover expenses.

Funding through External Partnerships

Medicaid waivers. As mentioned above, one way we have found to employ student supports is through partnerships with community service providers who offer services using Medicaid waiver funds. This process involves an agreement with the service provider in which they employ our undergraduate students to provide services to PSE students with ID and be paid for doing so with Medicaid waiver funds. The provided services have included community networking (for participating in courses), supported employment (for jobs or internships while in the program), supported living services (for independent living skills), and personal assistance (to assist with personal hygiene and similar daily living skills).

Medicaid is a joint federal–state partnership, and funds are managed within the states, often through local management entities (LMEs) or health maintenance organizations (HMOs). The state and the LME/HMO define the nature of services and determine for whom services may be provided. In many states, acquiring Medicaid waivers to support persons with ID living in the community can be very helpful, but requires navigating a complex system. Because the waiver funds require certain eligibility criteria be met, not all PSE students will qualify. But for those who have qualified, we have been able to use these funds to help with our support costs for some students while they attend college.

Medicaid waiver funds have aided many UP students and graduates in acquiring supports while in the program and as they move back into homes and jobs in their own community. One of our recent graduates now living in his own apartment and working full-time in the community received Medicaid waiver support to provide various home and community-based services.

Vocational Rehabilitation. As with Medicaid waivers, each state has a Vocational Rehabilitation (VR) office and regional offices and counselors distributed around the state. VR uses its funds to support persons with disabilities to achieve employment. Some state VR offices will fund items such as tuition, meal plan, room and board, assistive technology, glasses, hearing aids, driving assessments, and books, but others will offer more limited funding, depending on state and local policies. Although we have experienced variation with VR funding allotted, the funding has been a good source of support for some students, usually providing partial or full tuition.

Accessing VR support while in college can also help the student transition back to the community. Having a VR counselor while a student often allows the student, family, PSE staff, and the VR counselor to map out long-term support and employment opportunities when the students return to the community. As students graduate, if they have established a relation with VR while in college, it may be easier to receive support for employment and related services, such as transportation, when they are back in the community.

Achieving Sustainability

When the UP Program began, initially with no funding and no assigned personnel, we referred to it as a pilot program. Later, when we received grant funds, it was called a grant project. Today, it is called one of the "gems" of Western Carolina University, and is a fully accepted and valued program by virtually everyone in the university community. Perhaps more importantly, it has been financially supported internally for several years.

Many PSE programs have started in a similar way. They were proposed and developed by a few key people, were started with grant funding or some other special source of funding, and they have managed to find an accepted place in the host university or college. For the UP Program, and for other PSE programs, though, continuity was never guaranteed, and still may not be. For many, sustaining the program beyond its initial start-up has been and continues to be a concern.

When the UP Program was funded with a TPSID grant for a five-year period, we realized we had succeeded in designing a legitimate program, but we also realized for the program to succeed, we would need to launch an ongoing public relations campaign. And so we did, beginning on day one. Ten key efforts we made to sustain the program are presented below.

1. Become a successful program. We first determined the values that would guide our program, and then we worked hard to implement practices based on the values. We wanted our students to be fully included, participate in the academic and social environment of the university, and learn to work on jobs of their choice in a competitive environment. We sought people to work with us who had the same values and who shared our passion about offering a high-quality program, regardless of the effort required. We made a commitment to the program, and we made every effort to live up to that commitment.

2. Be visible and be a good citizen. We forged paths into every nook and cranny of the institution. Our staff and our students were in classes, in residence halls, in the dining halls, in clubs and organizations, and in offices throughout the university. If we realized there was an area we had not been in, we found a way to get there. One of our early successes was placing a UP student as a work-study student in the provost's office. Throughout our presence in various locations, we placed great emphasis on the demonstration of appropriate social behavior and how to fit into existing social structures.

3. Avoid becoming a liability. But there were doubters and those who questioned the appropriateness of our presence. We had a sense that some were waiting for us to make a mistake, and in fact we were once told that we were one mistake away from being kicked off campus. Although that is probably not true today, it probably was true when the program began. As much as we cringed at the thought, we knew that we could not afford to put the program in jeopardy because of careless or dangerous events.

4. Fit into the existing system. As both a philosophical and practical matter, we have avoided having the term "special" attached to our program. In as many ways as possible, we have used and worked within existing university structures and policies. The benefit of this strategy is that key players in the university recognize our program and operate their offices with consideration of our program and its students. This means we don't have to constantly explain who we are, what we are, or why we are here.

5. Focus on relationships. In a healthy relationship, all participants benefit. When we place students in classes, or in work settings, or in social organizations, we want the key individuals who are helping to make the placement successful to benefit from it as much as we and our students benefit. We reinforce and celebrate their involvement, give them praise, present them with awards, and make sure there is a broad audience that appreciates their efforts. This is not to say that they work with us for this recognition, but it no doubt helps to forge a strong, symbiotic bond.

6. Look for and reinforce champions. And from such bonds, we often develop program champions, including administrators, faculty, staff, and students, who are happy to stand up and tout the merits of our program . . . and say we are a "gem" of the university. Among our greatest champions have been some of the leaders of our student body. Because they were willing to push back against some of the "powers that be," a few rules were changed and UP students were allowed to participate in formal commencement exercises, replete with caps and gowns, despite not actually receiving a college degree.

7. Ally with other PSE programs. Many other PSE programs have had experiences similar to ours and we have learned from many through our participation in conferences and consortia. Our state is fortunate to have the North Carolina Postsecondary Education Alliance, an organization for all PSEs in the state. Our participation in this has helped us and other programs gain recognition by some in our legislature and administration. Ultimately we believe this alliance will provide us with the political fortification to secure top–down state funding.

8. Build in PSE-based scholarship. Colleges and universities will always value scholarly activities, and creating reputable scholarship based on the PSE program can add to the value of the program as features of the university. Since the inception of the UP Program, we have published more than 20 papers in professional, refereed journals, and made well over 150 presentations at state, national, and international conferences. Not only have these academic products shown the value of the program, they have also shown our administrators and our academic evaluation committees that we remain serious scholars engaged in meaningful work.

9. Leverage the value of the program. We often look for sources of funding to support the UP Program, but we rarely find them, and when we do, the funding is usually very limited. But because we have such a valuable, model program, we leverage the program to seek grant funding that is *based* on the quality of the program. In other words, because we have a successful PSE program, we try to persuade funders that we will do a good job with related projects. We recently have had two projects funded using this strategy, one for $300,000 and one for $1.25 million. Although these funds cannot be used to directly support the program, we let our administrators know that we would not have been funded *without* the UP Program.

10. Make your case for internal funding. During the last years of grant funding, we began to present our case for internal funding with the appropriate individuals. We made points to them based on the above strategies and outcomes, and told them what funding would be required and for what expenditures. Ultimately what resulted is approximately the budget presented in Table 4.2. We knew the "dream budget" was not possible, but we received enough support to keep the program operating. To do this, as there was no line in the budget for a PSE program, the university and our college, the College of Education and Allied Professions, were able to "find" the necessary funds by "shifting" money around. In other words, our champions supported us!

Final Thoughts

As we have focused on success and sustainability, we continuously reflect and evaluate our program operations with the intention to streamline and maximize our potential. We must be willing to make changes and be flexible, pursue funding opportunities, and continue to make positive connections. We realize that being transparent with needs and avoiding questionable activities will help with more long-term system integration and sustainability. Additionally, we constantly demonstrate how the program aligns with the university mission and overall future plans. We believe that programs will prevail when success and passion are shared among more than a few individuals who understand and value the outcomes achieved.

This chapter has addressed several important topics related to funding and program operations. Based on our experiences and reflection with this topic, we have had financial abundance during some years of program operations with additional staffing resources as well as several cuts. Importantly, though, we have not decreased the number of students we have served each semester despite our financial resource availability. While money is important to providing stability and security, having passionate staff members who understand their roles and the mission also helps drive the motivation and outcomes. Many passionate individuals in the field are not doing this "job" for the money. They do it to make a true difference. If this remains the primary mission along with the long-term sustainability efforts, many programs can do a lot more with less.

Note

1 VR funding for PSE participation varies from state to state. Currently, in North Carolina, this funding is limited.

Reference

Martinez, D. C., & Queener, J. (2010). *Postsecondary education for students with intellectual disabilities*. Washington, DC: George Washington University HEATH Resource Center. Retrieved from https://heath.gwu.edu/files/downloads/pse_id_final_edition.pdf

Part II
Major Components

5 Recruitment and Admissions Procedures

Admissions Considerations

In previous chapters, we have discussed issues of why, what, how, and who should go to college. In this chapter, we discuss how to recruit qualified applicants with ID, and how to objectively decide who should be admitted to a college PSE program, and what to do about those not admitted.

Admission procedures can be difficult when there are no test scores, grade point averages, or essays on which to base an evaluation, but still an admission process must be fair and objective, and ultimately should result in the admission of students who are most likely to be successful in the PSE program. It is important to remember that college applications and admissions procedures are often very emotional experiences, and unhappy applicants and their families sometimes lodge complaints with higher-up university officials. For this and many other reasons, this process for students with ID must be fair, honest, and transparent. Ultimately it may be necessary to defend decisions about who was accepted into a program, and who was not.

Table 5.1 provides an overview of the procedures we have used in the UP Program. It indicates that there are three key components to the process: Outreach and recruitment, systematic review, and final evaluation and selection.

Table 5.1 UP Program Recruitment and Admissions Procedures

Outreach and recruitment →	Systematic review →	Final evaluation and selection
• Developing visibility • Community outreach • Open house	• Application materials • Initial reviews and ratings • Review by the admissions committee • Selection of top applicants	• Invitations to orientation camp • Conducting orientation camp • Accepting new students • Supporting unaccepted applicants

Outreach and Recruitment

Developing visibility. As traditional students and their families search for colleges that may be right for them, they typically look at resources such as the *Fiske Guide to Colleges* (Fiske, 2018), the *Best 384 Colleges* (Princeton Review, 2018), or the *collegevine* (www.collegevine.com). Like traditional college-seeking students, those with ID and their families are also becoming more sophisticated about researching and selecting a college or university PSE program most suitable for them. It makes sense, then, that PSE programs wishing to attract the most qualified students with ID should begin by developing the visibility of their program with the purpose of increasing their applicant pool.

Perhaps the most useful way to develop visibility is by having the PSE program listed in the *Think College* database (www.thinkcollege.net), as this is where many will turn when searching for a program. The *Think College* database includes a variety of PSE programs in the United States and Canada, and provides details about program characteristics and contact information. The website allows potential students and their families to identify PSE programs in specific states and learn about the various features and characteristics of programs.

Think College encourages programs to contact them in order to be listed in their database. This may be done by going to their website and sending an initial email about listing the program. Newly developing programs should consider this as an essential step and should be sure that the PSE program is not only included in the database, but that the correct information about the program is provided.

It is also important, and perhaps goes without saying, for a PSE program to have its own website that provides key information for potential students and their families. Interested persons should be able to learn about the PSE program and communicate with PSE personnel through email. Our own website, up.wcu.edu, allows interested persons to learn about the essential features of our program, and about some of the students who have attended the program. On our website we describe program features, policies, costs, and how to contact us.

Another way to develop visibility is by attending state and national conferences. Throughout the history of the UP Program we have gained much visibility by attending various statewide and national conferences, and have almost always been accompanied by our students with ID and our natural support students. This allows students with and without disabilities to share their stories with audiences made up of families, students, school personnel, and service providers, always increasing the number of people who know about our program and attracting potential students to us.

One such conference we frequently attend is the annual *State of the Art Conference* on postsecondary education for students with ID, now held at different locations across the United States. It is attended by many current PSE program representatives, as well as by current and future students with ID and their families. Programs that wish to gain more visibility should attend this conference and perhaps apply to make a presentation about their program. Participation in the conference across several years will not only gain visibility for a PSE program, but it will provide up-to-date information about other successful PSE programs.

Community outreach. Although national visibility is important, we have found that reaching out to communities in our state is essential to recruiting high-quality students. There are several ways this can be done. Although our website is helpful, we have found that actual contact in more traditional ways is often better. In our state, some families and students in more rural areas have limited internet access, so we send brochures and information using "snail mail" to those who contact us by mail or phone.

For different occasions and events, we will also use live representatives for outreach and recruitment. This might include our staff attending school district transition fairs, or participating in state meetings and conferences. We have also asked current or past students and family members to represent us, especially those living near to the meeting or conference venue. These representatives can be very effective because they can share their firsthand experience, which they often enjoy doing, and in exchange potential applicants enjoy hearing. If personal attendance is not possible, we will share recruitment videos and brochures that may be distributed and shown at transition fairs or informational meetings.

Another direct outreach resource may be staff from the PSE's university or college admissions office. Personnel from this office often attend high school and community recruitment activities as part of their normal duties, and when doing so they can provide information about the PSE program. To help them, PSE personnel should provide them with videos and printed information about the PSE program.

As discussed in previous chapters, collaboration is essential to the success of a PSE program and so program personnel should be sure to network with as many community and school programs as possible as part of the outreach process. Contact information for school district special education directors, high school principals, and guidance counselors across the state should be maintained in order to send out information about the PSE program on a regular schedule. These individuals will have more direct access to students, parents, and teachers, and will be able to provide them with program information. Other contacts should include statewide family support networks, University Centers for Excellence in Developmental Disabilities (UCEDDs), and community agencies that provide direct services to individuals with ID and family members.

Open house. Offering an open house event allows students and their families to take a very close look at the key features of the PSE program and facilitates more meaningful interactions between the program and potential students and their families. Preferably the open house for the PSE program will take place as part of the open house for the college or university. Typically, university admissions offices have a well-developed system for welcoming and coordinating open house events, and we have found co-planning activities and agendas with this office has maximized our recruitment efforts while making us less "special" as a program.

For an open house to be successful, several actions must be taken. To begin, the program should notify all those families and students it has had contact with in the past year about the open house, and encourage them to attend. To do this, it is important to maintain the contact information of all those who have inquired about the program and to use this list to inform them and invite them to an open house. Creating listservs and using services like Mail Chimp to organize sending mass email updates has helped us capture and send out news before open house events.

Next, when planning our open house activities, we have found it to be helpful to involve a range of individuals to share information and some of their personal experiences about the program. We typically invite some of our current and past students with ID, their parents, and some of the student supports to speak to visitors, to show them around campus, and to engage with them informally. In addition, we have asked university administrators, faculty, employers, residential living personnel, disability services staff, and transportation providers to share information with visitors. To prepare these individuals for their roles in the open house, we ask them not only to share information about their relationship with our program, but to speak to visitors personally about what they view as the best features and benefits of our program.

During the open house, we schedule an array of events so that visitors can gain a comprehensive view of the program. We also undertake efforts to learn as much about potential applicants who are attending the open house, including the students with ID and their family members. In essence, this is the beginning of our evaluation of applicants as much as it is an opportunity for them to learn about us. Table 5.2 shows a typical schedule for our open house activities.

During the opening session of the open house we provide an overview of the program and our expectations for students who attend the program as well as for their parents. Throughout the day we spend time with the visitors so we can get to know potential applicants and their family members. Visitors tour various residence halls and key campus locations, eat lunch, and chat in small groups with natural supports. We try to answer all questions about program operations, the application process, and ask current students and families to share stories.

The open house event concludes with videotaped interviews of all potential applicants and their parents. During the interview, we ask about life goals, why going to college is important, and what kind of life after college is desired. We ask our natural support students to conduct

Table 5.2 A Sample Open House Schedule for the UP Program

8:00–8:30: REGISTRATION AND CHECK-IN – Check-in will take place in the Ramsey at the "UP Program" Registration table near O section on the concourse. At check-in, guests will need to reserve an interview time slot and campus tour time for the afternoon. UP Guests must complete online registration PRIOR to Open House to receive a lunch voucher.

8:45–9:50: UP PROGRAM OVERVIEW – Meeting in the Hospitality Room of Ramsey. Guests and families will learn more about the University Participant Program from staff and hear firsthand experiences from parents and students.

10:00–10:30: WELCOME SESSION – University speakers. Please find a seat in the W-V section near the floor of the arena in the Ramsey Auditorium. Cat-Tran pick-up will be out through the tunnel and transport to Blue Ridge by 10:45.

10:45–11:45: TOUR OF RESIDENCE HALLS – Tours with UP students. Cat-Tran will provide transportation from Blue Ridge to Norton Halls and then to UC Theater.

11:45–12:30: UP PROGRAM INFORMATION SESSION – Meeting in the UC Theater located on third floor of the University Center. Students and guests will learn more about residential living, accessibility resources, and faculty involvement.

12:30–1:45: LUNCH – Students may redeem their lunch voucher at our Courtyard Dining Hall or UC Food Court.

1:45–3:15: VIDEO MEETINGS AND TOUR OF CAMPUS

- VIDEO MEETINGS – For scheduled video meetings, please meet on the third floor in the Grand Room of the University Center. The videographers will come get you from the Grand Room at the following times: 1:45 pm, 2:00 pm, 2:15 pm, 2:30 pm, 2:45 pm, or 3:00 pm. Please attend the video meeting time and room location selected at Registration and Check-In.
- TOUR OF CAMPUS – Students and guests will be guided through a campus tour by current enTOURage guides. Please wait in the Grand Room for the campus tour. Tour 1: 1:45–2:30. Tour 2: 2:30–3:15

3:15: QUESTIONS AND REMAINING VIDEO/DISCUSSION

*Parking is available at Ramsey. There will be directional signs, enTOURage guides, and UP volunteers to help direct guests to specified locations. Look for UP volunteers and staff to assist you throughout the day in the Ask Me...What's UP shirts. Ride the Cat-Tran shuttle back to your vehicle. Cat-Tran pick-up is located near the Courtyard Dining Hall.

---

the interviews and serve as videographers. We let applicants and their parents know that we expect honest and open answers and that the videos will be considered as part of their application materials if they decide to apply to the program. When visitors are leaving the open house, we try to thank everyone personally and remind everyone of the upcoming application deadlines. After all visitors have left, we gather informal feedback from natural supports on potential applicants and their families, asking them about their impressions of individuals who might be considered good applicants for the program.

Systematic Review

Application materials. Application materials should serve to provide the most comprehensive portrait possible of the applicant as well as their family support system. Although different PSE programs may have a need for different materials, the UP Program requires the following items be submitted. These materials are required in December of the year preceding potential admission:

- **Completed university admissions application.** Like all college students, the university needs demographic and other relevant information about all students applying to the university.
- **Resume.** This should list and explain relevant experiences including paid and unpaid work experience, community service, clubs, unique skills, honors and awards, etc.
- **Three letters of recommendation.** These should not come from family or friends, but from teachers or other professionals and should provide an honest description of the applicant and give examples of relevant experiences, abilities, interests, accomplishments, and support needs.
- **Recent psychological assessment.** This should include relevant diagnoses, cognitive strengths and limitations, and areas of behavioral or psychological concern.
- **Most recent Individualized Education Program (IEP).** The IEP should include present level of academic achievement and functional skills as well as transition goals.
- **Signed program agreements.** Agreements include statement of agreement, financial resource plan, proof or acknowledgement of guardianship, and release of exchange of information, assistive technology needs, photography and video permission, and video interview questionnaire for potential applicants. These can be found on our website at up.wcu.edu.
- **Personal skills inventory.** This assessment provides a listing of skill levels and support needs for daily living, social, communication, and personal care adapted from the Domain Skills Inventory through the Colorado Department of Education (CDE, 2014).
- **Applicant and parent videos.** These are usually recorded during the open house but may be recorded at the applicant's home. The videos include answers to three broad questions: What the applicant wants to do before, during, and after attending college.
- **Other products showing honors or commendations.** The applicant can share relevant achievements or accomplishments that might show unique abilities or characteristics that separate them from other applicants.

Initial reviews and ratings. As applications are received online or by mail, they should be organized and examined for being complete. It is the program's decision to request any missing material, or discard incomplete applications, but we view complete applications that arrive on time as an initial sign of commitment.

The initial review of application materials is conducted by one or two UP staff members and has two purposes. First, it is a binary assessment to determine whether the person should be considered for further evaluation and consideration based on program requirements. Second, it is an initial step to rank order applicants based on relative strengths and weaknesses.

At this stage we review materials to determine if the applicant meets the disability requirement of the program (i.e., has an ID); if they are encumbered by any characteristics that may be detrimental to the program and that would preclude their admission (e.g., a history of aggressive behavior, theft, dishonesty); and if they could potentially benefit from the program (based on previous life experiences, is the applicant interested in learning, being included, and being as independent as possible, and are these characteristics supported by family members). We are not concerned with the developmental level or support needs of the individual as long as we feel the program can accommodate the applicant, or if the applicant will be able to bring their own support services to the program through Medicaid waivers.

A program staff member and/or another person familiar with special education terminology and psychological reports should review the application materials to make the initial assessment. Using two or more persons, if possible, will reduce the amount of time to review applications and, if necessary, allow a reliability assessment for marginal cases. In the UP Program, we have found it helpful to use a review form to collect applicant information systematically and objectively as application documents are reviewed. Although we enter this information in an online survey as we review applicants, the hard copy format is available by the senior author upon request.

Once applications have undergone initial reviews, discussions among the PSE staff can be undertaken to rank applicants that have not been eliminated due to more obvious concerns as indicated above. During these discussions, in addition to the application materials, it is very helpful to consider observations and the videotaped interviews made during the open house visit, including the comments that came from the student supports who spent time with the applicants and their families.

Review by the admissions committee. While the initial review allows the UP staff to rank order applicants, we feel an additional external review is also important. This allows us to have our evaluations confirmed or challenged by others knowledgeable about our program and the university. To do this we use an admissions committee comprising key university personnel and others, including the following:

- an undergraduate and/or graduate student
- former parents of program graduates
- director of financial aid
- administration representative from the College of Education and Allied Professions
- representatives of undergraduate admission
- representatives of educational outreach
- representatives of residential living
- director of accessibility resources
- faculty that have taught UP students
- employers who have worked with UP students
- representatives from tutoring and student success centers
- representative from counseling services
- representative of partnering community service providers.

The work of this committee usually requires a half-day time commitment with the entire committee meeting together. We set the date for the meeting as soon as we can, usually in late January or early February, and give members sufficient notice so they can put the meeting on their calendars. We strongly encourage all members to attend (we try to encourage their presence by serving lunch), but if they cannot, we ask them to send a representative from their office.

The meeting begins by giving a brief overview of the UP Program and our purpose, describing the types of students we serve, and explaining our admissions process. Committee members are reminded that all proceedings during the meeting are strictly confidential and nothing said in the meeting should be discussed outside the meeting or with anyone not on the committee.

During the meeting, we carefully present and discuss the top ten applicants identified during our initial review, but do so in alphabetical order, not revealing our own rankings. During the presentation of each applicant, one at a time, the UP director provides a verbal description of the applicant (along with a visual image) that includes the following information:

- name and age
- hometown
- disability diagnosis, intellectual disability level based on IQ, adaptive behavior ratings
- diplomas and school background
- special skills and interests
- job and other relevant experiences
- strengths and/or concerns about the student or the family
- future living and career goals.

Once all relevant information about an applicant has been presented and discussed, we then present the videos of both the applicant and their parents that were recorded during open house or submitted with application materials. Following the presentations and videos for each applicant, there is an opportunity for everyone to ask questions and discuss their impressions about the applicant and their family, including any concerns they may have. If necessary, committee members may have access to the original application materials, which we make available in the meeting, including the applicant folders, resumes, reference letters, etc.

Lastly, the applicant is rated by individual committee members. Using an admissions committee evaluation form created in Survey Monkey® (available by senior author upon request) and provided to each committee member on an individual laptop. Individual committee members are first asked to describe individual strengths of the applicant and any areas of concern, then to use a seven-point Likert-type scale to express their confidence about several characteristics of the applicant and the family. Confidence levels used in the assessment include *not confident at all, unconfident, somewhat unconfident, neither unconfident nor confident, somewhat confident, confident,* or *absolutely confident.*

The ratings are applied to the following items:

- This student's personality, interests, and goals will make them an asset to the WCU campus community.
- This student will represent WCU and UP Program favorably.
- This student will be responsible in classes, at work, and in a wide variety of social situations.
- This student can cope with change/remain flexible in a dynamic college environment.
- This student will NOT exhibit challenging or dangerous behaviors in campus settings.
- This student will succeed in college environment; socially; academically; vocationally.
- This student will strive to develop the skills necessary for independent living.
- Upon graduation this student will be competitively employed.
- This student's parents/guardians will meet all UP Program requirements and expectations.
- This student's family will support transition into full employment and independent living.

Members complete these ratings for each applicant after they are presented to the committee, going from one applicant to the next. Typically, the presentation and evaluation of each applicant during the meeting requires 10 to 20 minutes.

Selection of the top applicants. The intended outcome of the admissions committee meeting is to identify seven or eight applicants who will progress to the final stage of the admissions process, which is participation in the orientation camp, described below. Therefore, after the committee members exit the meeting, the UP staff reviews their evaluations in summary form. Based on these evaluations, seven to eight applicants are rank ordered by the UP staff and are invited to attend the orientation camp, which usually occurs one month after the admissions committee meeting.

Final Evaluation and Selection

Invitations to orientation camp. The seven to eight applicants selected for advancement to the next level of consideration – participation in our orientation camp – receive an email indicating this decision. In the message, we explain that camp is the second and final phase of the admissions process, that it will occur over three nights and three days, and that "adequate performance" in camp is the final consideration for admission to the UP Program. We want the invitation to make it clear to the applicant and the family that the applicant has not yet been accepted, and that ultimate acceptance will be dependent on how the student performs in camp. In the email, we also give parents detailed information about the cost of our program. The message lets parents and the student know we are close to making a final decision, and it allows them to reflect on their degree of interest and commitment for attending our program.

Conducting orientation camp. The orientation camp takes place in the spring prior to the fall semester in which new students will enter the program. Students arrive on a Wednesday afternoon and stay until Saturday afternoon. The parents are asked to arrive Saturday morning so they can participate in meetings about the program and their responsibilities should their son or daughter be admitted.

The main purpose of an orientation camp is to conduct an *in situ* assessment of how an applicant will conduct themselves on a college campus and in different college environments and activities. Therefore, camp activities include a lot of "try ons," such as living in a residence hall, attending classes, eating in the dining hall, etc. A second purpose of the camp is to learn more about the applicant and what the applicant wants to gain during the college experience. This is the "getting to know you" part of the orientation camp. For this part of camp we use a person-centered planning process that allows applicants, sometimes for the first time, to express their own preferences about what they want to learn and do in life. The key components of the orientation camp include the following:

Trying on staying overnight (without parent supervision). The overnight stays are very important to include if a residential program is offered. We have found that some applicants who have not stayed away from home overnight without family members may have a difficult time with the consecutive overnight stays during orientation camp. On the other hand, staying for a few nights in a college dorm room allows some applicants to show a high degree of independence and reliability. So this experience allows the UP staff as well as the applicant and the parents to determine if living away from home is feasible. Sometimes it shows a clear strength, sometimes it shows a weakness.

Trying on college classes. Since a central component of going to college is attending classes (at least for most students), we like to make sure that applicants attend at least two college classes with their peers without disabilities during orientation camp. To do this we have our campers choose three classes related to their interests and then we contact the instructors regarding their attendance and usually have them attend two of the three.

Noting how an applicant participates in classes can help us make a final decision about whether they might benefit from the program. We can also learn something about the interest of the applicant in the class topic, and whether we will need to help the applicant develop any goals that will help make class attendance more meaningful.

Trying on a part-time job. The third major activity of the college camp is engaging briefly in a part-time job. When in the UP Program, students must work at least ten hours a week in a part-time job or internship. To see how applicants fare in a working situation, we ask campers to indicate three job choices. Their choices are typically based on past job experiences, interests, and future career goals. Working with available employers, we arrange for each camper to work four to six hours during the camp period. Observations of the applicants during work time allows us to assess their ability to stay focused and engaged on a job, and also provides insight into future career interests and possibly goals that might be developed to help them learn to be better employees.

Trying on the fun part of college. One of the most important parts of the orientation camps is the applicants' involvement in college-level social activities. These events are mixed into camp life throughout the applicants' stay on campus. Through these activities we have a chance to assess applicants' social maturity and personal skills. We learn if students will be engaging, aware of others' feelings, and willing to try new experiences. It gives us an opportunity not only to better judge how the applicant will fit on campus, but also to identify potential goals, especially as related to social behavior and communication skills, when interacting with college peers. Typical social activities have included attending concerts, bowling, cooking, karaoke, swimming, and many more college-age appropriate campus activities. It should be noted that we do not usually have to create special activities for the campers, but instead arrange for them to engage in activities that are already occurring on campus.

Trying on the serious part of college. Finally, we want applicants to know that attending college also has a serious side that requires mature, adult behavior. Part of the way we do this is by inviting our campus police and safety personnel to come and explicitly share strategies for staying safe on campus and to provide emergency training procedures with our potential students. This also allows our campus police and emergency personnel to meet each student before they arrive on campus. Our intention is to initiate a process through which our students with ID will remain safe and react appropriately during any emergency that may occur if they end up living on campus. As we have noted elsewhere, safety is always a concern for students and their parents, so we take proactive steps to maintain a safe environment and also review the WCU Student Code of Conduct together carefully (Westling, Kelley, & Prohn, 2016).

Getting to know you. One of the most critical parts of the orientation camp is the opportunity it provides for the UP staff to get to know the applicants . . . and for the applicants and their families to get to know us. The three nights and days of camp allows an up-close view in both directions. By the end of camp, we want to know if the applicant is a good fit for the program; and the applicant and the family need to know if our program is right for them. Both parties learn much through the activities and interactions we have described. However, there are some additional specific undertakings that allow us to get to know the applicants and for them to leave camp with a plan for the future . . . whether they are accepted into the program or not. These are briefly described below.

Initial person-centered planning (PCP) meetings. With the experience we have had with the applicant during camp, we are ready to guide them through a PCP meeting to help them develop an initial PATH plan (Pearpoint, O'Brien, & Forest, 1993) and *academic roadmaps*. For those who will be accepted into the program, this will serve as the starting process for their first semester, which will occur in the fall. For those not accepted, this plan can help them progress with mapping out future activities. This PCP process allows them to personalize future goals, interests, college classes, extracurricular activities, and career aspirations.

Technology assessments. As we spend time with the applicants, we also learn about how assistive technology devices and supports might be useful for both daily life and academic participation. We will often allow an applicant to try different kinds of devices, support them as they learn to use it, and then share with families what we have learned about how their son or daughter might benefit from such a device.

Parent Meetings

As much as it is for the applicants, orientation camp is also for families. At the end of the week, while students are still doing activities with their peer supports, program staff connect with families and provide them with orientation and networking opportunities. We recognize that while applicants need support in transitioning to a PSE program, so do family members. During meetings with parents, we focus on two topics. First, we discuss our memorandum of understanding with parents (see Chapter 14) so that they have a clear expectation of their responsibilities if their son or daughter is accepted. Then we allow the parents of current applicants to have a discussion with parents of current and previous UP students for the latter to share lessons learned before, during, and after the program. We will also introduce parents to our university orientation counselors, who provide training to all incoming university students and families.

Accepting New Students

On the final afternoon of orientation camp, we hold individual, face-to-face meetings with applicants and their family members to discuss the camp experience. For all students and families we point out our perceptions of strengths and weaknesses demonstrated during camp; offer our views of important goals that will lead to more independence and adult success; and, most importantly, let each applicant and their family know whether they have been accepted into the UP Program for the coming fall semester.

Obviously, for students not accepted, these meetings are difficult and can sometimes be emotionally laden. Certainly it is not easy to tell applicants when they are not accepted. But the meetings provide a time for individuals and families to reflect and to consider if there are goals or next steps that should be pursued, and other options they might pursue in the next year.

Once accepted students and families have been formally notified, our program then works with the Office of Admissions to start the official admission process. As with all other students, entering the university requires several administrative steps: Immunization holds must be released, application fees must be paid, resident hall agreements and deposits must be secured, meal plans must be selected, and students must register for classes. We also make sure that we share the residence hall packing list, review the university's code of conduct, make arrangements for fall internships, and discuss budgeting and the use of checking accounts and debit cards. For many students, we must also work with them and their families to make sure adult services provided through Medicaid waivers or support from Vocational Rehabilitation is brought into the university setting.

When move-in day finally arrives, it is a most memorable and exciting moment for everyone. It is at this time that both students and parents realize that a real transition in life is occurring and the move toward less dependence and more independence has begun. Soon after students arrive, we work with them to establish their individual schedules so the semester can begin. Subsequent PCP meetings are also scheduled to allow everyone to know when they can connect again to talk about progress and support needs on a monthly basis (see Chapter 10).

Supporting Unaccepted Applicants

In the process we have described in this chapter, there are two points in time when an applicant and their family may learn they have not been accepted. The first comes after the initial review of the applicant by the UP staff and the admissions committee, and the second comes after the orientation camp. At both times, for unaccepted applicants, we attempt to provide supportive information and resources so that the applicant and the family may learn from the application process and maybe find other avenues to successful adult life. In many cases, we recommend working on goals that will make the applicant more likely to be successful if they apply again to the UP Program, something that happens quite regularly.

If applicants do not move forward after the initial review, an email is immediately sent informing them of the decision. The email is rather brief, reminding the applicant and the family of the admission requirements and the competitive admission process we use. We let them know that they may re-apply for admission, but more importantly, we let them know about supports in the state and in their surrounding community that may be helpful. We realize that many applicants and families are searching for next steps and are looking for resources available after high school. Although we cannot offer them a spot in the UP Program, providing these resources in a timely and well-thought-out manner is important. If the families follow up with a phone call, we try to offer a sympathetic and professional ear, and provide more elaboration of other options.

If applicants are allowed to participate in the orientation camp, but are not among those finally accepted, as we explained above, we meet with them to inform them of our decision. Again, this is a difficult task, and even more so because it is face to face. The key to this interaction is to be professional and sincere, and let the applicant and the parents know that there are other options, one of which is to reapply for the following year. What is often helpful is to provide very specific goals that the applicant may work on in the intervening year. These goals are often the goals we would have worked on in the UP Program, such as getting a job and doing it well, interacting socially with others in an age-appropriate manner, and showing greater independence in making daily decisions.

After emails or direct notice of non-acceptance are given, subsequent emails or phone calls are likely to occur. When they do, it is important to be delicate and open. Some of these will be pleasant and some may not be as pleasant. It is important to remember not to take these responses personally and to remain as professional as possible. Students and families who were not accepted are welcomed to stay in contact and be among the visitors at the next open house.

Final Thoughts

We feel that college programs for students with ID should be as meaningful as for any other student. Part of having a meaningful program is admitting students who are likely to be successful in the program and after completing it. Therefore, we must have a process for finding and admitting students who will achieve these desired outcomes. Although some PSE programs have more lenient admission standards and practices, our view is that our standards and procedures have served us well and should remain competitive.

Not only do we feel that good students will do a better job in college, but we feel that by seeking the most qualified student, we will influence families and students to strive for greater success, whether or not they pursue a PSE program. That is one part of our mission, and it is a message we have shared with parents of younger children with ID (Westling & Kelley, 2015).

References

Colorado Department of Education (2014). *Domain skills inventory and skill tracker.* Retrieved from https://www.cde.state.co.us/cdesped/tk_tab07_teachertransitionteam

Fiske, E. (2018). *Fiske guide to colleges.* Naperville, IL: Sourcebooks.

Pearpoint, J., O'Brien, J., & Forest, M. (1993). *PATH: A workbook for planning positive possible futures.* Toronto, Ontario, Canada: Inclusion Press.

Princeton Review (2018). *The best 384 colleges, 2019 edition: in-depth profiles & ranking lists to help find the right college for you.* College Admissions Guides.

Westling, D. L., & Kelley, K. R. (2015). *Preparing your son or daughter for college: suggestions for parents of children with intellectual disability.* Retrieved from Kelle Hampton's blog at https://kellehampton.com/2015/04/preparing-your-son-or-daughter-for/

Westling, D. L., Kelley, K. R., & Prohn, S. M. (2016). A tiered approach to promote safety and security in an inclusive postsecondary education program for college students with intellectual disability. *DADD Online Journal, 3*(1), 160–171.

6   Living on Campus

Living the dream is what we all aspire to, and for a young person with ID, having their own room on a college campus is about as good as it can get. Unfortunately, this component of a college PSE program is not too common, although it is becoming more so . . . as it should. Our experience with the UP Program has taught us that living on campus greatly increases learning opportunities, and more importantly, it allows more opportunity for personal development through self-discovery. We hope this chapter will assist programs as they move to develop or improve successful on-campus residential opportunities for students with ID.

Weighing Potential Benefits and Risks of On-Campus Living

The transition away from home brings newfound independence for everyone. However, many individuals with ID are faced with greater obstacles and less opportunity when it comes to living in residence halls in fully inclusive college housing. More specifically, among the approximately 264 current PSE programs, only 89 (33%) offer housing options (Think College, 2018). Several factors have been suggested to limit on-campus residential living for individuals with ID. These include limited living space on college campuses, policies that allow only full-time or degree-seeking students to live in residence halls, and liability concerns. In some cases, lawsuits have helped gain access to on-campus living options, but have also caused some college administrators to become hesitant about offering PSE programs for individuals with ID.

We think it is important to consider the benefits and risks associated with offering an on-campus living experience to individuals with ID. By doing so, we hope to inform existing and future PSE programs so they can consider the significance of offering residential programs and issues requiring caution.

Benefits of residential programs. Any student who has moved from a family home into a college dorm room or apartment can attest to the benefits associated with the move. If they were to speak candidly, they would say: You can come and go when you wish, at any time you wish, and with whomever you wish; you can keep your space as you want it, in any style you want it, and with nearly anything you want in it; you enjoy some degree of privacy, and, for better or worse, there is generally no one to tell you what to do, when to do it, or with whom to do it. In short, living on a college or university campus means having a large dose of freedom.

The same is true for individuals with ID. There is no doubt that having such personal space and latitude can cause concern for parents, the PSE program staff, and many college or university officials. But for the student, it usually brings a life that has never before been experienced. It is one of the main ways that adolescents learn to become adults, because ultimately there is no freedom without responsibility, and being a responsible person is necessary for being a mature adult. But in addition to the benefits that on-campus living brings to *all* college students, it brings some unique opportunities for college students with ID, such as the following:

- **More opportunities for situational learning.** Many of the personal goals established by and for our students in the UP Program are more readily achieved when they have an opportunity to practice them on a daily basis in a real-life situation. By living on campus, students have many opportunities to demonstrate responsibility for daily living skills, personal and social skills, domestic housekeeping skills, etc. In addition to targeted goals, there are an indeterminable number of opportunities to incidentally learn social and functional skills, with peers providing informal instructional sessions and feedback on appropriate and inappropriate daily living activities.
- **More opportunities for self-determination and decision-making.** One of the major goals being promoted by us and most PSE programs is increasing opportunities for self-determination and personal decision-making (Wehmeyer & Abery, 2013). Living on campus in one's own space presents an ideal situation for a student with ID to exercise in self-determination and decision-making. Notwithstanding the need for periodic support, independent living provides plenty of opportunities for students to make many daily choices.
- **More opportunities to engage in different aspects of campus life.** An active college campus is a virtual smorgasbord of interesting and fun opportunities for living and learning. Students who live on campus can become engaged in ways that they could not otherwise experience if they did not reside on campus. They can get involved in student clubs and organizations, fraternities and sororities, interest groups, religious organizations, and attend any number of athletic events, concerts and plays, and social and cultural presentations. All of these events give them numerous chances to expand their worldly knowledge, develop social and personal skills, and enlarge their circle of same-age peers and acquaintances.

- **More opportunities to develop relationships.** Being immersed into a living and learning community can offer bonds with other students and greater opportunities for learning and campus engagement (National Survey of Student Engagement, 2011). Further, living on campus allows nearly an unlimited number of opportunities to develop friendships and acquaintances, many of which will continue throughout life. This is especially important for people with ID, who are often socially isolated or who have relatively few opportunities for social relationships beyond a limited circle of family and friends (Wilson, Jaques, Johnson, & Brotherton, 2017).
- **Increased maturity and positive effect on attitudes of others.** And finally, with the development of more social relationships between students with and without ID, comes increased independence and social maturity (Hafner, 2008). And the more socially mature the students with ID become, the more likely positive attitudes toward persons with ID will result. We found that the more traditional college students know about students with ID and interact with them, the more accepting they are of these students and the program as a whole (Westling, Kelley, Cain, & Prohn, 2013). So positive on-campus interactions are likely to benefit not only individual students with ID, but also the concept and practice of including persons with ID in the community.

Risks of residential programs. Although there are clearly many benefits to offering the chance for students with ID to live on campus, we have also learned about some risks. These do not imply that residential programs should be avoided, but they do suggest that in some cases precautions should be taken. The risks outlined below should be considered and discussed carefully during the development of PSE programs so everyone can proactively anticipate them, try to prevent them, and handle them if they arise. Notwithstanding the significance of these risks, we feel compelled to point out that many of these are also risks for traditional college students:

- **Emotional reactions and challenging behaviors may occur.** Sometimes, when first living on their own, students worry about being alone and away from home, and behaviors may surface that are indicative of homesickness. Sometimes students may act out, may be offensive to others, or may even be aggressive or exhibit self-injurious behaviors. Usually the passage of time will help with these feelings, but if the behaviors are serious, they will need to be addressed through discussions or a behavior intervention plan (see Chapter 13).
- **Engaging in use of illegal substances.** As we said above, students have much more opportunity to make choices, which is a good thing, but some of these choices may be dangerous, and that is a bad thing. It doesn't mean we should take choices away, but it does mean that

at some time, supported decision-making may be helpful (Shogren, Wehmeyer, Lassmann, & Forber-Pratt, 2017). For example, experimentation with alcohol and illegal drugs can not only get the student in trouble with the school's administration and law enforcement agencies, but in some cases may conflict with current medications.
- **Parental concerns and demands may occur.** Sometimes there is hesitation on the part of family members to let go and allow for the independence that comes with living away from home. Although this is not uncommon for other college students, what may be a little different with family involvement with students with ID may be the issue of guardianship or conservatorship. If this exists, parents may demand prerogatives not usually demanded by other parents. For example, they may want their son or daughter to report to them nightly, or they may even want to put a camera in the dorm room. To address such issues, it is a good idea for PSE programs to work with their university legal counsel to discuss appropriate ways to deal with such demands.

Strategies for Developing and Operating Residential Programs

As noted earlier, PSE programs that offer on-campus housing to students with ID are a minority of all existing PSE programs. However, we feel there is much value to these programs and recommend that existing and future programs make efforts to develop them if at all possible. To do so, we suggest collaborating with key campus partners; preparing and assessing students for on-campus living; and putting in place a residential support system that will allow students with ID to be as independent as possible, but also to live with the same degree of comfort and security as other college students.

Connecting with Campus Partners

Perhaps the most important part of developing an on-campus residential program is having buy-in and collaboration with key campus partners. It is probably safe to assume that many PSE programs that do not have an on-campus living program have met resistance from some key administrators or other influential persons on campus. Therefore, if a plan is being developed to pursue a residential program, connections with important partners are essential. In Chapter 3, we included many of the most important on-campus collaborators and the roles they play. With these partners, it is important to keep an open door policy, build mutual trust, and have regular communication. Their support for developing a residential program can be critical, and their ongoing support after the program is developed can be important for its success.

Assessing and Preparing Students for Residential Living

It is important to understand that it is a huge step for individuals with ID to take up residence in a college or university dormitory or apartment when they have never been away from home without family members. Although they often find the idea appealing, it can be surprising and sometimes disturbing in several ways. Therefore, as part of the admission process we discussed in Chapter 5, we provide an orientation camp before admission. This not only allows us to see the student away from the family in an overnight context and evaluate their potential for independent living, it allows the student to assess their own ability with regard to living away from home. Therefore, we suggest that offering orientation camp experiences can be most beneficial to assess a student's potential for living on campus, and to give the student a taste of doing so.

We have learned that having an orientation camp before final commitments are made by either party helps everyone involved. It is a chance to "try on" college before the first day. Many colleges offer orientations for traditional students and their families, so this is not necessarily a special service. In fact, the camp could be offered as part of an existing residential program that already provides overnight orientations.

In our experiences, we have had students with ID come and attend camp and realize that going to college and living on campus is a little more than they could handle, at least at that point in time. These students and their families have often stated how they appreciate the experience before getting in too deep, and especially before paying tuition and fees. On the other hand, some students truly relish the orientation camp experience and demonstrate they are totally ready to experience more living independence, even though they may need to develop additional skills to do so. For these students and their families, the camp experience is a valuable activity and an important step to gaining more adult independence.

Providing a Residential Support System

Before students with ID move into their campus rooms or apartments, it is necessary to consider how to provide them with an appropriate level of support. We have found that when looking across PSE programs, the type and degree of support provided varies widely, including taking a "hands-off" position regarding support. However, we feel that to some extent support is necessary even though it should be the minimum amount required. To provide this support, we use two kinds of personnel: residential assistants and residential supports.

Residential assistants. Colleges and universities that offer on-campus residences for their traditional students usually rely on residential assistants (RAs) to oversee the daily operations and activities within residence halls. These individuals are usually upperclass students who have a high degree of maturity and whom can be counted on for guidance and direction by the other students living in the residence.

Of course RAs can provide support to students with ID, but this support will generally be at about the same level as it is for all other students in the hall. The RAs are carefully selected for their maturity and experience, but they will not likely have any particular training or information related to students with ID (unless it is provided by the PSE staff). Their role is mainly to ensure the safety and security for all students and thus they must complete training to stay well informed about campus life, safety issues, and university regulations. Their expertise and skills should be valued as part of a support system, but they cannot be overused to provide exclusive support to students with ID. Still, checking in periodically and staying in touch with residential staff about their concerns is important.

Residential supports. To supplement the support available from RAs, we have used some of our undergraduate students to serve as natural supports in the residence halls. Typically these residential supports are strategically placed in rooms or suites with, or in the vicinity of, students with ID, and provide support that may be beyond what an RA would typically provide. Table 6.1 shows the types of support they most often provide.

Just as with RAs, it is important that residential supports be selected carefully. They should be interviewed to determine their compatibility with students with ID, and trained to provide appropriate support. Consideration should be given to how personal characteristics of the residential supports and the students with ID will interact. Being a residential support is not a role every college student desires . . . or should have . . . as it requires a commitment of being available overnight and on some weekends. Therefore, it is important to be above board in the recruitment and interview process with regard to duties and time commitments.

Table 6.1 Residential Supports' Responsibilities and Activities as Needed

- Rehearse monthly fire and tornado drills with students.
- Encourage students to keep clean rooms according to a self-developed checklist.
- Prompt students to set alarm clocks and help with time management.
- Mediate shared living spaces.
- Provide personal care or hygiene support.
- Assist with room keys or identification cards when lost.
- Perform simple first aid.
- Help complete maintenance reports.
- Help with move-in and move-out protocols.
- Provide updates on living goals during PCP meetings.
- Develop visual cues or task analyses for routines and complex tasks.
- Monitor medication taken daily and weekly if necessary.
- Celebrate birthdays and special events.

Table 6.2 Potential Interview Questions for Residential Supports

- Why do you want to be a residential support or suitemate?
- What do you consider as your strengths and weaknesses when working with peers and with individuals with ID?
- Describe your typical day and what it looks like. What do you enjoy most about your day? What do you enjoy least?
- How do you plan to grow in this experience?
- How would you react if a parent accused you of not monitoring medication use?
- What would you do if a student is sick or you are sick while sharing closer living conditions?
- How would you support a student who becomes fearful during a fire or tornado drill?
- What would you do if a student has trouble with personal hygiene routines?
- How would you handle an underage student drinking alcohol?
- What would you do to mediate someone having trouble with personal boundaries?

Many of the residential supports we interview and select are student supports who may have already worked on a regular basis with our students with ID. They have typically started out volunteering as unpaid supports and work into paid natural support positions. Based on our experiences, many students are not primarily focused on the stipend they receive for being a residential support, but they are truly seeking to support students with ID to help them achieve their independent living goals. During the interview of potential residential supports, we ask several key questions to probe their commitment as well as their problem-solving skills. Examples of these are presented in Table 6.2.

Supporting Families to Support Residential Living

More and more families are realizing the value of a PSE program for their son or daughter with ID. Considering this opportunity in the abstract is very appealing, but for some, maybe most, the realization that their son or daughter will be living outside the family home, out of their sight, and with less of their influence, can be stressful. Often the result of this is that family members attempt to find ways to be virtually or actually present and to continue their traditional parental roles. While this is admirable, it may also stifle the opportunity for the student to acquire more independence.

Because of this, we have found that it is sometimes important to encourage parents to find the right degree and kind of support to provide, but to make sure they are not impeding the opportunities for the student to learn and develop important abilities and skills associated with independent living. To do this we have used several strategies:

- Parents have been asked to limit their communications and contacts with their son or daughter to a pattern more common to parents of traditional students, such as texting or calling a limited number of times per week.
- They have been strongly encouraged not to visit their son or daughter too often, and to never "drop in" unexpectedly.
- Parents are required (through our parent MOU, see Chapter 14) to provide for the financial and material needs of their son or daughter, but they are encouraged to require personal responsibility of them to manage a budget and take care of meeting their own needs.
- We make sure we inform parents of the multiple steps we take to make sure their son or daughter is safe and secure. It is natural for parents to worry about their children regardless of their age or ability, but it is also necessary for them to understand that an independent life cannot be achieved if a person is always living in a bubble.

There is a role that parents and families can play, and it is an important one. But part of that role is knowing when to step back and let the student begin to do things on their own to develop their independence.

Minimizing Risks and Preparing for Emergencies

As we explained earlier, there are some risks associated with offering an on-campus residential program, and emergency situations are almost certain to arise. In our program, we do a few things to increase safety and mitigate against the risks, and we prepare so we can be ready for different kinds of emergencies.

In order to keep students safe and secure while not infringing on their opportunities to be independent, we use a multi-tiered safety support system (Westling, Kelley, & Prohn, 2016). The tiers of this system include: (1) relying on the campus security system that is in place to protect and keep safe all persons on campus, and keeping them informed about the students with ID on campus; (2) proactively addressing issues of safety and security with our students with ID, such as keeping them informed about the code of conduct and campus safety policies; and, (3) responding to unique issues or conditions in which one of our students may pose a threat to others, or be threatened by others, or be a threat to themselves.

Examples of actions at the second level include explicitly educating everyone about ways to avoid exploitation, promoting and practicing campus safety and emergency procedures, and having an on-call emergency hotline so students can contact our program staff 24/7. For this last action we emphasize to each student the importance of knowing how to use a cell phone, using it appropriately for an emergency situation, and answering it appropriately if and when the student is called by a PSE staff member. An example of taking action at the third level might be an occurrence of one of our students being stalked on campus, or one of our students harassing another student personally or online. In any case where we would perceive potential danger to one of our students or to another associated with one of our students, we would engage with appropriate campus officials to address the issue.

Sometimes there are emergencies that may or may not include issues of safety or security but that require preparation in advance, and quick attention if they occur. In general, all colleges and universities maintain a high degree of readiness for emergencies, but most do not make preparations specifically for students with ID. These students may need more practice in order to be more confident about what to do in certain events, or who may need support for events that are less common among traditional students. We have found that many students with ID may have a harder time focusing or remaining calm when things are more chaotic than usual, and some may also have sensory or routine issues that might interfere with their ability to respond appropriately. Still others may have challenges related to daily needs that are not emergencies per se, but require some uncommon attention.

Perhaps erring on the side of caution, we have undertaken steps that we believe will be helpful in the event of an unplanned, potentially dangerous event. Some of the situations we have faced and proactively prepared for are presented in Table 6.3.

Although there may be heightened concern among some for individuals with ID living among their peers on a college campus, there are no identified differences in legal requirements for these students to do so (Plotner & Marshall, 2015), nor have we located any data that suggests

Table 6.3 Responding to Emergencies

- **Fire and tornado drills:** Rehearsing the proper protocol between UP students and residential supports
- **Campus lockdowns:** Rehearsing the proper protocol with RAs in residence halls
- **Unknown visitors in residence areas:** Reviewing the protocol at the beginning of each semester used by all students for allowing guests into residence areas and quiet hours for all students; teaching students to check the peep holes or asking who is at the door before opening
- **Lost keys and identification cards:** Following protocol for reporting lost keys and retracing steps to try to find keys or cards; having students understand the cost associated with lost keys and cards as well as where to request replacements
- **Medical emergencies:** Educating our campus emergency medical team about any unique circumstances or conditions with consent from students and their families; mapping out and teaching the emergency plan with phone numbers programmed in cell phones ahead of time
- **Minor first aid needs or sickness:** Providing residential supports with emergency kits that help in these minor situations

their presence raises risks for themselves or others. From all that we know, no campus can legally reject a student with ID from on-campus living because of their disability. Still, reservations may persist. We have found that the best way to address these issues is to invest heavily in the nurturing of our campus relationships and partnerships.

As we noted in Chapter 3, collaboration is essential and it is especially important for one of the most important aspects of going to college: living on campus. We strive to have everyone involved in on-campus living connected so they can plan together with us and provide valued input and expertise. We believe that investing in these relationships will help overcome reservations and proactively address concerns about liability.

Final Thoughts

This chapter has addressed several important topics about the development of on-campus living opportunities for students with ID. In doing so, we have tried to help programs consider the benefits and risks of on-campus living, and how to develop and manage such a program.

Based on our experiences, living and learning opportunities among same-age peers has allowed for greater progress to be made during and after program completion for achieving goals towards more inclusive community living success. College experiences and living away from home are some of the best vehicles for gaining confidence and exploring one's independence. This shouldn't really have to look much different for students with ID than for traditional college students. Taking time to map out the process and develop important support needs can make an important difference.

References

Hafner, D. (2008). *Inclusion in postsecondary education: Phenomenological study on identifying and addressing barriers to inclusion of individuals with significant disabilities at a four-year liberal arts college*. ProQuest Dissertations & Theses Global. Retrieved from http://ezproxy.lib.umb.edu/login?url=http://search.proquest.com/docview/288108493?accountid=28932

National Survey of Student Engagement (2011). *Fostering student engagement campus wide – annual results 2011*. Bloomington, IN: Indiana University Center for Postsecondary Research.

Plotner, A. J., & Marshall, K. J. (2015). Postsecondary education programs for students with an intellectual disability: Facilitators and barriers to implementation. *Intellectual and Developmental Disabilities, 53*, 59–69.

Shogren, K. A., Wehmeyer, M. L., Lassmann, H., & Forber-Pratt, A. J. (2017). Supported decision making: A synthesis of the literature across intellectual disability, mental health, and aging. *Education and Training in Autism and Developmental Disabilities, 52*, 144–157.

Think College (2018). *College options for people with intellectual disabilities*. Retrieved from http://www.thinkcollege.net

Wehmeyer, M. L., & Abery, B. H. (2013). Self-determination and choice. *Intellectual and Developmental Disabilities, 51,* 399–411.

Westling, D. L., Kelley, K. R., & Prohn, S. M. (2016). A tiered approach to promote safety and security in an inclusive postsecondary education program for college students with intellectual disability. *DADD Online Journal, 3*(1), 160–171.

Westling, D. L., Kelley, K. R., Cain, B., & Prohn, S. (2013). College students' attitudes about an inclusive postsecondary education program for individuals with intellectual disability. *Education and Training in Autism and Developmental Disabilities, 48*(3), 306–319.

Wilson, N. J., Jaques, H., Johnson, A., & Brotherton, M. L. (2017). From social exclusion to supported inclusion: Adults with intellectual disability discuss their lived experiences of a structured social group. *Journal of Applied Research in Intellectual Disabilities, 30,* 847–858.

7 Course Participation

At the core of a college education are the courses taken by matriculating students. While living on campus and participating in various social and extracurricular activities enrich life on campus and add to the educational experience, it is the courses taken by students that ultimately comprise their formal learning experience. In PSE programs for students with ID, this is also true. The courses students take will ultimately be the most definitive part of their college experience.

We classify the courses available to college students with ID into four types, which are shown in Table 7.1. In seeking, developing, or improving a PSE program, one or more of these types of courses will be made available through the program. The program developer or consumer will need to decide if courses that are offered, or to be offered, reflect the desired philosophy and values of the program.

In the UP Program, three of the four course types presented in Table 7.1 are available to our students with ID: audited courses, inclusive courses, and specialized courses. Audited courses are the same as credit-bearing courses except the student does not earn credit for taking them. This has the advantage of allowing course requirements to be modified to meet the unique learning needs of our students, and does not require the instructor to grade students with ID on the same scale as is used with traditional students.

Beyond auditing courses, we also offer inclusive courses that are non-credit courses. In these courses, we encourage (but do not require) students with and without disabilities to participate together. Three inclusive courses

Table 7.1 Types of Courses Offered by PSE Programs to Students with ID

Credit-bearing courses: Courses taken for credit and usually aligned with degree requirements.
Audited courses: Regular courses which may be taken without earning credit. There may be exemptions of some course requirements. Students must pay fees to audit courses.
Inclusive courses: Courses designed by PSE programs that can be taken by students with and without ID.
Specialized courses: Courses designed by PSE programs only for students with ID.

are currently offered in the UP Program: the PEERS course (on social communication and interactions), our "About Life" course (on intimacy and adult relations), and our weekly cooking times (where students can plan and cook meals together in the residence hall kitchens). These courses are beneficial both to students with and without ID and give students a chance to interact around important topics and learning experiences.

Finally, we also have one specialized course, SPED 493, in which students with ID are tutored one-to-one by our undergraduate student supports on specific skills the student with ID has identified as being important for achieving their unique goals. Topics have ranged from improving reading or math skills, to preparing to get a driver's permit, to money or time management. UP students usually spend about two to three hours a week in these individualized, one-to-one sessions taught by their same-age peers. This is the only course we offer in which students with ID are not integrated with students without disabilities.

Some PSE programs also enroll students in traditional courses and allow them to take the courses for college credit. While we see some advantages in this kind of opportunity, we also believe there are disadvantages. For various reasons, we have not pursued this route as an integral part of our program, although we have kept the door open for the possibility.

The following story about Sosha demonstrates a case of how our PSE program provided an opportunity for one student to acquire knowledge and skills necessary to pursue a meaningful life and career. In the remainder of this chapter, we discuss the strategies we use to achieve these outcomes.

Benefits of Students with ID Enrolling in Traditional Courses

Some PSE programs offer only what in Table 7.1 is called specialized courses. In these programs, students engage in their formal learning activities mostly with other students with ID, although they may also have some inclusive learning events, or what is sometimes referred to as "reverse inclusion." In many ways, these kinds of courses resemble the self-contained, segregated classrooms that students experienced in public schools. We believe that although there may be a need for some specialized coursework, that separate courses only for students with ID should not be the mainstay of a college education, especially one purporting to be inclusive.

In the UP Program, each semester, all of our students with ID audit about nine to twelve credit hours of traditional coursework. Students are advised to take courses related to their personal and career interests, and there are no limits on the courses in which they can enroll. This is because since the development of the UP Program, inclusion has been one of the cornerstones of our program philosophy. We believe that students with ID who attend college should be able to attend all aspects of college. Further, enrolling students with ID in college courses has several positive effects, including effects on the students themselves, *and* effects on others in the university community.

Meet Sosha

Sosha has shown interest in owning her own restaurant when she finishes her college experience. She enjoys working with people and has strong family support to achieve her future career goals. Sosha has completed her academic roadmap with various career interests and goals she wants to achieve in the two-year PSE program. With owning her own restaurant, she understands she has to develop a business plan and learn more about restaurant operations. She also knows she has to learn ways to market and promote her business to acquire the professional communication skills to interact successfully with employees and the public. For classes, some of her coursework includes: public speaking, interpersonal communication, first aid and CPR, hospitality and tourism, restaurant management, Facebook marketing, nutrition, intro to entrepreneurship, group leadership, and food and culture. For some of her individualized goals in these courses, the instructors and her support team members have met to review the big ideas from the course syllabus to establish her individualized goals and level of course participation. In her First Aid and CPR class, her ultimate goal is to complete all the required online modules and in-class drills to obtain her Red Cross and CPR First Aid Certification. She has requested an in-class support to read aloud the online modules and extra time for the in-class drills when possible. She expressed she will participate in all class discussions and group projects but has asked to write papers at a shorter length when possible and have extended time on bigger projects. The instructor, Sosha, her in-class support, and PSE program staff have all agreed on these goals and course participation levels at the initial meeting before the first week of classes. The instructor and all support team members have agreed to review and reflect on Sosha's progress in this class and her goals at her next monthly person-centered planning (PCP) meeting. If the instructor or in-class support is not able to attend the monthly PCP meeting, they will help document Sosha's class performance on her individualized goals through weekly surveys and by email to program staff before the meeting occurs. Goals are rated and the class plan is adapted or revisited as needed throughout the semester.

Benefits for PSE Students with ID

Just as it is for other college students, it is difficult to quantify the effects of taking a particular college course on students with ID. Nevertheless, our experience has provided us with sufficient observations and anecdotal reports to allow us to conclude that there are several specific benefits related to students with ID enrolling in traditional courses.

Knowledge acquisition. When most students with ID take college courses, they learn and retain some percentage of the core content of the course. They participate in class discussions, do group and individual assignments (albeit sometimes with support), and sometimes take course tests, often doing well on them. During and after the course, many times students will discuss the subject matter with UP staff members and their peers, and show evidence of knowledge about the course. Although it is not possible to say they have learned as much in the course as have other students (although we do not have data that bear on this question), it would clearly be wrong to say they have not acquired and retained some of the most significant course content and big ideas from the course.

Intellectual stimulation. In addition to specific knowledge acquisition per se, many students with ID enjoy and benefit from the intellectual stimulation provided by a college course through the various intentional and incidental learning experiences the course offers. Often these students have not had an opportunity to take courses of interest to them while in high school, so when they take college courses in areas ranging from art to history to public speaking, they often find the course to be intellectually stimulating and refreshing. They may not grasp all of the content, but what they do understand is often enthusiastically consumed. It is not uncommon that a student will develop sufficient interest in an area so that they want to take another course in the same area, or want to pursue a career in an area related to the course content.

Learning stamina. Learning requires energy, and sometimes we find that students with ID initially lack this energy. Participating in a class that may last an hour or more and that then requires out-of-class homework can be a bit fatiguing. But like other endeavors, with experience, interest, and the benefits associated with the activity, students usually develop greater endurance for engaging in formal academic learning. This is shown by being able to increase the amount of time they can engage in individual and group assignments, and the ability to finish assignments by due dates. We believe that "lifelong learning" should be a goal for everyone, but before this can occur for someone, they must be able to stay engaged in a learning activity for a sufficient amount of time. Taking courses increases the learning energy for students with ID and also helps them to develop responsibility for achieving demanding cognitive tasks within a time limit.

Knowledge application. There are two outcomes that all PSE programs should strive for: Graduates should attain community-based employment in a career area of their choice, and they should achieve a level of confidence that allows them to advocate for themselves in society. We have observed that the knowledge and intellectual activity acquired through college courses can contribute to both outcomes. Through their coursework, students have learned about career areas of interest and how to work in these areas. In some cases, they have already had an interest in an area and have learned more about it; in other cases, they have learned about a new area and have decided to shift career goals to that area. Also, through course participation, virtually all students have gained confidence. Many times, this allows them to "speak truth to power," including telling parents (and the UP staff) about the life they wish to have.

Worldly sophistication. Many students with ID benefit from college courses in a way we would like to believe all college students do: It makes them better and more knowledgeable world citizens. Although colleges and universities serve as a source of knowledge and skills for specific career paths, they also connect many young minds to our society and societies beyond ours. In our program, students have had the opportunity to learn about different cultures through courses and student organizations, and have even experienced short study abroad courses (Kelley, Prohn, & Westling, 2016; Kelley, Westling, & Prohn, 2017; Prohn, Kelley, & Westling, 2016). Unfortunately, there are few instances of people with ID having opportunities to learn about and understand broader world conditions and events, but participating in college courses presents such an opportunity.

Benefits for Others in the College Community

Having students with ID enrolled in courses with traditional college students provides benefits not only for the students with ID, but for other college students and for many faculty members as well.

Other college students. The students who work with the UP Program as natural supports for the students with ID often comment about the effect of observing the students with ID pursuing their academic goals, and they often share that they themselves have better attendance and academic performance because of the strong commitments demonstrated by the UP students. We believe, as our research and that of others has shown, that it is gratifying and rewarding for college students to provide personal tutoring, note-taking, and other kinds of support. For many, it confirms their interest in teaching or providing services for individuals with disabilities; for others, it allows them to experience an important maturation experience (Barron, Kelley, & Westling, 2017; Zafft, 2006).

Additional available literature also suggests a positive effect of college students with ID on others when enrolled in college courses. For example, Westling, Kelley, Cain, and Prohn (2013) and Sowell and Maddox (2015) found having students with ID in college coursework and campus life created greater acceptance and awareness with their peers without disabilities. Similarly, Rimmerman, Hozmi, and Duvdevany (2000) found more positive attitudes for college students who had tutored individuals with disabilities, while Casale-Giannola and Kamens (2006), and Culnane, Eisenman, and Murphy (2016) found having students with ID in courses brings greater purpose to the course and increases awareness and sensitivity toward persons with disabilities. Moreover, Griffin and colleagues (2016) found five common themes among peer mentors that worked with students with ID in college courses: (1) developing friendships, (2) experiencing personal growth, (3) increasing community involvement, (4) attaining experiences with people with disabilities, and (5) developing future careers related to people with disabilities.

College faculty. While college students see benefit in having students with ID in college coursework learning alongside them, faculty have also reported some benefits. This is important because faculty members are in pivotal roles to influence attitudinal change and facilitate overall student success, while serving as gatekeepers of college learning environments. Findings reported by Jones, Harrison, Harp, and Sheppard-Jones (2016) include faculty reports of academic, social, and personal gains for themselves and students. Faculty not only gained understanding from a student with ID's perspective, but learned new ideas and perspectives about the subject content, greater acceptance, and greater appreciation for diversity. Many faculty have repeatedly noted that having students with ID has helped them more constantly reflect on their own teaching practices and the accessibility of their course content.

Socially, both students and faculty have reported greater gains in awareness and acceptance of disability and an increased motivation to learn together. Gains have been reported in specific areas such as self-confidence, personal communication skills, recognition of learning potential, and self-worth. Faculty members have reported an opportunity to demonstrate and model the differentiated instruction, and promote other strategies for inclusion (Causton-Theoharis, Ashby, & DeClouette, 2009). Overall, many faculty express a favorable attitude about the development of PSE programs and the inclusion of college students with ID into college classrooms and campus events (Gibbons, Cihak, Mynatt, & Wilhoit, 2015).

Responding to Challenges Related to Course Enrollment for Students with ID

Although our personal experiences and available literature show clear benefits of enrolling students with ID, challenges to doing so still abound, and likely will continue. One of the biggest challenges are simply the unfounded dispositions and attitudes of key individuals. Unfortunately, some college administrators and college faculty have questioned why individuals with ID should be included in typical college courses given their presumed learning limitations. Or they have questioned how these students can be included effectively when typical college course content is designed to be rigorous and challenging. In fact, traditional course content *can* be a real challenge, but it is a challenge that can be effectively addressed.

Even though most college courses are designed to be demanding, we propose that there are three important facts that should be considered pertaining to enrolling students with ID in these courses, especially when they audit the courses.

First, in any college course you will find students with a wide range of ability. Some easily master the subject, but some are quite content just to earn a passing grade. Therefore, it is erroneous to say that a certain level of ability is required for all students who take a course. Additionally, we suggest that the motivation of the student is often a more significant factor than the student's intellectual potential for being successful in a course.

Second, the way in which the course content is delivered by the instructor affects how much is learned by each student in the course. Some instructors manifest an old-school attitude that implies, "I will teach the course in any way I want, and it is the responsibility of the student to learn the course content." On the other hand, many feel, "I should try teaching in a way that all students learn the essential course content." These latter instructors know that the way in which course content is delivered, the way they teach, and the way requirements are structured, will affect how much every student benefits from a course. Therefore, many college instructors today follow the principles of Universal Design for Learning (UDL). This approach is intended to make course content accessible for all learners, including those with diverse learning abilities (see UDL ON CAMPUS, http://udloncampus.cast.org/home#.W7-5lvlRepo).

Finally, we suggest that it is not actually necessary for everyone taking a course to learn the same thing or acquire the same knowledge as everyone else in the course. As a matter of fact, most colleges and universities allow some or all of their courses to be audited or taken without credit for any individual who wishes to pick and choose the content they want to acquire. For instance, a person might like to learn the rudiments of a foreign language, but not want to memorize the rules of grammar of the language, or be able to speak the language as fluently as a professional interpreter. Nevertheless, for a fee, this person could join the class and enjoy learning those aspects of the language that are relatively more important.

With these realizations, we draw three important conclusions:

1) All students enrolled in most courses can acquire *some* of the course content, even if all do not acquire the same amount.
2) The instructional approaches used in a course, based on the teaching philosophy of the instructor, can have a significant bearing on what all students learn.
3) It is possible to uniquely design the learning outcomes for individual students as long as earning traditional course credit is not a desired outcome.

Steps for students with ID to achieve success in traditional college courses

Based on the conclusions we have drawn, we propose using four steps so students with ID can benefit from audited enrollment in traditional college courses:

- Identify those courses of interest and relevance to the student.
- Identify the instructors of those courses who use methods that facilitate learning by *all* students in their classes.
- Collaborate with the student and instructor to individualize the course.
- Provide the student with natural support in the course so they will be successful.

Identifying Relevant Courses

Advising students with ID on which courses they should take should be based on three broad questions: What career path does the student wish to pursue; what other personal interests does the student have (outside their career interests); and what other special learning needs does the student have?

Student advisement should be based on previous career assessments and interviews with the student to determine their interests and needs. In the UP Program, we work with each student to develop an individualized academic roadmap when they first enroll in the program, and then update the roadmap as necessary based on interactions at PCP meetings. It is not uncommon that as the student progresses through the program, their interest becomes more focused, or differently focused, and the choice of course topics becomes clearer.

When the student's interests are known, the college course catalog (which includes course descriptions) serves as our primary resource to help students select courses. Using the catalog, soon after admission, we work with students, families, and our advising center to compile a list of courses that can be used throughout the program. Throughout the program, we use our PCP meetings to reconsider, and if necessary to update, courses relevant to the student. This means students will not be locked into courses that may not align with their career goals or interests. To assist in understanding the courses, we have formed collaborative relationships with our advising center and faculty members who teach the courses of interest to our students.

Prior to each semester, during a designated advising time (our university sets aside an "Advising Day"), PSE program staff reviews the academic roadmaps of each student, including the list of possible courses, and then compiles the related courses in which the student may have interest.

Although we do not use a pre-specified list of courses, we have found that some courses tend to be of particular interest to many of our students and are often included on lists of potential courses. These are useful as choices, especially when the student has just started the program and may not know the direction they wish to pursue. Some courses we often suggest include courses on public speaking, first aid and CPR, nutrition, health and wellness, career majors and exploration, and leadership courses. Further details are provided in Chapter 10 in relation to person-centered planning and academic roadmaps.

Identifying Cooperative Faculty

Perhaps like most programs, when the UP Program was beginning, we found it important to have personal interactions with those faculty whom we identified to teach the students in the program. We thought it unfortunate that there were still many people who possessed misconceptions and stereotyped images of individuals with ID, but sometimes we found this to be the case, even with college professors. So, when faculty members were not aware of our students, or were hesitant about having them in their courses, personal contact and communication was necessary to explain the characteristics of the student, how the student could participate in the course, and what was expected of the professor. At this writing, we have placed students with ID in over 265 different courses across all our colleges with more than 160 faculty members. As awareness has been spread, we often find little hesitation or resistance. Such an improvement in on-campus attitudes has been reported by others (Plotner & Marshall, 2015) and will no doubt occur for other PSE programs over time.

Nevertheless, there will be times when course instructors will require an orientation from the PSE staff in order to accept students into their class. Therefore, after a course has been identified for a student, if necessary, we suggest engaging in three steps.

- Inform the faculty member that a student with ID wishes to take their course.
- Explain that the student will audit the class and discuss and agree upon what the student will do in the course, based on what is required of other students in the course syllabus.
- And describe the kind of support the student will have while in the course.

One thing we have never done, and have rarely had the need to do, was force an instructor to accept a student with ID. While some might argue that it is the right of a student with ID to be included, and we agree they have a good point, the ultimate pushback from the instructor and college or university administrators might ultimately make the effort counterproductive.

At this time, we are fortunate that because we are not usually talking to a first-time faculty member, the reception is uneventful. This will likely be true for all successful programs as they achieve longevity. Initially, however, the course instructor may have to be supported in order to accept a student with ID into the course.

Individualizing Traditional College Courses

The benefits of having a student audit a course are that the student does not have to meet all the requirements of the course (tests, projects, reports, etc.); does not have to be graded like students taking the course for credit; and can complete requirements of the course that are meaningful but within the learning potential of the individual. So the first step that should be taken when a student with ID is enrolled to audit a particular course is to establish individual goals for and with the student. This is done by reviewing the syllabus to identify course goals for all students, and then identifying those relevant to the student with ID. Aligned with the individualized goals will be the activities the student will be completing in the course.

Course accommodations. After identifying relevant goals and activities, depending on the nature of the course, various accommodations may be provided to the student in order for them to have better access to course content and participate more fully in the course. Note that this does not mean that the course content is being modified, but that instructional procedures may be made in order for the student to be able to learn more in the course. For example, a student may take a test orally instead of in writing, or a student may listen to a recording of a lecture more than one time. In this way, the course content is not watered down, but the student's needs are addressed through these kinds of accommodations. Additional accommodations might be made by providing the student with different kinds of assistive technology that they are comfortable with and trained to use. Some of our students have used handheld audiorecorders, LiveScribe pens, or accessibility features built into their laptops.

The Office of Accessibility Resources (or the Disability Services Office), present on virtually all university and college campuses, can help establish required documentation for requesting accommodations for students. Some of the more common accommodations from this office include note-takers, audiobooks, extended time on tests, and/or testing in a separate room. In order for these accommodations to be provided, however, the students must choose to self-disclose their disability to this office. Beyond these kinds of accommodations, the student and program staff can propose course participation activities with instructors.

Another helpful arrangement is for instructors to incorporate principles of UDL into their courses. As we said earlier, some instructors are willing to do so, while others may be more traditional in their teaching. We have found that reaching out to offer support to willing faculty members to use UDL strategies has been helpful, but we have also chosen to be strategic rather than forceful with our outreach. A few of our efforts that have been helpful have been: (1) providing online resources for faculty members to read on their own, (2) having summer institutes in partnership with our university faculty support center on UDL topics, (3) setting up informal mentorships among faculty in colleges or departments, and (4) having brown bag lunches or focus group meetings from time to time.

We have sometimes found that it is helpful to have short meetings at the beginning of the term to address course-related issues with instructors so the student can fully participate and be comfortable in the course from the beginning of the term.

Establishing platforms for communication and homework support. At times homework can be one of the most frustrating areas for all college students, including students with ID. For many students with ID, homework has commonly not been a part of their school requirements, and when taking college courses, they sometimes have difficulty in completing this responsibility. We have found that the more structure and resources that can be provided, the more apt the student will be to engage in challenging college course homework. Here are a few ways and resources we have found helpful to provide more meaningful learning experiences and help maintain positive attitudes, especially related to homework completion.

1) Create an e-learning platform such as Blackboard to provide an online agenda book for everyone (student with ID, in-class support, PSE staff) to connect. We use the discussion board threads to create a thread for each class our students audit.
2) Host a place for documents that are being worked on over time to be housed for easier retrieval or to work on again if not finished in one homework setting. We have found attaching work in progress to the discussion threads helps alleviate lost papers or files.
3) Train and connect everyone on how to use and post to the discussion board as work is updated. It is primarily the responsibility of the PSE student to update the material, but the in-class support and the PSE staff need to monitor this progress.
4) Post syllabi for each course in one place for easier retrieval and review along with academic calendars with color-coded assignment deadlines.
5) Create hard copies of color-coded folders and binders to store important papers for each class. This allows the student to stay more organized with handouts and organizing separate files for each class.

Student accountability for course performance. We are often asked how our students, who are auditing courses, are graded. Because UP students are non-degree-seeking university students, they will receive an official transcript and the course will appear on the transcript. But it will be identified as an audited course and therefore will not have a grade or credit hours attached to it. However, this does not mean students are not held accountable for their work in the course. Their individual goals and course requirements for each course become part of the goals on their individual plan for college participation (IPCP) and they must complete at least 80% of these goals in order to complete the UP Program. Not completing individual course requirements jeopardizes their chances of successfully completing the program. Therefore, once goals and requirements for a course have been established, the student is expected to complete most of them and their progress is monitored during PCP meetings.

Using Natural Supports in Courses

Although many faculty are willing to provide support and accommodations for students with ID, we also use in-class student supports to help facilitate course accommodations and/or to support the student with ID to complete their course goals. While many programs provide in-class support in different ways, we have opted to solicit and recruit class supports who are already enrolled in the same class with the PSE student. This allows us to avoid an extra person going into the classroom making it awkward for the student with ID and all the other students in the class. The in-class support provides necessary assistance, but the student with ID is held accountable for completing the individualized course requirements.

Initial recruitment. The first step for initial recruitment of in-class supports is to gauge the comfort level of the PSE student about disclosing to the entire class that they are in the class. PSE staff must assess if the student would or would not be comfortable with any announcements for potential class supports to be made in the class in which they are enrolled. They may or may not want to identify or express their program association or disability, which is their option.

If the student is not comfortable with information being shared in the class, program staff should respect this decision and allow the PSE student to more informally find and ask someone in the class to be the in-class support for the semester. If they are supportive of sharing the need with the class, the program staff, with the instructor's permission, can share the need and give a general description of the roles and responsibilities for being an in-class support. Following the announcement and explanation, contact information of potential class supports can be quickly gathered for follow-up communication. Many instructors are also willing to help send out recruitment emails and information about in-class support roles and responsibilities to their students for further consideration.

Training. After a commitment has been made to provide in-class support, a contract expressing the responsibilities of the in-class support is developed and online training is provided. We use online training modules for our class supports and then a quiz to test the big ideas from the training module content. The in-class support training module covers topics such as: (1) an overview of the program and values, (2) how to interact and work with individuals with ID in class and during weekly homework sessions, (3) examples of how to review or teach course content in effective ways, (4) review strategies . . . there is always homework to do every week, (5) scheduling software overview, (6) Blackboard resources and ongoing communication platforms, (7) working with professors and documenting student progress, and (8) confidentiality.

Final Thoughts

As a PSE student engages in course participation, it is important to reflect on what is working well and what may need to be changed. Short and simple evaluations or quick emails among faculty, students, and class supports can help to assess overall progress and in-class behaviors, and can often alleviate miscommunication and end-of-semester issues. In addition, we have monitored academic progress by having weekly academic check-in meetings with PSE students. This allows us to help hold the student accountable for upcoming assignments or group projects, but also support them with accommodations they may need to understand course content better. The monthly PCP meetings also offer a platform for evaluation and accountability where faculty, supports, students, and staff connect to discuss overall class performance and assignments. During these monthly meetings, we also take time to share stories of success and showcase class projects together. While enrolling students with ID in traditional college courses presents one of the most challenging aspects of a PSE program, it can also be an important learning experience for everyone involved.

References

Barron, T., Kelley, K. R., & Westling, D. L. (2017, December). *Effects of interacting with college students with intellectual disability on natural supports.* Paper presented at the 2017 TASH Conference, Atlanta, GA.

Casale-Giannola, D., & Kamens, M. W. (2006). Inclusion at a university: Experiences of a young woman with Down syndrome. *Mental Retardation,* 44(5), 344–352. doi:10.1352/0047-6765.

Causton-Theoharis, J., Ashby, C., & DeClouette, N. (2009). Relentless optimism: Inclusive postsecondary opportunities for students with significant disabilities. *Journal of Postsecondary Education and Disability,* 22(2), 88–105.

Culnane, M., Eisenman, L. T., & Murphy, A. (2016). College peer mentoring and students with intellectual disability: Mentors' perspectives on relationship dynamics. *Inclusion,* 4(4), 257–269.

Gibbons, M. M., Cihak, D. F., Mynatt, B., & Wilhoit, B. E. (2015). Faculty and student attitudes toward postsecondary education for students with intellectual disabilities and autism. *Journal of Postsecondary Education and Disability, 28*(2), 149–162.

Griffin, M. M., Mello, M. P., Glover, C. A., Carter, E. W., & Hodapp, R. M. (2016). Supporting students with intellectual and developmental disabilities in postsecondary education: The motivations and experiences of peer mentors. *Inclusion, 4*(2), 75–88.

Jones, M. M., Harrison, B., Harp, B., & Sheppard-Jones, K. (2016). Teaching college students with intellectual disability: What faculty members say about the experience. *Inclusion, 4*(2), 89–108.

Kelley, K. R., Prohn, S. M., & Westling, D. L. (2016). Inclusive study abroad course for college students with and without intellectual disabilities. *Journal of Postsecondary Education and Disability, 29*(1), 91–101.

Kelley, K. R., Westling, D. L., & Prohn, S. M. (2017, November). *Benefits, challenges, and reflections of study abroad experiences.* Paper presented at the 2017 State of the Art Conference on Postsecondary Education and Individuals with Intellectual Disabilities, Syracuse, NY.

Plotner, A. J., & Marshall, K. J. (2015). Postsecondary education programs for students with an intellectual disability: Facilitators and barriers to implementation. *Intellectual and Developmental Disabilities, 53*, 58–69. doi: 10.1352/1934-9556-53.1.58.

Prohn, S. M., Kelley, K. R., & Westling, D. L. (2016). Studying abroad inclusively: Reflections by college students with and without intellectual disability. *Journal of Intellectual Disabilities, 20*(4), 341–353. doi: 10.1177/1744629515617050.

Rimmerman, A., Hozmi, B., & Duvdevany, I. (2000). Contact and attitudes toward individuals with disabilities among students tutoring children with developmental disabilities. *Journal of Intellectual and Developmental Disability, 25*(1), 13–18. http://dx.doi.org/10.1080/132697800112758.

Sowell, R., & Maddox, B. (2015) Added value: Perspectives of student mentors working within a university level inclusive education program. *Online Journal of Education Research, 3*(1), 1–10.

Westling, D. L., Kelley, K. R., Cain, B., & Prohn, S. (2013). College students' attitudes about an inclusive postsecondary education program for individuals with an intellectual disability. *Education and Training in Autism and Developmental Disabilities, 48*, 306–319.

Zafft, C. (2006). A case study of accommodations for transition-age students with intellectual disabilities. *Journal of Postsecondary Education and Disability, 18*(2), 167–180.

8 Career Planning and Job Training

Many adults with ID, compared with those without disabilities, do not enjoy the benefits of community-based employment. According to the United States Census Bureau, the employment rate for working-age adults without disabilities is over 70% (Winsor et al., 2017), but only about 17% of working-age adults with ID are employed in a community job (National Core Indicators, 2015). These data suggest that efforts must be improved if we want to have better employment outcomes for adults with ID.

Early employment is usually a good predictor of later employment. In fact, research demonstrates that when students with ID are employed while in high school, they are more likely to be employed later as adults (Carter, Austin, & Trainor, 2012; Luecking & Fabian, 2000; Mamun, Carter, Fraker, & Timmins, 2017; Test et al., 2009; Wehman et al., 2015). What's more, attending a PSE program is also associated with successful adult employment (Migliore & Butterworth, 2008). This is likely true because most PSE programs focus on successful employment as an important outcome of their program. In fact, Papay and Bambara (2011) surveyed PSE programs across the United States on the various services provided to individuals with ID and found that 67% of the PSEs listed improving employment opportunities through vocational training as their main purpose. So it is important that PSE programs know how to prepare students with ID for employment. This is the purpose of the present chapter: To discuss how vocational preparation should be woven into a PSE program for students with ID. Before doing so, let's consider the benefits associated with paid employment.

Why Community-Based Paid Employment Is Important as a PSE Outcome

When compared with no employment or employment in a sheltered workshop, the benefits of community-based, competitive, integrated employment for an adult with ID are numerous. Working in a regular job means higher wages, access to benefits, greater independence and economic self-sufficiency, more integration with people without disabilities, more opportunities to make personal choices and exercise self-determination, expanded career options, and increased job satisfaction. Additionally, when young adults with ID have jobs there is less need to rely on public benefits, there is a greater feeling of self-worth, and there is an overall improvement in quality of life (Wehman, 2013).

A key question, however, is: What leads to employment and the benefits of employment? Much of it comes down to the preparation of the individual and the expectation for success. For example, Test et al. (2009) reported greater employment success when students with ID participated in a sequence of courses defined by their career focus, received an education that combined academics and vocational studies, and participated in school-sponsored work opportunities. In another study, Carter et al. (2012) found that more positive parent expectations for success, along with other life experiences, contributed to community-based employment.

Recent data based on the federally funded TPSID projects show the important role that PSE programs can play in preparing individuals for adult employment. As we stated previously, employment while in high school is an important predictor of later employment. But Smith, Grigal, and Papay (2018) reported that 56% of students attending TPSIDs had *never* held a paid job prior to entering college. This makes employment and employment training while students are in PSEs essential. In another study, Smith, Grigal, and Shepard (2018) reported that youth with ID receiving PSE services as part of their Individualized Plan for Employment (IPE, a Vocational Rehabilitation plan) not only made gains in educational attainments, but landed jobs paying 51% higher wages than counterparts who did not participate in a PSE program. In yet another study of the graduates of Taft College's Transition to Independent Living Program, Ross, Marcell, Williams, and Carlson (2013) found that 78% of the graduates (or 87 of 125 graduates over a ten-year period) were employed in the community, with 80 of 87 making above minimum wage. From informal contacts with our own graduates, we have found that about 90% of them are employed in one or more community jobs within a year after leaving the program and working jobs around 20 or more hours per week making minimum wage or above.

All in all, these outcomes far exceed the job outcomes reported over the years for most adults with ID (Newman et al., 2011; Rusch & Braddock, 2004; Sanford et al., 2011; Wagner, Newman, Cameto, Garza, & Levine, 2005), strongly suggesting that it is important for PSE programs to focus on preparing students for jobs in the community after graduation.

Critical Steps for Achieving Post-Program Employment

Given the benefits of employment and the need to prepare for employment while in a PSE program, one of the most important services of the program should be for students to be employed *while in the program* and receive instruction and support that teaches appropriate job skills.

Employing an Employment Support Specialist

Because we consider job experience to be such a critical part of our program, we commit a one-half-time employment specialist to oversee job placement and support for the eight students with ID in our PSE program. This person is employed by the university as a "student support specialist" (as well as a half-time administrative assistant), and is a *Certified Employment Support Professional™ (CESP™)*, certified by the Employment Support Professional Certification Council (ESPCC).

Under the leadership of the employment specialist, during our two-year, four-semester program, students are placed in part-time jobs (or internships) for approximately ten hours a week, sometimes splitting their time between two placements. Their jobs may change from one semester to another as they explore their interests, or they may remain in a given position if they clearly express a strong interest in the position as a long-term employment goal. As a rule, if students are placed in an internship for one semester, we will not continue the student in the same position unless the employer converts the internship to a paid position. Steps taken by the employment specialist to determine job interests and place, supervise, and evaluate students in jobs or internships are presented Table 8.1.

Conducting Employment-Related Assessments

Different assessment procedures can help provide guidance to the PSE staff about the type of employment that may be most appropriate for an individual with ID, and therefore the type of training that should be provided while in the PSE program to achieve post-program employment. These assessments fall into two broad categories, formal and informal, and help us to identify

Table 8.1 Employment Specialist Duties and Responsibilities

- Collaborate with PSE staff, students, and families to identify career and related goals for students.
- Identify work sites or internship sites for PSE students based on career goals and interests and initiate contacts with employers.
- Help coordinate transportation options to and from work sites.
- Assist with hiring paperwork, interviews, and scheduling work hours.
- Place PSE students on jobs or in internships and specify working hours and other relevant arrangements.
- Conduct task analysis of each work-sited requirement.
- Direct student supports in supervision methods and interactions with PSE students.
- Evaluate PSE student's achievement of work goals.
- Participate in person-centered planning sessions to discuss student progress and provide feedback to students.
- Collaborate with UP staff, UP students, families, and community agencies to identify post-PSE job possibilities and facilitate job placement.

a student's strengths, preferences, interests, and needs on which to base the student's short-term training goals while in the program in order to reach long-term employment goals after the program. Based on the assessments, we try to identify between two and four career directions for each student.

Formal assessments are more traditional, usually norm-referenced assessments. They are intended to provide information about the ability or status of the student in comparison with similar individuals in the standardization sample. More common formal assessments related to employment include learning style inventories, academic achievement tests, adaptive behavior scales, aptitude tests, work performance measures, and personality tests. Informal assessments focus on a student's expressed interests, attitudes, and behaviors. They typically include incidental observations, structured performance trials in specific situations (similar to curriculum-based measures), and interviews with students. The results of informal assessments may be used to create anecdotal notes, and performance artifacts may be stored within individual student portfolios (Sitlington & Clark, 2007).

In the UP Program, we have used a combination of formal and informal assessments to help determine our students' career interests. These have included *Your Employment Selections: YES!* (formal; Morgan et al., 2000), *Brigance Transition Skills Inventory* (formal; Curriculum Associates, 2010), interviews (informal), and personal profile questionnaires (informal; Sitlington & Clark, 2007) to name a few.

We also gather input from the undergraduate students who serve as natural supports. Beginning with the initial visit to open house, during the orientation camp, and in the first few weeks of the program, we learn from the UP student's peers about various strengths, interests, preferences, dislikes, and areas requiring improvement. This information, generally presented at PCP meetings and in other informal contexts, along with our formal and informal assessments, helps us to understand the direction(s) the student might pursue with regard to employment, and to determine individual goals for successful employment to be achieved.

Teaching Students to Seek Part-Time Jobs

After the student and the PSE staff have agreed on one or more career areas and identified related employment learning goals, a search for part-time employment in one or two of these areas may be pursued. In the UP Program, our employment support specialist will take the lead role in working with the student on this activity, focusing initially on an area that is of greatest interest to the student in order to search for a job for the current semester. In later semesters, we usually move the student to another job in order to provide an expanded learning opportunity.

When seeking potential employers, we first explore work experiences that are the most inclusive and have higher-paying options. We have found that paid work is more meaningful to students than unpaid internships, so paid employment is always our first option. An additional advantage of paid work is that the employers will hold the UP student employees to the same standards as all other employees. If paid employment is not possible in a career area of interest to the student, we will explore the possibility of placing the student with a desired employer as an unpaid intern. However, this is not an option we desire, and as a rule, we will not allow a student to remain in an unpaid internship for more than one semester. We have often seen secondary school programs that have fallen into a vocational training trap by providing work experiences without pay. Therefore, if at all possible, PSE programs should avoid this.

The search for an appropriate job for a student (or if necessary an internship) should involve the student in every step of the process. The more the students are involved, the more they learn about job searches and about the specific duties and requirements of different jobs. This knowledge will allow them to reflect on their strengths and interests vis-à-vis the job duties, and also give them an opportunity to advocate for accommodations they may need to do a job. As we work with students to find jobs on campus or in the surrounding community, we teach them to use several resources.

Traditional job searching. Job searches today can be conducted online as well as through traditional newspaper want ads or posted notices. Therefore we work with our students to conduct searches using our university's online job search tool, other employment search engines, and the newspaper. These searches allow them to explore hundreds of jobs located on and off campus. Based on the searches, we help the student develop a list of jobs that might be of interest, help them understand the nature of the job and the job requirements, and discuss the pros and cons of different jobs with them, such as the working conditions, the hours of work, and how much a job pays.

Families and friends. Many individuals find employment through personal contacts, and this is also a possible avenue for students in a PSE program. Friends and acquaintances on campus (such as some of our natural supports) might have information about possible jobs that are relevant to the interest of the PSE student, and parents or other family members may also be aware of useful connections. Therefore, we assist students in communications with these individuals in their searches for jobs. Additionally, our families are also asked to help make a list of potential employers in their student's future living area that we can approach about current or future employment. This allows us to map future job opportunities to which the students may be able to transfer after graduation, while providing us with a clear picture of the job training the student will require while in the program.

Pool of former employers. Over the years the UP Program has been in operation, our students have been employed by more than 60 employers on and off campus. Just as many other university students are employed locally while in college, so are UP students. And because of this, many university-based and local employers have come to count on the labor of students to help operate their businesses. So it is not uncommon for employers to tell us that we should contact them when we are looking for a position for a student, and many times we do. However, this resource should be used with a bit of caution. First, we don't simply want to place the student in a job; we want the student to identify the type of work they want to do, and then find the best employer with the desired kind of work. Second, over-relying on the same employers might ultimately lead to burnout by the employer and eliminate a possible position for a future student who would be a better fit. For these reasons, going to previous employers is usually not our first option.

Assisting Students to Apply for a Job

Once the employment support specialist and the student have agreed on one or two possible jobs, we work along with the student and our *Career Services and Professional Development Office* to help students develop or polish their resumes and prepare application materials for the sought-after position(s). Many times, this university office can be an asset by helping the student practice interview skills and update resumes. They also might help with job searches and organizing job fairs that all students take part in each semester. Peer supports can also help by providing interviewing practice and helping with resumes. We have found it very helpful to video-record practice interviews and then play them back for the student to observe and reflect on. This can help the student identify areas that might need a little more practice before going to the interview.

When the student feels ready, with the employment support specialist assisting as necessary, an appointment will be made with the potential employer to submit the application and participate in an interview; or, alternatively, the application may be submitted online and a future interview appointment made. When the face-to-face meeting with the employer occurs, the student should take the lead, with the employment support specialist providing assistance only as necessary. Since the student has prepared beforehand for the interview, the interview itself should be more or less uneventful. The employment support specialist can provide support as necessary, but the primary communication should be between the student and the employer.

When the student is ultimately hired, it is important to make sure the employment support specialist assists the student to gather necessary documents for the employer such as their social security card, identification cards or driver's license, tax information, and/or direct deposit or routing numbers for bank accounts. Since we know we want our students to find jobs as part of the PSE program learning experience, we ask parents for these documents at the time of admission to the program. This hastens the employment process and allows the student to get paid in a timely manner.

Maintaining Positive Relations with New Employers

After a student has been successfully employed, there should be a brief celebration. The student should recognize the significance of having a job and how it enhances their status as an adult. But it is also important that the PSE program, and especially the employment support specialist, work to develop a good partnership with the student's new employer. Although for many college students having a job in college is just a way to earn extra money, for students with ID it is more. It is a significant learning opportunity that will bear on their future life in the community. The relationship between employers and the PSE program will likely benefit from the following steps.

Defining Critical Roles and Responsibilities

It is good practice to clearly define the roles and responsibilities of the employer, the PSE program, and the student in order to establish a positive working relationship and avoid unintentional miscommunication. In our program we do this by meeting with employers and asking them to sign a memorandum of understanding (MOU) listing responsibilities and roles for the employer, the PSE program, and the student. The MOU is then signed by the employer, the employment support specialist, and the student, making clear the expectations for all parties.

One of the important elements of the MOU is the schedule for the student and for observation by the employment support specialist or by one of the students who provides natural supports. The employer should know when the student will work and when a program supervisor will appear to provide one-to-one assistance with the student. Additionally, to support the employer, as we also do with our faculty teaching our students in their classes, we encourage our employers to connect with some of our previous employers in order to share ideas and network.

Creating and Implementing a Job Task List

After the MOU is signed, we have found a useful next step is to create a job task list, or a task analysis of the job requirements, based on input from the employer. The specificity of this list will depend on the student and the job. In general, the more complex the job is in relation to the student's ability, the more specific the task list should be. It is important that the employer agreed with the content of the task list, and the student understands the steps on the list. Adding figures or symbols can sometimes be helpful if the student's reading ability is limited. We often use Google images or pictures that the student self-selects. Most of the time these task lists are laminated and used each time the student is on the job. Sometimes we will use apps such as *First Then Visual Schedule* or recording devices for the task in lieu of paper lists.

The primary reason for the task list is so the student can ultimately complete the job independently by following the list. It is also a useful tool for the employer, the employment support specialist, and natural supports who may be assisting the student. If we determine a student is not making adequate progress on learning the job skills, we will use the task list as a data collection system so we can assess the steps in the task that the student is having difficulty with versus those which are being performed independently.

Many times it is important to discuss with the employer exactly how the student is expected to complete each step on the task list, and any assistance, modifications, or accommodations the student may need to complete all or some of the steps on the list. Many employers or co-workers can serve as natural supports in this process, or if not, other student supports can provide assistance. This is a process that can vary with the workplace and the employer. Sometimes the employer wants the PSE program to arrange for support while the student is on the job, but in some cases the employer does not wish an outsider to come into the business, and will provide support from within the work environment.

Ultimately the task list is meant to allow the student to be more independent. They should be able to rely on the task list instead of having to rely extensively on co-workers and supervisors. By the completion of the program, we would like all students to be able to perform their desired jobs with minimal reliance on human supports.

Developing, Supporting, and Monitoring Job-Related Goals

As noted in Chapter 1 (Table 1.1), vocational success is a major outcome of the UP Program as well as other PSE programs (Papay & Bambara, 2011). In order to reach this goal, the student with ID must have several sub-goals (or objectives) that, if achieved, will allow for on-the-job success.

Developing Job-Related Individual Plan for College Participation (IPCP) Goals

We have found that two kinds of IPCP goals are important, and we collaborate with the student to make sure these are included on the student's plan and discussed regularly at the student's PCP meeting. The goals include: (1) the skills necessary to appropriately complete the job; and (2) social skills (often referred to as "soft skills") necessary for appropriate interactions with the employer, other employees, and customers or other individuals in the work environment.

Goals are developed based on input from the employer, student, the UP employment support specialist, and the natural supports. We usually begin with an initial list of goals, and then discuss them with the student at PCP meetings during the term based on input from the student and other key persons. This is a fluid process that can change based on the work tasks assigned or other circumstances, such as when the employer might need the student to be present. As the student progresses, some goals will be achieved and so noted, others will continue to need work, and some new goals may be added if the need arises.

Monitoring and Improving Job Performance

Documentation of a student's work performance is a critical need. It allows us to know areas the student is performing well in, and areas that need improvement. Sometimes monitoring also points to the need for accommodations or job modifications, and often it tells us that supports can be faded as the student shows greater independence.

The job task list, as well as the soft skill goals developed for and with the student during PCP meetings, serve as the basis for job performance evaluation. Initially, the employment support specialist will collect performance data and give the student feedback and support. However, as soon as possible, undergraduate students who serve as natural supports will take over this role, collecting performance data, and giving the student with ID both support and feedback on their job performance. The natural support student will often be a co-worker employed at the same location as the student with ID.

The employment support specialist conducts biweekly observations at the job site, and most of the time observations are unannounced. This allows them to observe the student in the work environment, suggest strategies to improve performance, check in with the employer, and assess how the natural support is doing. The visits can sometimes help identify the need for assistive technology that might help improve work success. Most importantly, these visits also allow the PSE staff to make decisions about fading support, as discussed below.

Occasionally issues will be raised by the employer about unsatisfactory job performance. The employment support specialist will make efforts to address these concerns, and ultimately they are likely to be discussed at a future PCP meeting. Usually the issue is resolved. However, if the student's performance does not improve, for either job-related skills or for social behaviors or skills, the employer has the right, as the student knows, to dismiss the student from the job using the same termination protocol as would be used for any employee. This is part of the agreement signed by the program staff, the student, and the employer. It is important for the student to learn while in the PSE program what is expected on a job site, and behaviors that are and are not acceptable by most employers.

114 *Major Components*

Providing Supplemental Instruction

Although we clearly believe that experience is the best teacher for both job skills and social skills, through our SPED 493 class, we provide individualized tutoring to help students acquire key job-related skills. Topics that are often addressed are included in Table 8.2. The specific topics addressed in the sessions are based on the most relevant needs of the student at a given time, and are often determined and discussed in the PCP meetings. Again, we use our undergraduate natural supports to provide some of the tutoring.

Fading Support as Students Learn Job Skills

As students show sufficient progress on a job, we fade the support provided to them. This is often encouraged by employers and the students themselves when students have adequately become part of the work environment and are engaging in job activities similar to other employees. Support may be faded for parts of the job, or for the entire job. The fading is determined based on the performance data across time. It has occurred as quickly as the first day on the job for some students, but for others fading may require an entire semester or may not completely occur. The fading process depends on everyone's comfort level and the student's overall work performance, including demonstration of appropriate social skills. We consider being able to work on a job with little or no support as a major accomplishment for a student and celebrate such an accomplishment at a subsequent PCP meeting.

Building Positive Relations with Employers and Co-workers

Assisting PSE students to find part-time jobs in career areas of interest, and teaching them how to be successful on those jobs, rests on securing the

Table 8.2 Job-Related Topics Taught by Peer Supports and Employment Support Specialist

- Developing a video resume
- Searching for a job
- Preparing for job fairs
- Filling out a job application
- Writing a cover letter
- Participating in a job interview
- Follow-up steps after an interview
- Starting a new job
- Changing jobs
- Important social skills when on the job
- Maintaining appropriate conversations
- Setting and respecting personal boundaries
- Using problem-solving skills
- Understanding yourself and advocating for job-related accommodations

cooperation of employers and co-workers. The employers must be willing to offer the student a job and support the student as they learn the job, and co-workers must be willing to interact appropriately with the student and sometimes provide support themselves. In fact, when possible, we will recruit co-workers (who are often undergraduate students themselves) who are willing to serve as a natural support within the UP Program.

Both employers and co-workers must understand that the part-time job is an important part of the student's learning experience and generally must invest some amount of time and energy in helping the student to succeed on the job. To help and support them do this, we attempt to maintain strong, positive relations. To do this we provide adequate support for the student on the job; we invite them to participate in the student's PCP meetings; and we offer them resources to help them better understand the purpose of our program and how to interact most effectively with an individual with ID. Examples of strategies for maintaining positive workplace interactions are presented in Table 8.3.

Final Thoughts

The ultimate goal of career identification and job training in PSE programs is for the student to find a desirable job in their chosen community after graduation. This requires a strong partnership be developed between the PSE program, the parents, and service providers typically in the selected

Table 8.3 Supporting Employers and Co-workers

- Demonstrate and reinforce natural interactions between employers, co-workers, and students.
- Encourage intentional and incidental instruction of the student by employers and co-workers.
- Occasionally remind employers, co-workers, and students of their respective responsibilities.
- Develop formal and informal opportunities for employers and co-workers to engage with other employers and co-workers to share ideas and strategies.
- If an outside natural support is used to supervise, make sure the employer knows the proper role of this person and what they can and cannot do.
- Encourage open and honest evaluative feedback from the employer; discourage "petting" or "letting the student slide" as a result of their disability.
- Be responsible for supplying any supplementary material, devices, or resources the student may require to do the job instead of relying on the employer to do so.
- If there are expectations beyond normal duties, such as providing letters of reference, assisting with video resumes, or completing evaluations, ask for this assistance in advance.
- Encourage employers and co-workers to attend PCP meetings and communicate with the PSE staff when the need arises.
- Ask employers to help identify other employers for possible future job sites.

community. The process begins when the student enters the program and culminates when a student lands a job that will begin after graduation.

It is important to start planning as early as possible during the college experience for making the transition from college to independently working and living in the community. Throughout the program there are many resume updates, job evaluations collected, career assessments completed, videos of work tasks collected, and meetings with other parents, Vocational Rehabilitation and Benefits Counselors to determine and educate students and families of their upcoming transition.

Family involvement and education have been key factors for soliciting and deciding on appropriate career paths. As program staff, we do our best to come alongside our students and families early in the process in order to map out their community and make visits when close enough to network or contact employers with them. PSE programs should continue successful vocational practices, seek additional funding, and most importantly provide individuals who have a solid foundation to blaze the trails with a greater quality of life along with the employment outcomes they deserve (see more in Chapters 12 and 14).

References

Carter, E. W., Austin, D., & Trainor, A. A. (2012). Predictors of postschool employment outcomes for young adults with severe disabilities. *Journal of Disability Policy Studies, 23,* 50–63. doi: 10.1177/1044207311414680.

Curriculum Associates (2010). *Brigance transition skills inventory.* North Billerica, MA: Author.

Luecking, R. G., & Fabian, E. S. (2000). Paid internships and employment success for youth in transition. *Career Development for Exceptional Individuals, 23,* 205–221. doi:10.1177/088572880002300207.

Mamun, A. A., Carter, E. W., Fraker, T. M., & Timmins, L. L. (2017). Impact of early work experiences on subsequent paid employment for young adults with disabilities. *Career Development and Transition for Exceptional Individuals,* Advanced Online Publication. https://doi.org/10.1177/2165143417726302.

Migliore, A., & Butterworth, J. (2008). Postsecondary education and employment outcomes for youth with intellectual disabilities. *DataNote Series, Data Note XXI.* Boston, MA: Institute for Community Inclusion.

Morgan, R. L., Ellerd, D. A., Gerity, B. P., & Tullis, M. D. (2000). *Your employment selections. YES!* Utah State University. Logan, UT: Technology, Research, and Innovation in Special Education (TRI-SPED).

National Core Indicators (2015). *Chart generator 2014–15.* National Association of State Directors of Developmental Disabilities Services and Human Services Research Institute. Retrieved from www.nationalcoreindicators.org/charts/

Newman, L., Wagner, M., Knokey, A. M., Marder, C., Nagle, K., Shaver, D., Wei, X., with Cameto, R., Contreras, E., Ferguson, K., Greene, S., & Schwarting, M. (2011). *The post-high school outcomes of young adults with disabilities up to 8 years after high school. A report from the National Longitudinal Transition Study-2 (NLTS2)* (NCSER 2011-3005). Menlo Park, CA: SRI International. Available at www.nlts2.org/reports/

Papay, C. K., & Bambara, L. M. (2011). Postsecondary education for transition-age students with intellectual and other developmental disabilities: A national survey. *Education and Training in Autism and Developmental Disabilities, 46*, 78–93.

Ross, J., Marcell, J., Williams, J., & Carlson, P. (2013). Postsecondary education, employment, and independent living outcomes for persons with autism and intellectual disability. *Journal of Postsecondary Education and Disability, 26*, 337–351.

Rusch, F. R., & Braddock, D. (2004). Adult day programs versus supported employment (1988–2002): Spending and service practices of mental retardation and developmental disabilities state agencies. *Research and Practice for Persons with Severe Disabilities, 29*, 237–242.

Sanford, C., Newman, L., Wagner, M., Cameto, R., Knokey, A.-M., & Shaver, D. (2011). *The post-high school outcomes of young adults with disabilities up to 6 years after high school. Key findings from the National Longitudinal Transition Study-2 (NLTS2)* (NCSER 2011-3004). Menlo Park, CA: SRI International.

Sitlington, P., & Clark, G. (2007). The transition assessment process and IDEIA 2004. *Assessment for Effective Intervention, 32*, 133–142.

Smith, F., Grigal, M., & Papay, C. (2018). *Year one employment and career development experiences of college students attending Cohort 2-TPSID model demonstration programs.* Boston, MA: University of Massachusetts Boston, Institute for Community Inclusion.

Smith, F., Grigal, M., & Shepard, J. (2018). Postsecondary education and employment outcomes for youth with intellectual disability served by Vocational Rehabilitation. *Think College Fast Facts*, Issue No. 18. Boston, MA: University of Massachusetts Boston, Institute for Community Inclusion.

Test, D. W., Mazzotti, V. L., Mustian, A. L., Fowler, C. H., Kortering, L. J., & Kohler, P. H. (2009). Evidence-based secondary transition predictors for improving post-school outcomes for students with disabilities. *Career Development for Exceptional Individuals, 32*, 160–181.

United States Census Bureau (2015). *American community survey.* Retrieved from https://www.census.gov/programs-surveys/acs/

Wagner, M., Newman, L., Cameto, R., Garza, N., & Levine, P. (2005). *After high school: A first look at the postschool experiences of youth with disabilities.* Menlo Park, CA: SRI International.

Wehman, P. (2013). Transition from school to work: Where are we and where do we need to go? *Career Development and Transition for Exceptional Individuals, 36*, 58–66. doi: 10.1177/2165143413482137.

Wehman, P., Sima, A. P., Ketchum, J., West, M. D., Chan, F., & Luecking, R. (2015). Predictors of successful transition from school to employment for youth with disabilities. *Journal of Occupational Rehabilitation, 25*, 323–334. doi: 10.1007/s10926-014-9541-6.

Winsor, J., Timmons, J., Butterworth, J., Shepard, J., Landa, C., Smith, F., Domin, D., . . . Landim, L. (2017). *StateData: The national report on employment services and outcomes.* Boston, MA: University of Massachusetts Boston, Institute for Community Inclusion.

9 Developing Campus Membership through Extracurricular Activities

Being a real college student usually means being fully engaged in campus membership, that is, being involved in a variety of extracurricular activities that go beyond attending classes. For many students, it is a part of going to college that will be of the greatest significance and remembered for the longest time. Campus membership includes such activities as participating in special events, joining campus organizations, engaging in college celebrations like homecoming and fraternity weekends, attending athletic competitions, participating in intramural sports, hanging out in off-campus gatherings, and any number of other formal and informal adventures.

Some of the activities and events that have occurred on our campus in which students with ID have taken part are listed in Table 9.1. Students participating in other PSE programs may participate in similar activities on their campuses. Along with the activities listed in Table 9.1, we have noted some special considerations for the participation of students with ID in the activities.

Why Campus Membership Is Important

While some activities in Table 9.1 might be considered non-essential for some college students, we suggest that they are an important source of learning for college students with ID. Many adults with ID are not very involved in social activities. For example, many do not see friends on a regular basis, have a significant relationship with another individual, or participate in recreational activities out of the home (Newman et al., 2011). Additionally, many do not plan for leisure time, are not able to drive or use public transportation, and do not engage in social organizations. So for college students with ID, who are in a very formative period of life, these types of experiences while in college are important learning opportunities that may bear on their future quality of life.

Participation in many extracurricular activities presents multiple chances for informal, observational, and incidental learning. More importantly, these experiences create an expectation that activities beyond working or going to school are an important part of life. They can also

Table 9.1 College Events and Considerations

University clubs: This can include clubs, marching band, dance teams, campus sports, etc. **Intramural sports:** Playing sports on small teams with all other college students	• Unintentional roadblocks with GPAs • Auditions/tryouts: Think outside the box and network to share how all students can help level the playing fields • Liability for injuries • Sportsmanship and following the university code of conduct • Spontaneity with weather, scheduling, and game cancellations
Greek life: Students will want to pledge and participate in Greek life organizations	• Members sometimes need a GPA to be fully initiated into Greek life organizations • Activities and rituals that might make the student uncomfortable (e.g., sensory) • Understanding the work and hours required beyond the surface for joining Greek life • Unintentional miscommunications or parental hesitation when students may not be their own guardian
Homecoming: Where students are voted by the student body as homecoming king and queen **Graduation:** Participation in commencement ceremonies with all other students	• GPA requirements • Logistics with accessibility • Fear of defeat and competition • Certificate recognition rather than a degree • Find student voices and advocacy to support this campus activity (e.g., SGA)
Professional conferences: Traveling, attending and presenting at local, state, national, and international venues	• Cost of traveling and registrations • Liability concerns • Different routines
Study abroad: Taking trips out of the country to live and learn together about other services and cultures **Voting:** College campuses are known for student voice and democracy. Many campuses can have voting polls right on campus	• Liability concerns for traveling • Not having a GPA to officially register for study abroad coursework • Traveling in unfamiliar territory with airport security and different routines • Special considerations for guardianship and voting rights • Supporting decisions while educating students on their voting rights, accommodations at the polls, and about candidates in fair and impartial manner

help students learn and apply specific skills such as budgeting, managing shared spaces, reading social cues, organizing transportation, navigating campus safely, and sometimes learning about the natural consequence of social behavior. Although many PSE programs focus on areas such as academics, personal skill development, and career training, we suggest that full campus membership that includes numerous extracurricular activities is an essential aspect of going to college.

How to Facilitate Campus Membership

Our approach, as with all other aspects of our program, is to simply ask, "What do other college students do on campus and how does everyone go about accessing these opportunities? How can we make these opportunities look the same for students with ID?" With this tenet in mind, we pursue several strategies so that students are able to enjoy full campus membership. These are discussed in the following sections.

Know What Is Available

University or college personnel who are intricately involved in a PSE should spend many hours in contact with college students with and without disabilities. This connection, along with what is posted on the school's website or through social media, becomes an important source of information about various organizations, events, and activities occurring on and off campus. Some of these will be established and ongoing, like fraternities, sororities, and clubs; others will be special events, like concerts or weekend camping trips. Most likely, many will be of interest to students, including those with ID.

When we work with students to develop their weekly schedules, we ask them what is coming up that they plan to attend, either in the near term or in the future. Usually they have a list of activities or events already in mind. For example, a couple of years ago, two of our students decided they wanted to run for homecoming king and queen. They did so on their own, campaigned on campus, and garnered enough votes to win!

We also ask our student volunteers who are working as natural supports what is of interest. We generally don't have any difficulty in finding a variety of activities that students can pursue, based on their individual interests. Additionally, we keep our ears open about on-campus organizations so we know in which of these students might like to participate. While our primary purpose is to be able to share information about these organizations with our students, we are also interested in knowing what kind of reputation the organization has. For example, if a fraternity has a history of being put on probation for under-age drinking, we want to be able to share this information with a student who wishes to rush this particular fraternity.

Prepare to Pay the Cost

One key ingredient to having genuine campus membership is for students in the PSE program to know the cost of various activities and be prepared to pay the cost. It is important that PSE students pay the same fees as other students to gain access to campus activities. Some of these fees will be built in to the fee structure that will be paid at the beginning of a term, others will occur as the activities or events occur.

Paying normal fees is not only a necessity based on university requirements, it also better ensures that students in the PSE program are viewed as having the same rights to on-campus benefits as do all other students. We do not want students in the UP Program to be viewed as charity cases, and we do not think this is appropriate for any PSE program. When our students' parents pay their tuition and activity fees, the students receive student identification cards like everyone else. When special events require additional fees, we work with the student to make sure they understand the cost of the event and understand how it affects their budget. If we can start this process well enough in advance, often the student can plan a financial strategy to attend the desired event.

Use Peer Supports

Having a strong network of peers who provide support for students with ID also provides a great resource to enhance opportunities for extracurricular participation. Networking with peer supports who are already participating in campus activities has been our best strategy for opening doors to campus membership for our students with ID. We have found that the more presence the students with ID have "out there" around campus, rather than being isolated in a separate setting, the more involved they become in campus organizations and activities. The goal is for them to be as integrated as possible, including in organizations and activities that are of interest to them.

Develop Key Partnerships

On most campuses, there are various student groups and organizations with unique purposes, and many times their purposes lead to opportunities for PSE students, or even result in a potentially beneficial partnership with the program. These groups include academic clubs, fraternities and sororities, honor societies, religious organizations, interest clubs, and similar organizations. Many times students with ID learn about these organizations through their connections with natural supports or through friends in the organizations, and often they wish to join the organization, or are invited to participate. Sometimes when this occurs, even though it provides a valuable opportunity, our program personnel have had to intervene to make the membership or involvement possible. For example, some student organizations require that members be full-time students with grade point averages and these requirements, if not waived or modified, could be a barrier to students with ID.

Beyond individual connections with our students, student organizations often want to form a relationship or alliance with the PSE program, or "do something" for the program. This can be beneficial to the program because it might provide needed funds, or human resources. But at the same time, it can be a throwback to the idea of raising contributions for "the handicapped." A PSE program can benefit from the intention, but we believe the activities should be conducted so that they are mutually beneficial and so that the partnering organization isn't creating a "pity party" or using the organization to promote its own goodness. We try to avoid this by stressing the idea that we operate based on the principles of normalization and inclusion, and welcome involvement that respects these values. Two examples of this type of relationship are worth noting.

We have often benefited through relations with students in our Honors College who need to complete contracts to fulfill their obligations in coursework. These students will come to us with the purpose of providing some form of service to the program so that they can then present their project to their counselors or professors. When they do, we examine our ever-present list of needs and try to identify a project the student can pursue. For example, some honors students have helped jumpstart great ideas such as our "weekend warriors," in which our students with ID can choose to explore their community together on the weekends or even find ways to give back to the community. This type of project was beneficial to the honors student and the Honors College, as well as benefited our students, and in doing so enhanced everyone without demeaning anyone.

Another group we have worked with and achieved mutual benefits is our Center for Service Learning (CSL). This office connects students who are pursuing service projects with worthwhile organizations or groups in need of support. The CSL identifies projects for students as well as weaves service learning into various dedicated courses. Many of the natural supports involved with our UP students have found their way to our program through our CSL. The value they contribute to the program is immeasurable, and the nature of their relationship with our students demonstrates and upholds the values of our program.

Become Your Own Organization

The group of students who volunteer as natural supports in the UP Program formalized itself by becoming a recognized student organization (RSO) on campus. They call themselves the PushUPs. By becoming an RSO they become more visible and can actively connect the UP Program and students to other campus organizations.

They meet monthly with all campus organizations to represent our program and students. The advantages of this formality include having students working together to build awareness and also collaborating with other organizations across campus.

Consider Transportation

Even a relatively small campus like ours and its surrounding rural community requires consideration be given to how students will be able to travel to the destination they wish to reach. For many PSE programs, this likely means that students should learn to use the on-campus or public transportation system. When this is the case, learning goals in these areas should be built into the students' individual learning plans.

With a PSE program in a more rural setting, we have not been able to rely on public transportation, although we do have a very reliable on-campus transit system. Therefore, if our PSE students are attending events on campus, they either ride our "Cat-Tran" or walk to the event. Some students use apps like *Companion and Life360* to share their location with PSE staff. If they do not choose to use a location app, we encourage them to text or call in to let us know where they are from time to time. Ultimately many students learn to navigate campus independently and safely without the presence of a natural support. This means they can rely on campus landmarks, use their cell phones to communicate, use crosswalks safely, understanding time, and following stranger danger procedures. We also admonish them to follow the advice of our campus police, who encourage the use of the buddy system for night-time travel with all college students.

If off-campus travel is needed or desired, sometimes our natural supports drive UP students, and sometimes the UP students can drive themselves. The only other alternative is the use of a "door-to-door" community transit system. However, this option is limited to operating only for abbreviated hours, Monday through Friday, and sometimes weekends are a prime time for transportation needs because of jobs, service learning activities, or community outings.

Share Valuable Experiences

Finally, we continue to promote campus and extracurricular activities for UP students as part of their individual plan for college participation (IPCP) goals. Just as class and work goals are important, so are campus membership goals. Each month, we work with students to have them share their extracurricular learning experiences as part of their stories of success in their person-centered planning (PCP) meetings. Many students share their success and photos of campus activities with great pride as they have truly felt a part of genuine learning experiences among their peers. Additional discussion at the monthly PCP meetings also includes exploring further campus events and brainstorming additional ways to manage their time and schedule all the campus activities in which they wish to participate.

Lessons Learned through Campus Membership

As we stated at the beginning of the chapter, there are many lessons that can be learned through the various activities and events that occur outside of the classroom. Three learning areas that we believe are most important for students with ID are discussed below. Involvement in non-required activities gives students a chance to develop skills in each of these areas.

Discriminating between Needs and Wants, Responsibilities and Wishes

Often students with ID enter a PSE program without a great deal of experience in distinguishing between what is necessary for them to do, i.e., their responsibilities, and what is okay for them to want or want to do, but are not really essential, i.e., their wishes. If mature individuals cannot make such distinctions, they will not do very well in managing their life. Having a robust list of activities for which students are responsible (such as going to class, completing homework, and doing a job), and another list of optional activities (such as going to a movie or hanging out in the coffee shop), allows students to learn the difference between the two sets of activities and prioritize their actions.

Teaching students with ID about prioritization, and then managing their time effectively, can be a challenging and ongoing task. We attempt to do so by providing visuals and using frequent and explicit instruction to make these skills more concrete. One strategy we have used is to make a two-column chart with them while looking at their weekly schedule. An example of such a chart is shown in Table 9.2.

In the first column, the "have to" column, we work together with the student to list all weekly campus activities that are required in the program. This list is completed first. In the second column, the "want to" column, the student takes the lead in identifying various events and activities that they would like to do in the coming week. Not surprisingly, the second column is often the longer list. But like all college students, we ask them to decide on their priorities. For example, when there is a lot of homework to get done to meet a deadline (as shown in column 1), it might be necessary to wait on going to a movie (as shown in column 2). We point out that going to a movie is more fun than doing homework, but doing homework is a responsibility, whereas going to a movie is a wish.

Learning Time Management

Many students with ID also have had limited experience in effectively managing the use of their time. This could be for several reasons.

Table 9.2 Prioritization Chart

Have to . . .	Want to . . .
Attend classes	Cook meals
Attend jobs and/or internships	Game nights
Complete homework	Community trips (e.g., bowling, movies)
Weekly schedule meetings	Girls' and guys' nights
Shower	Religious activities
Sleep	Club or chapter meetings
Person-centered planning meetings	Ball games and sporting events
Check and record meal plan balances	Concerts
Work and reflect on IPCP goals	Plays
Clean dorm and bathroom areas	Listen to music
Take out the trash	Arts and crafts
Arrive on time and contact supports	Go shopping
Check and reply to emails	Swimming
Answer phone calls and texts	Facebook and social media
Meet with your RAs once a semester	Help with research studies
Laundry	Travel to present at conferences

Although they may have been taught to tell time in school, there may have been less emphasis on using time efficiently. Or, there may not have been many situations in their lives in which it was necessary for them to make time-based decisions. Or, maybe there have never been real consequences related to intentional time management such as finishing a job on time, or meeting a deadline.

However, if we expect students as adults to live in the real world, learning to manage time, or to manage their own behavior to meet time requirements, is an important skill that should be learned and generalized. Being on time for work is important . . . if you want to keep the job; meeting a friend at a specific time is important . . . if you want to keep the friend; and engaging in any number of daily activities in a timely manner is important . . . if you don't want people to grow impatient.

Experiences that require students to know what *must* be done versus what they would *like to do* are also a great way to teach them the importance of time management and how to achieve it. Class comes before the fraternity meeting; homework comes before watching Netflix; and work comes before going out with friends. All of these responsibilities require an understanding of time, that time is limited, and therefore, that time management is important.

One area in which we have found time management to be most challenging is completing homework assignments. While there is no doubt many more interesting things to do, going to college in the UP Program requires that homework be completed. Yet sometimes students have a great deal of trouble remaining sufficiently focused and on task in order to complete their homework in a timely manner. To help them achieve this, we use three strategies.

First, we provide a lot of opportunities and sufficient supports for completing homework assignments. To begin, we make sure that adequate time is built into their schedule to give them multiple homework completion experiences. This also gives their peer supports many teachable moments to prompt them to stay focused and complete assignments.

Second, with these opportunities, we provide supportive resources that can help them manage their time. These include wall calendars for mapping out assignments, and apps (e.g., todoist, Reminder, Google calendar) to help them monitor the days, hours, and minutes they have to complete assignments. With these resources, we encourage peer-to-peer talks about prioritization and strategies that the peers find helpful to complete their work on time. Generally, we find this to be more effective than scolding, coddling, or cajoling.

Third, we remind the UP student that ultimately, as a college student, they have a *responsibility* to complete homework assignments in order to achieve their IPCP goals and complete the program. Further, we point out that if there are other activities that they *wish* to do, that managing their time to complete both their responsibilities *and* achieve their wishes is up to them. With this approach, many ultimately learn how important it is to get the homework done so they can do the other things they wish to do.

Learning to Make Good Decisions

Having a variety of activities and events in which students can engage beyond those that are required provides opportunities to learn to make good decisions. Self-determination is a basic tenet and goal of the UP Program, but making poor decisions can ultimately reduce an individual's quality of life, an equally important outcome for our graduates. So because there are various opportunities to participate freely, there are also various opportunities to learn how to make good decisions.

We recognize there is a fine line between helping students make decisions, and inhibiting their right to do so. While we do not wish to impose our values on students, we also want them to learn to develop and think about their own values when confronted with real-world dilemmas. When we have an opportunity to provide supported decision-making, we use four strategies to do so.

Make sure students are educated and aware. Our first duty is to help the student understand the issues and conditions involved in the situation. For example, an under-age student may wish to attend a fraternity party where there will be a great band and lots of interesting people, but where alcohol will be consumed. The student then plans to walk alone about a quarter mile back to their room after midnight. We feel it is important for the student to know that there are legal and safety issues involved, and that although the party will be fun, there will be many opportunities to get in trouble, intentionally or unintentionally, just as there will be for all students at the party.

Support students to list all possible options and the pros and cons of their options, including possible consequences. Using an undergraduate natural support whenever possible, students are asked to list in writing the consequences that might happen. For example, on the positive side the student might go to the party with a friend, meet some new friends, enjoy the band, and engage in some interesting conversation. On the negative side the student might drink too much (doing so illegally), get caught by the campus police, or get assaulted when walking alone back to the dorm. Given the variations in outcomes that might occur, the student should be encouraged to think about the "what ifs," how they might impact their life, and what options might be better.

Encourage students to seek input from same-age peers. In the above step, input from same-age peers is invaluable. The peers have often been in the same or similar situations, and can report on firsthand experience related to what the student with ID wants to do. The PSE staff should stress to peers that their job is not to make the decision for the student, but to provide accurate input about the situation in question, the positive and negative aspects of the situation, and the options that might exist. Ultimately, these conversations should be honest and allow the student with ID to gain accurate information about the decision to be made.

Teach the concept of moderation. An important aspect of learning to make good decisions is understanding the meaning of moderation. Moderation helps address behaviors that are not often reflected on by students with ID such as excessively texting or calling someone, over-using social media platforms, flirting or stalking behaviors, studying too much, sharing too many comments in class, and even food or alcohol consumption. Working with students to determine and set boundaries for these types of behaviors can create much better outcomes. This concept is important for various decisions made about campus activities and can be a key to overall success and positive social interactions.

Respect students' decisions. After there has been an opportunity for honest input and reflection, ultimately the student needs to make the decision. For many students, this is their legal right, and for others, we cannot and should not be parent substitutes. We see our job, and that of any PSE program, to educate, support, and guide students. Everyone will make mistakes, but it is important to recognize that risk is inherent in life and is sometimes required for learning to occur.

Learning Social Skills and Boundaries

An important area of learning that can occur through participation in campus activities is how to exhibit important social behaviors, especially how to be aware of the importance of social boundaries. In many cases, students with ID need to learn how to develop boundaries related to social interactions so that they may be more accepted by other students. Understanding appropriate boundaries allows everyone to remain more comfortable when interacting regularly in living and learning spaces.

We have found that proactively teaching social skills and providing knowledge about boundaries, particularly with regard to relationships or sexuality issues, can alleviate adverse outcomes, such as reports to the university's Department of Community Ethics. Three programs we have used to frame social skills instruction and to teach relational boundaries are *CIRCLES* (Walker-Hirsch & Champagne, 1991), the *Program for the Education and Enrichment of Relational Skills (PEERS)* (Laugeson, 2017), and our *About Life* curriculum. We offer these programs to our students in learning environments that include both students with ID and peers without ID. As they are not required for our students, they can be considered as extracurricular learning opportunities. Each is briefly explained below.

The purpose of *CIRCLES* is to teach social distance and levels of intimacy by using categories or levels to represent real-life relationships. There are six color-coded concentric circles that represent various behaviors, feelings, and actions at each level. For example, the purple self circle is the center and it is the more private circle. The blue circle surrounds the purple circle and represents the very close relationships, such as family members or girlfriend/boyfriend interactions. The outermost circle is the red stranger circle, meaning people we do not talk to or touch. Along with the color-coded circles, there are target words and visuals that illustrate the boundaries more for conceptual understanding.

PEERS uses more of a cognitive-behavioral approach with more structured teacher-directed lessons delivered in a group format. Typically, peers serve as social coaches among the larger group to step in and lead practice roleplays or generalization of newly learned skills. PEERS topics for young adults address issues such as maintaining conversations, trading information, using humor appropriately, social media etiquette, dating, and interview skills. With this instruction, students learn that conversation skills and tone matter with how you talk across different people you encounter on a college campus. Many note they talk and act differently among their boss or professors, while they can change their context some among their same-age peers (Laugeson, 2017).

Finally, *About Life* is a relationship class in which peers teach the students with ID about boundaries with relationships or what you do when you like someone. Typically, very mature *About Life* coaches (undergraduate natural supports) deliver the topics to discuss and teach, but also allow the students with ID to bring up topics they would like to talk about and about which they may not feel as comfortable discussing with their families or program staff.

We have found providing this opportunity to have weekly dialogue about these topics helps students understand relationships and may also decrease inappropriate behaviors that can appear when a student wished to initiate an intimate, personal relationship with another individual. *About Life* sessions also reinforce some of the concepts from CIRCLES and PEERS curricula as circumstances are brought up for discussion. Based on the overall needs of the individuals, *About Life* can be taught in small groups with only one sex present, with both sexes present, and in one-on-one arrangements if the student wishes.

Social skills for various campus activities and genuine belonging among same-age peers are so important to teach and review within and outside of actual social settings. The more instruction and practice that can occur, the more social learning opportunities can be enhanced with campus activities, within classes, and on the job.

Final Thoughts

We leave you with a sample of a powerful excerpt from *Belonging on Campus* and what campus membership and social justice can truly do to promote genuine social inclusion from one of our 2014 WCU UP Graduates. Thanks Kenneth!

> Attending WCU has given me more independence and new experiences . . . I live in the same dorms as my college peers . . . I am also involved in Greek life on campus. I chose this fraternity because they encourage us to do work in the community, and because of the diversity of our members . . .
>
> For me, inclusion is a lot like social justice – it is about having the same options and opportunities as everyone else. Because I've been included at WCU, I've met a variety of wonderful people. I've also had the chance to educate others about the wide range of personalities and abilities found among individuals labeled with ID.
>
> Kenneth Kelty

References

Kelty, K., & Prohn, S. (2014). Belonging on campus. *Think College Stories* (10). Retrieved from https://thinkcollege.net/sites/default/files/files/resources/kenneth_kelty_story_0.pdf

Laugeson, E. A. (2017). *PEERS® for young adults: Social skills training for adults with autism spectrum disorder and other social challenges*. New York: Routledge.

Newman, L., Wagner, M., Knokey, A. M., Marder, C., Nagle, K., Shaver, D., Wei, X., with Cameto, R., Contreras, E., Ferguson, K., Greene, S., & Schwarting, M. (2011). *The post-high school outcomes of young adults with disabilities up to 8 years after high school. A report from the National Longitudinal Transition Study-2 (NLTS2)* (NCSER 2011-3005). Menlo Park, CA: SRI International. Available at www.nlts2.org/reports/

Walker-Hirsch, L., & Champagne, M. (1991). The circles concept: Social competence in special education. *Educational Leadership, 49*, 65–67.

Part III
Implementation and Coordination

10 Person-Centered Planning and Weekly Scheduling

The Importance of Person-Centered Planning and Individualized Weekly Schedules

Person-centered planning (PCP) allows a PSE program to focus on the unique interests and learning needs for individual students. Although there is not a universal definition of PCP, the general idea is that it is individualized planning centered around a person with a disability and their environmental supports. In other words, the planning process involves looking at the supports that need to be in place (e.g., people, technology, routines) to enhance success and build on the person's strengths or interests to be productive members of their inclusive communities while enjoying a greater quality of life (Claes et al., 2010).

This is our purpose in using a PCP process in the UP Program. Our goal with PCP is to increase the likelihood of success during the college experience and afterward by first examining individual needs and desires, and then arranging the environmental conditions and natural supports that would best allow them to occur. We have observed how the PCP process has helped students with ID and their families as they navigate college and transition into community living arrangements, an outcome noted by Weir (2004).

In order for person-centered planning to be of value, the outcome must be engagement in meaningful activities. In our program, these activities are embedded into individualized weekly schedules for each student. Although planning individualized schedules requires a more intense process than planning one schedule for all students, based on the growth we have seen in our students, we believe it is worthwhile. Individualization provides a way to personalize activities for each student that improves critical social and communication skills, and helps them meet their individualized goals. Without detailed, weekly schedules, we do not think our students would be as connected to campus life and their communities as they are. Erin's story depicts the benefits of the PCP process and the use of weekly schedules.

> ### Erin's Story
>
> Erin was 23 years old with mild ID when she entered the UP Program. When Erin moved onto the college campus she was very shy. While she had had strong family support throughout her life, Erin benefitted from having peers support her and model independent living that ultimately led to successfully living in her community.
>
> Erin had attended a compensatory education program at a community college prior to being accepted into the UP Program. During several of her first and second semester PCP meetings, discussion centered on living in an apartment with supports after graduation. Unfortunately, sometimes during these discussions Erin began crying and saying she was not ready for that outcome. Over time, after achieving many of her short-term goals on campus and building strong relationships with her peers, she became much more confident in her ability to live away from her family.
>
> At the completion of her college experience, Erin signed a lease to rent an apartment with two undergraduate students with whom she had become friends while in the PSE program. She was also hired by a community agency to work one-on-one on an as-needed basis with other individuals with disabilities in their community, received a job working part-time as a teaching assistant at a local daycare (which was her career choice), and also worked part-time at a local grocery store, taking the city bus back and forth to both jobs. We saw tremendous changes in the behavior and attitude of this formerly very shy and timid young woman, and doubt this would have occurred without the benefit of the PCP process.

Using PCP Meetings in a PSE Program

The PCP process allows individuals to set more personalized goals and work towards achieving those goals. It can also facilitate higher expectations for individuals with disabilities as it allows them to realize their potential success in life, and also helps them to address fears and concerns proactively. There are many decisions to be made that require strategic planning and support during the transition to college and back into the community, and PCPs help individuals make these decisions.

Initial PCP Meetings: Learning about Students

In the UP Program, PCP starts as early as the admission process. During our open house, we ask applicants to answer at least three basic questions as we video their responses:

1   Why do you want to go to college?
2   What do you want to do during your college experience while you are in the UP Program? (e.g., clubs, coursework, internships)
3   What are your goals when you finish the UP Program in two years? (e.g., with employment, independent living, education, recreation/leisure)

As reported in Chapter 5, this video is used in the admissions process. From here, if applicants are accepted into the next admission phase, our orientation camp, we plan their camp experience with them based on their individual preferences and future goals. Then, as part of camp, we complete an *academic roadmap* (see Chapter 7) with each student. This PCP activity identifies personal strengths; who they would like to be in the future; interests, curiosities, and hobbies; desired skills; and specific career interests. The roadmap concludes with statements about, "By the time I leave college . . . I want to know/be able to . . . , I want to prove to others that . . . , and I want people to remember me as . . . "

Ongoing PCP Meetings: Contents and Procedures

After a student has been formally admitted to the program, we hold a PCP meeting with the student and key individuals every month. Table 10.1 shows a sample of how we organize PCP meetings throughout the program to address key issues.

As the student progresses through the program, monthly PCP meetings are held that include the student, and many of the individuals from the campus and the community listed in Table 10.2. Using chosen multimedia presentation software (created by the student and a natural support), the student leads a discussion addressing the following topics:

1   stories of success (i.e., a report on progress made on goals listed in IPCP)
2   what is working well (i.e., discussing strategies that have led to success)
3   what could be improved (i.e., reviewing goals that need more work)
4   next steps (i.e., where to go from here to increase independence and reduce support)
5   other items or questions (i.e., open discussion of various topics).

Following introductions, PSE students typically use the color-coded themes, picture prompts, and/or multimedia presentations to lead their own meetings focusing on the above topics. The student prompts the group with the topic areas and then calls on attendees with raised hands to speak about the topic. If a student has limited verbal communication ability, avatars or assistive technology devices and photos or videos can be used during meetings. The UP student works through the meeting agenda

Table 10.1 Organizational Timeline and Main Content for PCP Meetings

Meeting	Purpose	UP Program Timeline
Preadmission – UP camp experience	One to two meetings before and after UP orientation camp to review progress and goals	*February/March*: UP camp meeting to choose classes and work experiences preferred during orientation camp *March/April*: Post-UP camp meetings to review strengths, interests, and continued needs with future goals assessed during orientation camp
Pre-planning for first fall semester	Planning for fall work internships, fall coursework, and campus activities	*March–June*: Conference calls or video-conferencing with meetings (if families and students live a distance from the campus)
Monthly meetings during fall and spring semesters throughout the program	4–8 formal meetings to review progress and celebrate successes each semester	*August and January*: Send out meeting requests to everyone involved. Try to schedule when families and community agencies are most available or already coming to campus
Formal exit meetings during last semester	1–2 meetings to review: revisit academic roadmaps and PATH progress; community mapping options; roles and responsibilities of all parties supporting the individual on campus and in the future	*February–May*: Send out meeting requests to everyone involved on campus and within the community where individuals will be living and working when exiting the PSE program
Follow-up meetings	1 per semester or as needed	*January and August*: Provide additional resources during community transition – may also have to assign one program alumni per staff member to provide follow-up services

Table 10.2 PCP Meeting Attendees and Roles

Attendee	Roles
UP student	Leads meetings and reviews goals and progress made throughout their college experience and post community experiences
Adult community service providers	Community members who work for agencies (e.g., Arc or Turning Point Services) and supervise employees hired to provide services written in the individualized personal care plans
Parents or guardians	Provide background information and follow-up support to fostering independence and meeting individualized goals developed as a team
Natural supports (all undergraduate students from varied majors)	Provide natural supports as necessary to UP students in academics, work, social skills, recreation or campus activities
Suitemates (undergraduate students who live with UP students)	Provide night-time emergency care, daily living instruction, and assist as necessary with personal care goals or hygiene needs
UP Program staff	Provides updates and progress in areas of social participation, community participation, vocational success, academic participation, and personal development
Faculty and employers	Provide information and feedback on student's performance in courses and on the job or internship
Vocational Rehabilitation Counselors (VR)	Develop individual plans for employment and participate in future employment goals

until finished, offering attendees several opportunities to contribute. A UP staff member or a graduate assistant records the meeting minutes.

The PCP meetings are generally viewed positively by students, attendees, and UP staff. The students particularly like the PCP meetings as they are able to lead and talk about their stories of success and other relevant topics. As natural supports, undergraduate students share their success stories and areas needing improvement by talking directly with the UP students – not about them. Talking student to student, they use specific examples experienced together to help UP students appreciate successes and identify areas needing improvement.

The abbreviated minutes of a PCP meeting offer a useful look at a UP student's status at a given point in the program. The minutes include input provided by the UP student, natural supports, UP staff, parents, and other meeting attendees.

Developing and Using Weekly Schedules

We believe that achieving individualized goals developed through PCP meetings requires engagement in numerous learning activities during the time a student is in the UP Program. For this reason, unlike some PSE programs, our PSE program is characterized by weeks that are chock full of activities and learning experiences for our students, activities that begin early each day and go into the night. We are firmly committed to the notion that more opportunities for learning correlate highly with more positive outcomes. For this reason, every student in our program has an array of weekly activities that provide the context for achieving their individual goals. Some of the activities, like attending classes, working on jobs, and participating in other common routines, occur on a regular basis. But others, like inclusive group social and recreational activities, are newly identified from week to week. All of these activities are used to form a weekly schedule for each student in the program so the student can achieve their individualized goals. Once individualized weekly schedules are developed, natural supports are identified for each time-activity slot for which support is necessary. This process is aided by an online scheduling program called WhenToWork.

Using WhenToWork to Develop Weekly Schedules

Weekly schedules have always been the centerpiece of our program. Even though they can be very intense and time-consuming to develop, they are essential to our program's philosophy of inclusive participation. Initially, we used Excel to develop schedules and display schedules, with color-coding and later pictures to help our students with ID interpret them. However, in recent years we have used a more efficient online software program, WhenToWork,[1] that saves time and allows natural supports and other key players to stay connected on one platform. The program facilitates three essential functions: It allows weekly schedules to be built, it allows natural supports to indicate when they are and are not available to volunteer, and it allows schedulers to assign the student supports to time slots and activities in which support is required.

WhenToWork is an online scheduling system designed so employees (or in our case, natural supports) can enter their availability to pick up work shifts using red and green shading. In our program, we teach our natural supports to go online and indicate when they are available to provide support during coming weeks. We then build weekly schedules for the UP students (as discussed below) as an array of "shifts" in the program. Then, the natural supports who are available for specific shifts during a week are assigned to them, typically working one to two hours per week, but sometimes more. If they are so inclined (and many are), natural supports can also request additional unassigned shifts using the "tradeboard" feature in WhenToWork. We have found this scheduling software to be economical and able to accommodate a larger number of volunteers. It also allows our students with ID to use mobile apps with necessary voiceover assistive technology and color-coding to navigate or follow weekly schedules.

Using Natural Supports as Schedulers

Although weekly schedules are developed as shifts within WhenToWork, the program *does not*, of course, determine what our students with ID will be doing during a given week! The students themselves decide this, and they are aided by a select group of paid natural supports whom we refer to as "schedulers." A scheduler usually has the responsibility for developing schedules for one or two UP students.

Meeting with UP students weekly, a scheduler maps out required activities (e.g., classes, work) and works with the student to select other activities. Developing the schedules with a scheduler teaches students with ID to prioritize activities and to juggle fun choices with required activities, and results in a robust weekly schedule so PSE students will know what is coming up. It takes a patient person to serve as a scheduler, because deciding what to do among a great variety of possibilities can be an arduous and complicated task.

There are several reasons why we use undergraduate students as schedulers. To begin, college students with ID will typically share more interests and experiences with their undergraduate peers, and tend to be more comfortable working with them rather than with older staff members. The students often bond with each other as they research on- and off-campus activities that are usually better known to students than to the program staff. Second, the student-to-student process allows for more individualized scheduling, as opposed to all schedules being developed by one staff person. Usually different students have different activities they want to do each week, and using individual student schedulers allows more time for one-on-one meetings to better hear the student's voice and identify preferences.

Third, the natural supports who are assisting students during weekly activities have an opportunity to connect with schedulers to provide input on what worked well, what didn't work, and what might be considered in the future. This student-to-student connection is very useful as subsequent schedules are developed. Finally, using students to create schedules, of course, frees up time for the staff to engage in other important activities. Nevertheless, the program director reviews and approves each schedule. Once approved, the schedule is published so our many student volunteers can identify when they are able to provide support during the week.

A great deal of trust and confidence is placed in the undergraduate students who are schedulers. This begs the question: How can this heartbeat of the program be handed off to undergraduate students? The answer is that there must be an investment of time and training to assure effective schedulers. We have found that successful undergraduate schedulers typically:

1. pay attention to details
2. are good communicators and problem-solvers
3. can multitask and work puzzles well
4. check and respond to emails often
5. demonstrate patience and flexibility
6. are creative and can develop additional training resources
7. show good team-building skills and collaboration with others
8. show a willingness to learn program operations
9. understand that schedules should motivate students to reach their highest potential
10. understand the ultimate goal is to fade their input as much as possible so UP students can organize their own future schedules.

All the students we use as natural supports and UP students must understand WhenToWork and how to use it. Schedulers must know how to develop schedules and are given a managerial role in using the program. They are trained to create schedules, add new employees, color-code, import, and publish schedules. Training for other students who serve as natural supports for periods of time each week includes how to log in and set up accounts, adding information to stay connected, how to shade preferences and availability, reading schedule descriptions and details about shifts, requesting and confirming shifts, and connecting with students with ID to coordinate meeting them at specific times before or after shifts. When training students to use WhenToWork, we use numerous screenshots and demonstrations, and provide specific scenarios we have experienced over the years. UP students also receive training in a similar way during the UP orientation camp experience and during the first few weeks of the semester.

In addition to training our supports and students in WhenToWork, we also train them about resources they can access in our Blackboard e-learning platform to stay connected. Usually students already know how to navigate Blackboard because they use it for their courses. This e-learning platform houses several very important resources for everyone that works with the UP students. During training sessions, we devote time to highlighting these resources and when and why supports might need to access them.

In Blackboard we share resources such as the semester calendar, emergency protocols, volunteer manual, UP student profiles sharing some of their common interests and hobbies (with their approval), quizzes, behavior survey links, PCP meeting information, individual plans for college participation (IPCPs), discussion board threads for homework support, and strategies for working with individuals with ID. Along with the training, from the UP students that are willing, we offer video introductions explaining their hobbies, goals, and what they want to be remembered for while in college. This helps us introduce the students before supports actually work with them.

Throughout training sessions, we stress the importance of confidentiality and have new supports sign confidentiality agreements as they complete a final quiz after the initial face-to-face training is completed. Once all trainings and confidentiality agreements are secured, trained natural supports can start requesting shifts or shadowing other veteran supports with the UP students through WhenToWork.

Making Choices about Weekly Activities

Because self-determination is a main philosophical tenet of our program, as schedules are being developed, the scheduler and the student with ID work closely together so the latter individual can make choices about how to spend their discretionary time. This is, in and of itself, an important learning activity. Traditional college students can be overwhelmed sometimes by the various campus activities that are available, and students with ID are no different.

During scheduling, the student with ID and the scheduler look at a wide variety of events, activities, and locations that may be of interest and considered for including on the weekly schedule. Four broad sources are usually considered:

- **Scheduled campus events and activities:** These are usually arranged in advance and well publicized on campus. Examples are concerts, football or basketball games, festivals, etc.
- **Community-based opportunities:** These could include special events like art shows, but also could include restaurants, theatres, shopping centers, recreational facilities, hiking trails, etc.
- **Recently developed or organized events:** These types of activities occur spontaneously and usually draw students' attention through posters placed on campus or social media notices.
- **UP Program activities:** These include several events developed by the UP staff that are presented in inclusive contexts and that are optional for UP student attendance.

To help the student and scheduler plan each week, and to keep ourselves informed about ongoing activities, at the beginning of each semester, we develop a UP master calendar that includes all known university events and activities. We review several calendars that are available that provide dates for athletic events, club meetings, diversity events, holidays and breaks, and payment deadlines. In addition to the university activities, we include on the calendar dates for the events developed within our program. These include recreational nights, cooking club meetings, weekend warrior events, and service learning activities. We also include on the calendar planned monthly PCP meetings, and monthly *Check and Connect* meetings that are used to communicate with our natural supports about different issues.

Beyond what is included on the calendar, students may identify activities that are of interest to them as they learn about them from

Table 10.3 Schedule Planning Template

UP Student: _____ Date: _____

Activity	When?	Where?	Contact?	Cost?	Transportation:
	What day? What time?		Who are you going with?		How are you going to get there?
EXAMPLE: Whee Sign Club	Sundays 6–7 pm	Dogwood Room UC	Name of person Email/phone number	No cost	Walk on campus
Shopping at Walmart	Saturdays 10–11am	Walmart Plaza (off campus – 4 miles)	Support's name and number	Need debit card for list of items	Car with support or Cat-Tran taking other students to Walmart

in-class announcements, flyers, the online campus life engagement system, emails, social media, invitations from other students, etc. We have found that by using written scheduling templates such as is shown in Table 10.3, or manipulative items, that students with ID can learn how to manage their time and work more effectively with schedulers to plan their weekly activities. A snapshot capturing the essence of a weekly schedule meeting is shown in Table 10.4.

As our students with ID have progressed through the program, some have advanced to a point that they wish to create their own activity within WhenToWork (i.e., instead of the scheduler). For these students we have created task analysis or video tutorials to help them do so. If students can learn to do this, it then becomes possible for them to structure and schedule their lives after graduating from the program.

Table 10.4 Weekly Schedule Meeting Snapshot

It is the beginning of the week and everyone is already overwhelmed. So we begin focusing on questions like, "What do you have to do versus what do you want to do this week? How can you make the most of your time?" This may require some additional planning and structure to make it all work together. For individuals with ID, this may also take additional repetition and more visual supports. In our program, students work with their scheduler an hour per week to map out the upcoming weekly schedule together. Here are some of the main ideas and topics they might cover in their weekly schedule planning meetings:

- checking and replying to important emails
- reviewing or submitting any timesheets for the week with paid work internships
- reviewing discussion board or agenda binders for homework deadlines
- using wall calendars, binders, and resources to determine any upcoming tests or accommodation needs
- taking medications regularly and noting any needed schedule reminders
- personal hygiene and well-being: reflecting on the amount of sleep obtained, showering daily, and doing laundry
- budgeting and checking meal plan balances using the semester meal plan charts and noting any meal details on the schedules to help serve as reminders
- reviewing IPCP goals and seeing which ones might need to be worked on more with peers in the upcoming schedule week
- filling shifts and activities together and learning appropriate ways to ask others to do things together (our students know this as filling their orange shifts)
- for weekend planning, asking for their completed weekend activities and supports
- any special appointments to note on the schedule (e.g., speech, counseling, group meetings, tutoring sessions, special events)
- reviewing decisions made with activities selected and scheduled based on the "have to" and "want to" activities for the week

---

Making Changes in Weekly Schedules

We create weekly schedules for each student one week in advance in order to ensure that every week is full of many learning activities, and to assure that students have the supports they require to participate in these activities. However, we realize that inevitably there will be changes that must be made in the schedules during the week they are implemented. Actual "schedules" of college students tend to be very spontaneous and when life is happening, things get complicated. Given that in one week a student with ID may have more than 50 planned events requiring the presence of a natural support, the chances of a change occurring at least once in a weekly schedule is very high.

Planned weekly schedules can change for various reasons, but three that are most common are: (1) the student with ID decides they would like to do something different than what is on the schedule; (2) the natural support student encounters a situation that prevents them from providing the planned support; or (3) an event or activity is cancelled. While any of these would not necessarily result in a dilemma for a traditional college student, for a student with ID, such changes can be confusing, or perhaps worse. Therefore we have developed contingency plans for such unexpected, but fairly common, occurrences.

First, a key tool that we use is an emergency UP cell phone. This phone is carried 24/7 by a designated UP staff member or scheduler, and its number is known to all UP students, the natural supports, and the program staff. We consider it a safety net tool that is not to be used lightly, but to be used when necessary. We require that all UP students are able to call the emergency number, and also require that they answer their cell phones when called.

Second, every day there is a designated "scheduler of the day" who monitors the WhenToWork tradeboard. This individual can screen requests for changes made by natural supports, and can send out mass emails searching of other supports to fill any gaps that may occur. The email address and phone number of the scheduler are published so that all UP students and all natural supports know on a given day who to contact for a change in a schedule.

Third, the WhenToWork program has a tradeboard. This allows natural supports to remove themselves from the work schedule, and to let other supports know that there is a shift that needs to be covered. It also allows natural supports to see where there is a need for a support to fill in for a time and activity.

With these tools, we have protocols to be followed by UP students and natural supports if they wish to make changes in their schedules. For the UP student, this requires that they first examine the WhenToWork schedule to see what changes they wish to make. They then call, text, or email the scheduler to let them know what change is desired. The scheduler will then determine if there is a need for support, who should provide the support, and make arrangements for the change in support. The student then contacts the upcoming support, if there is one, to let them know their change in plans. Safety and security is important, but so is spontaneity and choice-making. During the first semester and beyond, UP students work with their schedulers directly and also learn what activities are more mandatory (class, work) and optional (concerts, club meetings) that can be changed spontaneously.

If a natural support is unable to provide support at a time they have committed to do so, they are also asked to follow a protocol. This includes the following steps:

- Post a drop notice on the WhenToWork tradeboard as soon as possible. The later the notice, the more difficult it is to find another support to fill in.
- Send a text to the scheduler of the day to inform them of the need to drop a shift. If no response is returned, call the emergency number. If there is no answer, leave a message. Make sure you receive notice that your message has been received.
- If the change is going to occur soon, try to find a replacement support person to fill in. If successful, let the scheduler of the day know who the person is. The substitute should make an entry on the tradeboard.
- If a substitute is found, inform the UP student about the change.

These tools and protocols allow students with ID to be more flexible with schedule changes while allowing the program to maintain relative safety and security for students. If there is an occurrence when an expected support does not show up, UP students are instructed to call the support and then notify their scheduler to adjust shifts as needed. Conversely, supports are instructed to contact the emergency phone if they cannot locate a student after an allotted amount of time has passed. All student volunteers must have a cell phone and provide their numbers in WhenToWork to stay accessible to program staff and other natural supports.

Systematically Fading Support

As our weekly scheduling system implies, our philosophy is to provide an adequate amount of support so that students can be as included as possible as they learn new skills. However, it is also important that we fade that support as UP students demonstrate their confidence and begin mastering skills to become more independent.

For support to be faded, UP students need to show efficiency, or at least emerging independence, in the use of specific safety skills. These include: answering cell phones consistently, using time management strategies, interacting appropriately with others, choosing and wearing appropriate clothes for the weather, crossing the street safely, respecting personal space, telling the truth, and understanding stranger danger. Supports help observe and document these skills in weekly surveys that they then share with UP students at their PCP meetings.

In formal trainings and in informal discussions, we stress to natural supports that they are *support* persons and must avoid enabling dependency by UP students. We do not want the UP students to become overly reliant on the presence of a supporting student, but only to ask for help as they need it. We teach UP students to do all tasks as independently as they can before requesting assistance from any support person. Overall, feedback from the supports at monthly PCP meetings helps us determine how much we can fade support.

Final Thoughts

PCP at the college level can be a vehicle for increasing the overall quality of life for individuals with ID. It allows students with ID to lead their meetings and weekly activities while allowing the natural supports (same-age peers) to be involved in their routines. It also encourages family involvement along the way for lifetime advocacy efforts. These ingredients – the individual with a disability taking the lead, involvement of peers, and parental participation – are three necessary elements for successful transition planning outcomes. Without allowing individuals with disabilities opportunities to plan their own personalized roadmaps and weekly activities with everyone working together to provide necessary supports, the PCP process in any setting will not be as successful.

Clubs, classes, work, hiking, concerts, Greek life, intramurals, working out, you name it, college students are doing it. There are so many academic and social activities that occur daily on a college campus. Uniquely all students should be able to determine the level of campus involvement they wish to pursue each week. Some college students may want more time to study and be in their rooms, while others choose to enjoy more campus-wide activities and less room time. Many of the campus activities challenge self-discovery while building community across all college students. As discussed in Chapter 9, individuals with ID are no different and should have full access to extracurricular activities that enhance overall campus membership. Our role as a program is to help UP students facilitate their natural support systems at the level they desire while also honoring self-determination, choice, and voice. Scheduling can help all students connect for the common good to help students with ID and natural supports to share in their fully inclusive college experiences while providing a safety net when needs arise. However, self-determination and supported decision-making should be at the forefront of all decisions made with the PCP and scheduling procedures within any program.

Note

1 Other online programs that may be helpful include Humanity-ShiftPlanning, When I Work, and TrackSmart.

References

Claes, C., Van Hove, G., Vandevelde, S., Van Loon, J., & Schalock, R. L. (2010). Person-centered planning: Analysis of research and effectiveness. *Intellectual and Developmental Disabilities*, *48*, 432–453. doi:10.1352/1934-9556-48.6.432.

Weir, C. (2004). Person-centered and collaborative supports for college success. *Education and Training in Developmental Disabilities*, *39*(1), 67–73.

11 Recruiting and Coordinating Student Volunteers as Natural Supports

The concept of "natural supports" was developed in the 1980s as a way of integrating individuals with significant intellectual disabilities (ID) into community work environments with less reliance on professional rehabilitation workers (Nisbet & Hagner, 1988). The term implies individuals who would typically be present in an environment and who could provide support while there. A "natural support" for a college student with an ID is another college student without a disability who offers direction and assistance as needed. Natural supports can have many different terms, such as peer mentors, mentors, academic or educational coaches, job coaches, etc. In this chapter and within our program, we use the term "natural supports" as the roles they engage in are unique. This chapter will cover the benefits, limits, and roles of natural supports, how we recruit and coordinate natural supports in our program in a variety of capacities, and how we provide ongoing support, appreciation, and accountability to our natural supports.

Benefits of Natural Supports

There are many benefits to both natural supports and students with ID. Having natural supports allows students with ID to be fully included and engaged in all areas of campus life they wish to share together. Natural supports have assisted many UP students as they choose to engage in a variety of campus activities. While participating in these activities, natural supports provide age-appropriate models while socially reinforcing appropriate behavior or redirecting inappropriate behaviors. Natural supports also share the benefit of introducing students with ID to their friends and acquaintances to enhance and expand social networks.

There are also benefits for natural supports who work with students with ID. Being a natural support can help them better understand the nature of disabilities with firsthand and/or practical experiences. Natural supports can also develop a better self-concept and appreciation for the importance of human relations. Additionally, motivation for seeing students with ID do well in college and in life can be gratifying knowing they had a role in their support system. As the gratification occurs and practical experiences occur more frequently, natural supports often decide on career paths related to teaching or providing services to people with disabilities because of the college experiences they share together. Overall, natural supports also show others and experience the firsthand benefits of inclusion for individuals with ID as they provide a more inclusive service delivery structure in their future professions, and ultimately more acceptance in their workplaces and/or communities.

Limitations of Natural Supports

Natural supports serve so many roles. They are part friend, part teacher, and part caregiver, but not fully any of these. The friend part means that the natural support can be relied on and trusted. The teacher part means that they can explain or show the student with ID how something might be done. The caregiver part means that the natural support will make sure the student with ID is safe and doing what is socially appropriate like others their age.

However, there are limits to each part they sometimes play. As a friend, no matter how much effort is placed, the natural support is not likely to fully interact with the student with ID as would happen with a long-time friend, although this may evolve and develop over time. As a teacher, the natural support cannot utilize all the tools of a teacher because they may not be prepared to provide formal instruction in the current environment, although these skills and teachable moments may also be learned over time. And finally, as caregiver the natural support cannot provide all the attention that is needed because they do not have this level of responsibility (Westling & Kelley, 2018).

Roles of Natural Supports

Within the UP Program, natural supports often engage with UP students in "shifts" through the WhenToWork scheduling system that range between one and several hours (see Chapter 10). During this time, they provide support to UP students when most needed and when it fits in their own schedules. As a "shift" occurs, natural supports and UP students coordinate a meeting place and proceed to do the scheduled activity together. Often times, the UP students call or text the natural support based on the weekly schedule they have already created with their scheduler. Students with ID vary with support needs as some are more independent with some areas than others. Students with ID could request support when traveling around campus, attending and participating in classes, completing homework assignments, sharing meal times together, attending leisure or recreational events, personal hygiene, cleaning, laundry, supporting students on the job placements, and engaging in other on- or off-campus activities.

So with various natural support roles and not really feeling fully responsible for any of them, it can be tricky to recruit, train, and appreciate natural supports. However, fully inclusive programs do rely very heavily on same-age peers to serve in all these roles during their time shared with individuals with ID in the same college experiences (Kelley & Westling, 2013).

Initial Qualities and Recruitment Efforts with Natural Supports

In the UP Program, we have approximately 200 or more undergraduate students who serve as natural supports each semester. They serve in many capacities as friends, mentors, teachers, job coaches, residential supports, and caregivers. Some natural supports are paid while others are unpaid, but both serve very important roles. Out of the pool of natural supports, we have a small group of about 20 paid supports. It is great to have this volume of natural supports that we can call on for around-the-clock hours as needed. Many natural supports actively work with our students at least two hours a week, with some requesting up to 15–20 hours per week because they enjoy sharing more college experiences and memories with UP students.

As we recruit, we look for desirable qualities and characteristics in natural supports. Some of the characteristics include ones that are positive and energetic, caring and considerate, honest and trustworthy, responsible and dependable, and discreet and confidential. Overall, natural supports have qualities that demonstrate a good attitude towards their own lives and others' lives and see good in everyone while they work hard to reach their goals and make honest efforts. They are caring and considerate as they show concern with the well-being of others and their feelings or strengths, but show dedication to the improvement of their own lives and the lives of others. They are honest and trustworthy as they give accurate and reliable information and do not intentionally mislead or imply incorrect information while understanding they are a role model to others. They are responsible and dependable because they show more mature behaviors and have an understanding in the role they have to be reliable, cooperative, and accept responsibilities since others are counting on them. They are discreet and confidential because they know when to keep things given in confidence as well as not initiating or spreading rumors or sharing harmful information with others that doesn't need to be shared.

We get a lot of questions about our recruitment of natural supports and where they come from within the university. There are many ways we have invested in recruitment efforts. Without natural supports, our program would truly not be where it is today and as inclusive as it has been over the last decade. We have made it our mission to have UP students with their same-age peers and not taught directly by our program staff

100% of the time. This was a value we had in designing the program's mission that we have continued to hold very strongly. There is a significant value in facilitating natural supports that encourage students with ID in meeting or exceeding shared goals or connections. So how do we recruit natural supports each semester? Our university takes pride and values community and service learning among the student body. Some universities (including ours) has a Center for Service Learning. This was the first place we presented our program to and they welcomed us as a vital school and community partner. This office is responsible for coordinating and keeping an updated database of service learning opportunities on campus and within the surrounding communities. Their efforts and commitment to partner with us have been a great endeavor for everyone involved. Many times if students need to partake in service learning and do not have transportation at the college, they can recommend our program as an option since it is on campus and there are also weekend hours available to meet other work or class schedule demands. Additionally, we have learned to network with other colleges and programs to provide internship experiences and opportunities that offer firsthand experiences providing direct support to individuals with ID. This serves as a great partnership among both parties for interns needing to complete a significant number of hours towards graduation requirements and also getting to know our students by spending sometimes between 10 and 32 hours per week with them in various college experiences. Next, we solicit partnerships across colleges for graduate assistantships who help us with research and program operations. The graduate assistants typically come from related service fields beyond special education. We currently work with graduate assistants from communication sciences and disorders (speech), psychology, and most recently higher education and student affairs. With appropriate budget negotiations, both programs benefit and learn from each other through the direct experiences and opportunities. Other unique ways we recruit natural supports is through the agreements with AmeriCorps or Golden Leaf Scholars. These are time-limited hours, but provide great leaders who have shown great commitment to our students. Furthermore, we recruit from several other venues such as honors contracts and service projects. While these types of recruitment do not always involve as many direct support hours with students, they have provided us with very genuine projects and innovative ideas (e.g., weekend warrior activities, recreational therapy nights, orientation and retreat trainings, adapted materials for classes and program operations).

Many programs have also shared several innovative ideas and recruitment efforts with us over the years. One important yet simple recruitment effort is presence and representation at as many campus events as possible. These might include open houses, semester kickoff events, information, career fairs, etc. While our program has had little money for marketing, we have chosen to invest in posters that can be displayed at these events

152   *Implementation and Coordination*

and throughout the year along with designing brochures with our university creative services team. Other ways we have creatively approached recruitment for natural supports is by becoming a recognized student organization (RSO) on campus (i.e., the PushUPs). This allows our natural supports to network and connect among each other to recruit and share their valued experiences working with our program. The RSO is also able to reserve rooms in our university center for no cost when we have events, fundraise at various times across campus, work directly with our student government association, and host events with other student organizations. Requirements for us to continue to be an RSO include meetings with other student organizations once a month and establishing bylaws with relevant officers, such as an RSO student president, vice president, secretary, treasurer, and faculty advisor.

More traditional ways we have also found helpful with recruitment efforts that many programs also use include partnering with classwide service learning projects and/or service hours. This might involve classes in and out of special education. We have developed classwide partnerships with faculty teaching in recreational therapy, special education, social work, nursing, psychology, parks and recreation management, and leadership courses. Additionally, once these classes are actively volunteering with our students, word of mouth with more informal networks and previous interactions with individuals with ID sparks interest and many requesting initial training to work with our program after hearing about their friends' experiences. Other more familiar ways of recruitment include use of social media and email groups to make announcements and provide transparency when we have specific support needs (e.g., carpools, clubs, common religious interests). Many students read social media a lot more than their student emails, so we have chosen to be present on these outlets as well.

Finally, and maybe more unique to some, our program staff are also part of the university faculty. This allows us to teach courses and design projects that provide direct learning experiences between college and UP students in our program. One college class we have had approved is a seminar and practicum called Postsecondary Education for Students with Intellectual Disability. This is an undergraduate elective course where students serving as natural supports to UP students design weekly lessons to work with the UP students once a week and then they present their learning experiences together at local and state conferences.

Braided Funding Sources with Paid Natural Supports

While most of the ideas mentioned above are ways to recruit unpaid natural supports, we have also found ways to recruit and braid paid natural support options. Paid natural supports traditionally come from our pool of existing unpaid natural supports who have already completed the required training to work with UP students. Other ways we have also increased our program support is through our community agency partners who hire, train, and pay undergraduate students who work with UP students receiving Medicaid waiver or state funded services. Agencies partner to learn about our program operations and we schedule and help write the goals along with them once the paid natural supports are hired. Additionally, we have maximized limited resources by hiring undergraduate students who qualify to receive work study funding each semester. This allows them to work just like our other non-work-study students to receive the same wages and training, but from a different funding source. Overall recruitment of paid and unpaid natural supports can be a significant time commitment, but it is one worth the investment and benefits it brings to the students.

Coordinating Natural Supports

Now that we have shared ideas on initial recruitment of natural supports, it is equally important to share how they can be trained efficiently and effectively to work with students on a daily basis. Students with ID may need support in several areas to participate in college. With the ever-changing college schedules for everyone and the overall concept of natural supports, we have chosen to train our natural supports in a variety of ways. As stated above, the roles of natural supports change frequently as they may assist with navigating campus, attending classes, helping with homework, eating meals together, attending leisure and recreational events, assisting on the job, assisting with goal development and daily routines, or engaging in other on- and off-campus activities together. While supports are trained in all areas, there will always be issues that arise needing problem-solving skills that may not have been covered in trainings. There is also a necessity for a group of paid natural supports that work with students more frequently on more delicate or earlier morning shifts that are harder to fill with unpaid natural supports. Reliable participation and routine is sometimes more necessary.

Paid natural supports take on more leadership roles with UP students as they work 10–20 hours per week. Some are designated as schedulers, academic supports who are enrolled together with UP students in classes, suitemates who provide overnight care as needed, job coaches, providing transportation on and off campus, teaching lessons related to individual goals, homework and organizational skills training, serving as coaches in About Life (relationships and social skills instruction), and helping with personal hygiene needs. We have found having more paid supports in these capacities promotes greater consistency, but have also been flexible in allowing some promising unpaid natural supports to cover these more demanding shifts. This allows us to also assess the performance of unpaid natural support in these roles if there are available openings with paid natural support positions.

Training Natural Supports

So how do you train unpaid and paid natural supports in all these various roles? It is not an easy task, since many new supports come in each semester or trained ones also graduate each semester, but here are a few considerations and ideas. While online training has its place, we prefer to do initial orientation trainings with new volunteers face to face. This allows dialogue and questions back and forth as well as allowing our program staff or veteran natural supports doing the training to fully vet incoming supports. The initial training lasts 1.5 hours and covers a lot of information. The larger topics include an overview of the program, expectations and roles of natural supports, the use of WhenToWork scheduling software, resources and ongoing support in the e-learning platform (Blackboard), a variety of protocols for working as a team, strategies for working with individuals with ID, documentation requirements, frequently asked questions, and learning profiles with introductory videos of the UP students. As many of the service hours are typically tied to class requirements, there is a level of accountability and professionalism that must be honored among all unpaid and paid natural supports.

In addition to initial training, paid natural supports receive more in-depth trainings both in face-to-face and online formats once hired. Paid natural supports have opportunities each semester to attend professional development trainings structured or planned based on current student needs. Some professional development trainings we have offered across semesters relate to: About Life (relationships and social skills), person-centered planning, sign language basics, teaching effectively with daily living skills such as cooking, laundry, and cleaning, homework and testing accommodation support, and assistive technology. In addition to professional development trainings, paid natural supports also attend or choose at least two of five "Check and Connect" meetings across the semester. These meetings last for one hour and we discuss and brainstorm solutions for working with UP students and natural supports to provide consistency when tackling challenging behaviors or skills needing to be taught more consistently and systematically. It is important to facilitate these meetings with efficiency and formality to avoid unintentional "gossip" with issues discussed and focus on being productive to generate solutions. These meetings have gained positive momentum among natural supports feeling like they have been heard and supported as they also acquire more skills and resources to be more successful.

Schedulers also participate in additional trainings. They have biweekly schedule meetings to connect with other schedulers and program staff to be as efficient as they can be using WhenToWork and moving UP students towards designing their own weekly schedules. We have a retreat each semester to co-plan and work out details for the upcoming semester and coverage needs.

In addition to the trainings described above, it is important to continue providing ongoing support and accountability to natural supports. Several ways we have offered the ongoing support is to set up an e-learning system such as Blackboard as an organization (not a class) where you can enroll or delete users. Once natural supports have access to our program Blackboard organization, they have access to the scheduling system and numerous resources. This e-learning platform serves as a hub where natural supports can (1) complete their weekly behavior surveys after working with the students, (2) support and be involved in monthly person-centered planning meetings with access to a master list of all the PCP meetings scheduled for the semester, (3) know the UP students' goals or areas to work on within their individual plans for college participation (IPCP), (4) access to review various academic and semester calendars, and (5) post and have access to upcoming homework and assignment deadlines on the discussion board.

Accountability and Evaluating Natural Supports

With natural supports going all different directions, having accountability systems and procedures is also a necessity. While personality sometimes can influence work performance, many times, if given resources and rationale, there is usually improvement in behavior. Overall, our program teaches the supports about "being present" with students and not on their phones while looking for ways to intervene or remediate support as needed. They are trained to look for and intervene in the teachable moments. We train using relevant problem-solving scenarios and activities that include videos, role plays, and cross-mentoring of veteran supports to new supports. However, despite all the training and scenarios given, accountability procedures for natural support roles and responsibilities should be assessed regularly. At the beginning of the semester, we provide paid natural supports with a written document they sign listing their roles and responsibilities. We review this as a team and make sure everyone understands the difference between roles of paid and unpaid natural supports. At midterm and during Check and Connect meetings, paid natural supports are reminded to review and assess themselves on how they are doing with their roles and responsibilities as paid natural supports. Many reflect monthly during these meetings and develop solutions for areas to improve and how they will exceed expectations. At the end of the semester, the program staff give paid natural supports a self-evaluation survey (see Table 11.1) that evaluates their overall work performance. The paid natural support self-evaluates and gives examples to support how they rated their work performance. Once the self-evaluations are complete, the program staff (typically the staff member managing day-to-day operations) meets with paid natural supports individually to discuss their evaluations and potential leadership roles if rehired in the next semester.

Table 11.1 Paid Natural Support Self-Evaluation and Individual Growth Plan

The UP Program paid support should self-evaluate EACH area below and ADD COMMENTS before meeting with the UP Program Co-Director. Continued employment is dependent on satisfactory performance as a paid support. Please complete this survey at least 48 hours before your scheduled meeting time.

Q1: Your name:
Q2: Date of Completion
Q3: Email Address:
Q4: Total Number of Check and Connect Meetings
Q5: Total Projected Number of UP behavior surveys
Q6: Total Number of PCP meetings
Q7: Total Number of Professional Development sessions

Work Performance

Please rate yourself on the following criteria based on your work performance for this semester. COMMENTS ARE REQUIRED WITH EXAMPLES ILLUSTRATING HOW YOU MET THIS SELF-RATING.

Ratings: Exceeded Expectations, Met Expectations, Some Improvement Needed, Substantial Improvement Needed, Unresponsive to this Expectation

Q8: DEPENDABILITY

The paid support worked the hours scheduled each week for the entire semester, met UP students ON TIME, was PRESENT during the shifts (following schedule descriptions listed), did not drop shifts from the tradeboard without finding replacements, kept availability updated and shaded in w2w, notified UP staff of schedule changes, and was accessible as needed.

Q9: LEADERSHIP/ENGAGEMENT/INITIATIVE

The paid support was engaged in person-centered planning meetings/goals, provided academic, vocational, and social skills instruction opportunities, and attended extracurricular events with UP students.

Q10: JUDGMENT/PROFESSIONALISM/INTEGRITY

The paid support exercised good reasoning, made good decisions to support or benefit UP students, and demonstrated honesty and respect in the work environment (including all scheduled shifts). SELF-EVALUATE HOW YOU DID WITH CONFIDENTIALITY.

Q11: INNOVATION/COMMUNICATION/TEAMWORK

The paid support communicated new ideas or concerns to the team and understood and/or applied teamwork/communication strategies to actively contribute to the success of the program, other UP Program volunteers, UP students, and families.

Q12: PROFESSIONAL DEVELOPMENT/CREATIVITY

The paid support attended professional development sessions and implemented strategies learned to improve work performance while collecting data on UP student performance.

Q13: PROBLEM-SOLVING/ORGANIZATION

The paid support understands the goals and outcomes of the University Participant Program and was able to help in developing any alternative solutions when needed in a timely manner.

OVERALL PERFORMANCE RATING

COMPLETE QUESTIONS 14–16 IF YOU FEEL YOU ARE ELIGIBLE FOR REHIRE.
PROFESSIONAL GROWTH PLAN FOR NEXT SEMESTER
Based on your work performance this semester, explain specifically why the UP staff should rehire you next semester over other paid supports and active volunteers.
Q14: How can we (UP Program staff) help support your growth in these areas described above?
Q15: If rehired, based on our current activities, needs, and schedules, which areas do you feel you could lead best? Rank them from MOST/TOP CHOICE AS (1) to LEAST/LAST CHOICE AS (9) interested based on your strengths, preferences, comfort, and leadership style.

- vocational training (job support, applications, resumes, interviews)
- academic access (homework or class support)
- personal development (PCP leader)
- community participation
- suitemate for upcoming semesters
- training new UP volunteers and/or fundraising for UP
- health and wellness
- About Life: relationships
- weekend warrior/snow coverage

Q16: Do you feel you should be eligible for rehire next semester?
Yes or No with comment box
*By checking 'yes' this serves as my electronic signature to say I hereby completed this self-evaluation to the best of my ability and feel I have given the most honest and reflective answers about my work performance for this semester.

Handling Conflicts with Natural Supports

Unfortunately, we cannot always live in a harmonious world with natural supports interacting with one another for all hours of the day. There will be conflicts to address. Sometimes more conflicts arise on some days than others. However, there are several actions programs can take to minimize conflict and frustration. First, there has to be an open door policy. This means someone is actively listening and seeking solutions alongside sometimes frustrated natural supports. The program staff that works with natural supports needs to have a developmental approach and positive demeanor to handle conflicts. It should be dealt with fairly by facilitating and soliciting all perspectives to generate solutions together. Second, it is important to show appreciation to natural supports for what they do, but not "play" favorites. Having favorites will only result in more hostility. Third and most importantly, it is important to be more direct and have less talking without all parties represented. If you have conflict or issues with work performance among natural supports and they have been given multiple resources or opportunities, this should be addressed quickly before it spirals. Ultimately, program staff should stress the importance of working as a team and what that truly involves. They should also serve as a role model for this to natural supports and handle conflict with love and compassion, but help facilitate or uncover the root of the problem to keep things moving in a positive and productive manner. Along with compassion and love, there has to be a focus and investment of efforts towards reaching and empowering the next generation.

Showing Appreciation

Without natural supports, there will not be as many valuable and inclusive learning experiences. Therefore, it is important to take time (especially in this generation) to show appreciation and celebrate uniqueness with natural supports. Within the UP Program, we have decided to do this in many ways which have evolved into new program traditions. We have kickoff meetings and end-of-semester celebrations. We have appreciation weeks and small tokens of thanks across natural supports during stressful times in the semester. We complete numerous nominations for community engagement awards along with pictures or certificates or small tokens of appreciation for significant program involvement. We feature volunteers of the month on our program website and social media outlets as well as recognizing a UP Support of the Year annually at events or college-wide awards ceremonies. And last but not least, we have a tradition of making an end-of-the-semester volunteer video of memories made together to share with classwide partnerships and on our social media.

Final Thoughts

Natural supports are the crucial key ingredient for full inclusion that deserve time and investment. Programs cannot function without their dedication and commitment. Professionally, we also promote opportunities that matter or can turn into larger professional development or leadership opportunities. First, we strive when travel money is available to take natural supports and UP students to co-present and share their college experiences at local, state, national, and international conferences. This helps guide and connect them to others in the field as they explore their purpose and future career paths. Many graduates have stayed connected and found their future jobs in the same career paths in postsecondary education. Second, it is important to give students a chance and multiple opportunities to be leaders. Get to know their strengths and talents to invite them to do leadership activities within and sometimes outside of their comfort zone. Take time to genuinely commend or support them as they request feedback or assistance along the way. Third, as a program, do not be afraid to provide training in more non-traditional ways. This could be online, through videos, playing Kahoot games, using smartphones or apps, skits, and role plays to name a few. These creative trainings have made lasting impacts on our natural supports. Fourth, be transparent with your "to do" task list with natural supports. Although this may seem unnatural at first, it can be effective. We have found as a small staff that we cannot do all that needs to be done without having enough hours in the workday. Therefore, finding ways to delegate and allow for more student leadership of the program operations has been a key factor in moving things along over the years with and without funding. Fifth, be transparent and supportive, but do not hover. The newer generation has great ideas so take time to embrace and trust them to share their ideas. Encourage creativity and be open and flexible to change for the better. Support, but be willing to step back when the students have it under control and then express the value they provide to the students and program. Finally, you never really know when natural supports are gathering seeds to their future careers. They are watching and learning from you. Be the role model you didn't really know you were or intended to be. Many natural supports may change their career paths or majors based on the interactions or experiences they encounter with you, your PSE students, and overall program experiences. Invest time into the next generation and keep the connections open after they move on and graduate. After all, they are the next generation and will be what is supporting students with ID in their future jobs and communities beyond the college experiences.

References

Kelley, K. R., & Westling, D. L. (2013). A focus on natural supports in postsecondary education for students with intellectual disabilities at Western Carolina University. *Journal of Vocational Rehabilitation*, 38(1), 67–76. doi: 10.3233/JVR-120621.

Nisbet, J., & Hagner, D. (1988). Natural supports in the workplace: A reexamination of supported employment. *Journal of the Association of the Severely Handicapped*, 13, 260–267.

Westling, D. L., & Kelley, K. R. (2018). Full inclusion of college students with intellectual disability: Western Carolina University's University Participant (UP) program. In W. Plaute, S. Harter-Reiter, & R. Schneider (Eds.), *Inklusive Pädagogische Hochschule – Potenziale der Diversität für die Zukunft der LehrerInnenbildung*. Studienverlag.

12 Preparing for Post-Program Success

When someone goes on a trip or plans special events, this involves a great deal of time, detail, and organization. Similar to events and trips, there is always a destination or outcome to look towards. Many dreams and long-term goals also take effort and often times require orchestrated teamwork to make them happen. Having clear expectations and timelines established for post-program goals and outcomes can help increase overall success. This chapter will cover the importance of post-program planning, offers a timeline to promote post-program success, gives suggestions for data collection of artifacts each semester, provides family resources and workshops, and suggests a variety of ways for connecting families and students to future providers and community resources. The chapter concludes with sample data collection surveys to help gather follow-along and long-term data through a variety of ways and alumni events.

Importance of Post-Program Planning

Providing initial communication up front about post-program outcomes is a MUST with interested applicants and families that apply to PSE programs. The vision from the onset has to align from the very beginning of the partnership. We have found communicating very early during our open house event as well as the initial application process and then planning backwards to be two important ways to successfully prepare or plan for post-program success. To do this, having visuals for everyone to reference is important. Laying out clear paths keeps everyone on the same page and avoids unintentional miscommunication. As you have read in a few earlier chapters, we use the *academic roadmaps* in the UP Program to guide us. We also use the PATH model, as mentioned in Chapter 10, to provide more concrete ways to visually map out long-term goals and decide who will provide ongoing support to individuals with ID and their families. If everyone is not aware of the goals expressed by the student with ID and has their own agenda, this can be one of the biggest obstacles for post-program success and beyond. The clearer the illustrated path is mapped out in a visual representation, the more everyone can work together to achieve the common goals.

As with any plans made, there should be flexibility and patience with any sudden detours or allowance of someone changing their mind. This happens with many college students at pivotal moments who are also exploring future career paths. Many need to take time and reflect on their overall strengths, preferences, interests, and needs towards their future. While this is similar in many ways, offering more concrete and explicit visuals can improve post-program planning for young adults with ID. With some changes allowed, plans for the future should be reviewed and updated more than once a year or semester. As part of our monthly PCP meetings, we devote a percentage of the meeting time to future goals through our "next steps" part of the meeting, as noted in Chapter 10. This allows us to discuss as a team what's next and how we plan to work together to get there. However, while everyone has a seat at the table with the support team, it is important to note that planning and goal-setting should primarily be driven by the student with ID and what *they* want while team members *actively listen and support* as needed. When the students see opportunity and results for expressing their own goals and plans through self-determination and advocacy, they typically feel more ownership and responsibility to achieve the path they have set before them.

Proposed Timelines for Post-Program Success

With only four semesters and a few winter and summer breaks, we have found that every day counts. Within the UP Program, post-program planning begins at our open house meeting with initial applicants and families. We share with them the ultimate goals and outcomes we are striving for together, with examples and sometimes firsthand stories from our program graduates and families. This includes having inclusive and competitive community jobs (working at or above minimum wage for 20 or more hours per week) and living in inclusive community settings after graduation. This does not include going back home to live with family members, living in group homes, or congregated living arrangements. It does include having their own place or roommate, whether renting or becoming homeowners. We know these are ambitious goals, but ultimately setting higher expectations helps us all work together to achieve these post-program goals. Many of our students meet friends in college and then mutually agree to sign lease agreements together after graduation. With employment, a few graduates have had full-time jobs with benefits waiting on them after graduation that they have successfully kept for more than a year. Everyone's story and how they achieve the outcomes or timelines will be different. This is good to keep in mind as everyone works together, but ultimately having higher expectations for these outcomes should always be at the center of discussions and post-program planning. So, what does the semester timeline look like for a two-year program, and how do we work towards making every day count towards post-program success?

Implementation and Coordination

As stated previously, the first step in the timeline begins with sharing the expectations with interested applicants and families guided by our UP Program memorandum of understanding (MOU) in the open house materials. The MOU provides timelines for achieving success before, during, and after the program. Second, during our orientation camp, we work with students to begin the process of developing their *academic roadmaps* for what they want to do before, during, and after college. These roadmaps are completed separately with the students. Families are also given the roadmap to complete individually to bring back with them during the family part of the UP orientation camp. This allows us to assess how frequently everyone in the incoming support system have already talked about common career or future goals with everyone being on the same page. If not, it is a chance to have some initial discussions early on about what the student wants versus what the family thinks they want in the future. Third, during the family orientation, we discuss the MOU in great detail with help from our current and previous family members contributing to this discussion. Within the MOU, we propose the following timeline for preparing for post-program success along with the UP students.

1) At the end of the first semester, parents or guardians will help identify in writing eight seriously considered career option sites.
2) At the end of the first semester, parents or guardians will identify in writing eight seriously considered living arrangements in the community in which the student will reside after the UP Program.
3) At the end of the second semester, in collaboration with the UP staff, the original list given must be pared to an intermittent list of four high-probability career option sites and four high-probability living arrangements.
4) At the end of the third semester, the intermittent list must be pared to two very seriously considered career option sites and two very seriously considered living arrangements.
5) At the mid-point of the fourth semester, in collaboration with the UP staff, a specific career site and a specific living arrangement will be identified that the UP student can transition into no more than one year following graduation from the UP Program.
6) Parents or guardians must consistently work with our staff to identify employment opportunities during holiday breaks and the summer between the first and second year of the program.
7) Parents or guardians must provide a contact list of service providers, key community members, and agencies in their community that could provide support to the student during and after the UP Program.
8) If services or service providers change during the program, it is the responsibility of the parent/guardian and student to notify UP staff within a period of one week.

9) Continuation in the UP Program is also dependent on the requirements of the parents or guardians for identifying the career and living arrangements.

While this may sound detailed for the families and their involvement, we have found it helps guide them to planning ahead and also reflecting on what they can do to help prepare for the next steps. Having this timeline allows us to have productive conversations and goal-setting opportunities within monthly PCP meetings. Families review and sign the MOU at the end of the face-to-face family orientation retreat. As a program, we spend a lot of time reviewing and discussing this agreement so everyone has clear guidelines within the partnership and knows what we are working towards throughout the college experience and beyond. While families are working hard on these timelines, we as a program are also working hard to collect semester artifacts they can also use in their post-program journey.

Suggested Artifacts to Collect to Plan for Post-Program Success

Students who participate in the college should have exemplified experiences to highlight their overall strengths, interests, and work experiences during various parts of their college experiences. These opportunities should be captured and collected cumulatively to illustrate the learning achieved from students with ID. There are several suggested artifacts we have chosen to collect that relate specifically to post-program success. Some artifacts help the student, some help the program, and some help the future employers or community members that will join the student's support team after college.

During each of their work experiences, we request several items, such as reference letters and evaluations, from each of our employers and internship sites. This allows us as well as the student to learn what skills need to be remediated and what skills are a strength to highlight with future employers. In addition to these artifacts, we also ask employers to participate in video interviews and capture various footage of work sites to compile a short video resume. This is a concise way to share a variety of work experiences the UP students have had during their college experiences. The final video resumes are compiled in the final semester to present to future employers. Video resumes help share the student's strengths, preferences, and interests while being narrated by the student. At the end of the video resume, the student's contact information is displayed so they can use this artifact as a selling point with future employers (see Chapter 8).

Other artifacts we strive to provide to students and their families are career assessment results and work accommodations that have demonstrated greater success for them within the workplace. The students get copies of the career assessments, and electronic/hard copies of their updated resumes with job, volunteer, and conference presentations listed.

In the final semester, we update their *academic roadmaps* and PATH plans. Additionally, some students transitioning to similar jobs they might have had while in college also take their task analysis or work charts from previous job sites to adapt or use in their new, similar job sites. Finally, any additional certificates or milestones (e.g., American Red Cross CPR and First Aid certifications, ServSafe® trainings, work samples) are also included in UP graduate packets to take to new work and community settings. With independent living, we also collect recipes and task analysis they can take and use in their future apartments or homes. Uniquely, during the third semester, we also send out a senior survey to all our upcoming graduates that have worked with us during their time at Western Carolina University. The survey asks about where they will be living and their five-year plan to gauge continued interested or support to our students in shared job sites or communities (see Table 12.1).

As all these artifacts are collected for students, our program simultaneously networks with the currently enrolled families by coordinating with our previous parents of our UP graduates to come back and mentor each other.

Table 12.1 Senior Support Survey

The UP Program is proud of our senior supports. You're moving forward to impact your community. We also know the community will become the primary support for graduating UP students.

We're hoping to gauge the way you'll be impacting your community and whether you'll be able to continue supporting UP graduates after you leave WCU.

Q1: Name

Q2: What is your five-year plan? Where would you like to be living and what would you like to be doing (work, etc.) five years from now?

Q3: Where do you plan to live immediately after graduating from WCU?

Q4: What post-WCU jobs are you seeking or planning to seek? (please list)

Q5: If I live relatively close to a graduated UP Program alum, I am willing to live with the former UP student.

Yes

No

Maybe

Q6: If I live relatively close to a graduated UP student, I would be willing to provide the following support (check all that apply):

Community outings/activities

Recreation

Religious events

Personal care

Work

Volunteering

Transportation

Meals

Morning routines

Evening routines

Other (please specify):

Suggested Family Workshops

Some of our greatest lessons learned for post-program success have been working with families throughout the college experiences. This is a big transition for many families to navigate for young adults with disabilities. Many families express the unknown and fear that awaits them after the program ends. They truly want to do what is best, but sometimes resources are limited or they simply need additional resources or understanding to get to the next level. Many are told repeatedly how much their son or daughter cannot do rather than focusing on what they can do. We have found that parent-to-parent mentor meetings offering various topics are good time investments to dissolve some underlying myths or fears. Parents who have been there can share their lessons learned along the way with parents just beginning their transitions back into the community. Several workshop topics that our parent mentors have facilitated towards post-program success include:

1) transportation
2) social security income/disability benefits
3) Medicaid waiver and community-based services (working with LMC/MCOs)
4) lessons learned (from families and students that made successful college-to-community transitions)
5) social planning and keeping in touch with college networks (more remotely)
6) strategies for continuing after college (e.g., scheduling resources, facilitation of PCP meetings in the community, community mapping)
7) living on your own (advice from UP graduates and families)
8) finding a job and keeping it (working with employers and Vocational Rehabilitation).

Making the Connections in the Community

Beyond parent workshops and mentoring, there are a few other ways we have strategically helped make connections in the community. Our program personnel strive to stay current with available community resources and remain present at advocacy meetings with families and students transitioning to existing resources in their community. This helps everyone learn together and have a unified voice for post-program planning. We invite several community agencies and providers to connect with us along with traditional agencies like Vocational Rehabilitation before the last semester of the program. Each month, at least one staff member on our team devotes some time to researching a community agency or service (or attends relevant webinars) that might be relevant for UP students. As a staff, we try to get on every listserv we can to interpret and pass along relevant resources to our families and students. While each student and family are different, taking time to map out community resources available through informal and formal networks is worth the time to help them connect and transition back to their communities. Overall, we advocated and eventually worked out a unique follow-along service opportunity through our local management entity/managed care organization (LMC/MCO). This allows our graduates to have follow-along support on their jobs and in the community by hiring natural supports they choose to help them transition and continue to meet their goals. This agreement allows us to provide qualifying graduates and family members with supported employment and personal assistance services in their communities. Based on our experiences, this agreement and resource over the years has truly given more comfort to students and families embarking into more competitive jobs and inclusive living opportunities. With some families and students receiving more services and resources than others, we have creatively worked with others to help with community mapping and networks at graduation or birthday celebrations to have community members that want to be involved who simply commit or sign up for monthly outings with students rather than bringing traditional gifts to parties. This allows for commitments to be made for those who choose to make a difference, but also allows the student to continue generalizing and networking the use of skills learned in college specifically with planning weekly schedules and appropriately asking others to do things with them in their community. Ultimately there is not one protocol to follow when connecting graduates and families to future resources. This process has to be individualized, but should also remain at the forefront of planning post-program success. While we navigate the individual paths after college completion, we have also found value in investing our time in keeping college support networks open among our alumni and families that wish to continue in this support system while collecting follow-along data.

Collecting Follow-Along Data

As with any follow-along procedures, we strive to gain 100% response rates, but this can be difficult depending on the circumstances. While many families are great about providing the UP staff with their son and daughter's post-program status for at least two years after program completion through surveys, phone calls, and emails, some still disappear or do not wish to respond. This is typical among all college graduates and can be because of many reasons that are sometimes harder to predict. Luckily, we have a higher percentage of students and families that choose to stay connected. We have attempted to develop a standard way to gather the post-program outcomes of our graduates, which helps our continued program evaluation and potential future funding opportunities (see Table 12.2).

In addition, as funding allows, we have also hired external evaluators to conduct focus groups with students, families, faculty, and employers.

Table 12.2 UP Program Follow-Along Survey for Recent Graduates

1. Are you 18 or older?
   - ☐ Yes
   - ☐ No (if no, say "thank you, but we can't continue")

2. You understand that I am going to ask you questions about [former UP student]. Do you agree to participate?
   - ☐ Yes
   - ☐ No (if no, say "thank you, but we won't continue")

3. What was the month and year your son or daughter started the UP Program?

   August, _____

4. Did your son or daughter remain in the UP Program for the entire two-year period?
   - ☐ Yes
   - ☐ No. If no, what happened? (record here):

   _____

5. At any time after leaving the UP Program, has your son or daughter had one or more paid jobs (part-time or full-time) in the community?
   - ☐ Yes
   - ☐ No

6. What is the minimum number of hours per week your son or daughter has worked on a job since leaving the UP Program? _____ What is the maximum? _____

7. What is the longest amount of time your son or daughter has maintained employment on a paid job in the community after leaving the UP Program?
   - ☐ 1 month or less
   - ☐ 1 to 6 months
   - ☐ 7 to 12 months
   - ☐ Longer than 12 months

8. What is the total number of jobs (part-time or full-time) your son or daughter has held since completing the UP Program? This includes multiple jobs held at once or consecutively.
   - ☐ 1
   - ☐ 2
   - ☐ 3
   - ☐ 4
   - ☐ More than 4

9. In any of the jobs your son or daughter held, was he or she promoted or assigned to take on more responsibilities than at the beginning of the job?
   - ☐ Yes
   - ☐ No

(continued)

Table 12.2 (continued)

10. Has your son or daughter maintained continuous, community employment since leaving the UP Program?
    - ☐ Yes
    - ☐ No

11. Has your son or daughter been fired or laid off from any job since finishing the UP Program?
    - ☐ Yes
    - ☐ No

12. Does your son or daughter currently have a paid job in the community?
    - ☐ Yes
    - ☐ No

13. At this time, if your son or daughter is presently working at a paid job in the community, what kind of work does he or she do?

    _____

    From the list below, identify the area that seems most appropriate for the job:
    - ☐ Computer, mathematical, architecture, engineering, and science occupations
    - ☐ Education, training, and library occupations
    - ☐ Arts, design, entertainment, sports, media occupations
    - ☐ Healthcare practitioners and technical occupations
    - ☐ Protective service occupations
    - ☐ Food preparation and serving-related occupations
    - ☐ Building and grounds cleaning and maintenance occupations
    - ☐ Personal care and service occupations
    - ☐ Sales and related occupations
    - ☐ Office and administrative support occupations
    - ☐ Construction and extraction occupations
    - ☐ Installation, maintenance, and repair occupations
    - ☐ Production occupations
    - ☐ Transportation and material moving occupations
    - ☐ Military-specific occupations

14. At this time, if your son or daughter is presently working in a paid job in the community, what are the number of hours per week he or she is working?
    - ☐ Less than 10 hours per week
    - ☐ Between 10 and 20 hours per week
    - ☐ Between 21 and 30 hours per week
    - ☐ Between 30 and 40 hours per week
    - ☐ More than 40 hours per week

15. How much is your son or daughter currently paid?
    - ☐ Below minimum wage
    - ☐ Minimum wage
    - ☐ Above minimum wage

16. What is your son's or daughter's current annual income range?
    - ☐ $5,000 or less
    - ☐ $5,001 – $10,000
    - ☐ $10,001 – $15,000
    - ☐ $15,001 – $20,000
    - ☐ $20,001 – $25,000
    - ☐ $25,001 – $30,000
    - ☐ $30,001 – $35,000
    - ☐ $35,001 – $45,000
    - ☐ $45,001 – $60,000
    - ☐ Over $60,000

17. On your son's or daughter's current job, are benefits provided (e.g., paid vacation, health insurance, retirement) as part of the job?
    - ☐ Yes
    - ☐ No

18. If your son or daughter had one or more jobs in the community after leaving the UP Program, how much was the job related to the vocational training he or she received in the UP Program?
    - ☐ The job was very similar to the vocational training received in the UP Program
    - ☐ The job was somewhat similar to the vocational training received in the UP Program
    - ☐ The job was not similar to the vocational training received in the UP Program

19. Which of the following benefits does your son or daughter receive, if any?
    - ☐ SSI (Social Security Income)
    - ☐ SSDI (Social Security Disability Insurance)
    - ☐ Medicaid
    - ☐ Medicare
    - ☐ Private health insurance
    - ☐ None
    - ☐ Other

---

20. Which of the following best describes your son's or daughter's living arrangements immediately AFTER completing the UP Program?
    - ☐ Lived in the family home with parents and/or other family members
    - ☐ Lived on family property but in a separate apartment, house, or mobile home
    - ☐ Lived in foster care or with a host family
    - ☐ Lived in a group home, ICF/MR, or other congregate living facility
    - ☐ Lived alone or with roommates in a supervised apartment, house, or mobile home
    - ☐ Lived alone or with roommates in his or her own apartment, house, or mobile home
    - ☐ Other

(continued)

Table 12.2 (continued)

21 Which of the following best describes your son's or daughter's living arrangements CURRENTLY?
    ☐ Lives in the family home with parents and/or other family members
    ☐ Lives on family property but in a separate apartment, house, or mobile home
    ☐ Lives in foster care or with a host family
    ☐ Lives in a group home, ICF/MR, or other congregate living facility
    ☐ Lives alone or with roommates in a supervised apartment, house, or mobile home
    ☐ Lives alone or with roommates in his or her own apartment, house, or mobile home
    ☐ Other

22 Not including job-related activities, how often does your son or daughter CURRENTLY leave the home to go into community settings?
    ☐ Rarely or never
    ☐ Once or twice a week
    ☐ Three to four times a week
    ☐ Five or more times a week

23 How does your son or daughter travel around in the community? (check all that apply)
    ☐ Drives a car (has a driver's license)
    ☐ Walks or rides bike or other self-propelled vehicle
    ☐ Relies on parents, family members, or friends
    ☐ Uses public transportation, para transit, or taxi
    ☐ Uses transportation provided by an agency or organization. If transportation is provided by an agency or organization, please explain:

    _____

24 Which of the following financial skills does your son or daughter have? (check all that apply)
    ☐ Manages a debit/credit card (knows PIN; tracks spending, etc.)
    ☐ Manages a savings account
    ☐ Manages a checking account
    ☐ Writes checks
    ☐ Pays bills (i.e., rent, internet, cable, power, etc.)
    ☐ Other or more financial skills (please specify):

    _____

25 What is the best way to describe your son's or daughter's current relationship with a "significant other"?
    ☐ He or she is not currently involved with anyone
    ☐ He or she dates occasionally but is not seeing one person regularly
    ☐ He or she is seeing one person regularly
    ☐ He or she is engaged to be married
    ☐ He or she is married
    ☐ He or she is divorced, separated, or widowed

26 Does your son or daughter currently access any services to support living in the community? If so, what?

☐ Vocational services and job training
☐ Financial aid
☐ Educational assistance/supports/tutoring
☐ Reader or interpreter
☐ Occupational or life skill therapy
☐ Childcare or parenting skills training
☐ Psychological or mental health services
☐ Social work services
☐ Physical therapy
☐ Assistive technology
☐ Transportation services
☐ Medical for diagnosis
☐ Speech or language therapy
☐ Audiology services
☐ Orientation and mobility
☐ Respite care
☐ Adult day or adult recreation program
☐ Housing assistance or services
☐ Personal assistant/aide
☐ Nursing care
☐ Case management
☐ None
☐ Other (please specify)

27 In which of the following ways does your son or daughter regularly spend leisure time?

☐ Visiting family members
☐ Visiting friends or going out on dates
☐ Doing homework, household chores, cooking, or gardening
☐ Reading for pleasure or doing hobbies
☐ Shopping, hanging out, driving around, daydreaming
☐ Talking on the phone with friends
☐ Playing electronic games
☐ Using the computer for email or internet
☐ Watching TV or videos
☐ Listening to music
☐ Playing sports
☐ Doing organized activities with groups or alone
☐ Attending entertainment/events
☐ Looking for a job or attending college courses
☐ Working out, going to the gym
☐ Traveling, vacationing, going to summer camps
☐ Attending church or going to church-sponsored activities
☐ Volunteering or doing community service
☐ Other (please specify):

(continued)

Table 12.2 (continued)

28	ADDITIONAL COMMENTS OR INFORMATION
	Please feel free to tell us anything else about your son or daughter to help us better understand his or her life after the UP Program and how the program affected his or her life.
29	RESPONDENT INFORMATION
	Who answered this questionnaire? The former UP graduate's: ☐ Mother ☐ Father ☐ Both ☐ Legal Guardian

Thank you very much for answering our questions!

Their role is to collect their overall program satisfaction in order to see what we need to change with future graduates, program operations, and improve post-program success.

Staying Connected in the College Support Network

College is a time for all individuals to make lasting memories and friendships. So how can programs maintain these connections among college graduates? For us, traditional approaches and technology have helped enable more remote connections. From calls to FaceTime and social media outlets, staying in touch has been a little easier. Other more unique ways we have found to stay connected with our graduates and their families has been through inviting them back for alumni events such as open houses, class reunions, orientation camps, homecoming games, and even fundraising events. Additionally, our graduates and families are encouraged to help us visit high schools or transition fairs and share their firsthand college experiences with interested applicants and families. Our program also encourages graduates to co-present with us at conferences to share how college made a difference to the paths they are on now. This year, we also focused more fundraising efforts for scholarships and program operations by forming a booster club of families (current and past) who continue to work together on various fundraising efforts that our staff members simply do not have as much time to coordinate.

Final Thoughts

During our experience, we have united and invested both individually and as a group for the common good, focused on future funding and advocacy efforts to help change some existing policies that create barriers to independence for individuals with ID beyond their college experiences. Many of us continue to unite and have a common goal to explore more consistent funding streams with our families and students. There is importance in what we do and maintaining the networks and collecting data to show the successful outcomes are motivational reasons for doing what we do. It is important to focus on the outcome and lifelong goals that go well beyond the two-year college experience that will truly solidify and demonstrate how college experiences can and do make a difference for individuals with ID. Therefore, we encourage you as you develop your PSE programs to focus your efforts very early in the admission process on achieving post-program success.

Part IV
Special Issues

13 Providing a Safe Environment and Addressing Inappropriate Social Behaviors

During the years we have operated a PSE program, there are two issues that are often raised: How do you deal with safety issues? And, how do you deal with a student who exhibits immature or inappropriate social behavior?

In many ways the two issues are related. Some unsafe environments can increase the chance of inappropriate social behavior, and some unacceptable behavior can make a social environment less safe. So in this chapter we address both issues. Before we do, however, one point should be made. Safety and social behavior are issues relevant to *all* students on all college campuses. No one wants to live or go to school in an unsafe environment, and no one likes to associate with a young person who exhibits socially inappropriate behavior. Some people would argue that no special considerations need to be made about these issues for college students with ID, and in many ways, we agree. But there are two points that are relevant.

First, it's likely that parents of young adults with ID are more concerned for their safety than are parents of other college-age students because it is believed that the former do not always exercise good judgment with regard to issues of safety. If colleges are not able to say they are relatively safe, it will be difficult to develop and maintain a PSE program. Second, the social behavior of a traditional college student, as inappropriate as it may be, will not result in the institution being closed (although some specific organizations may be put on probation or sanctioned). However, the behavior of one student with ID can result in some people questioning the validity of an entire PSE program, perhaps making it difficult to maintain a program.

Focus on Prevention

As with most potentially difficult or undesirable situations, if there are strategies that can prevent an event from occurring, those strategies should be pursued. For both safety issues and behavioral issues, we try to reduce the probability of problems early in the program.

Reviewing Applicants

Although some PSE programs have a more or less open admissions process, as we discussed in Chapter 5 our process is relatively rigid and competitive. We want students who want to be in the program, who will work hard to be successful in the program, and who will benefit from the program. So as part of our admissions process, we carefully review the social and adaptive behaviors of our applicants during our initial review, and carefully search for indicators that suggest that an applicant might be harmful to themselves, to other students, or to the institution. We want to give everyone a fair chance to enter the program, but we are also cognizant that serious behavioral issues that have occurred in the past, especially if they are recent, are likely to occur again. Therefore, if our staff or our steering committee detects a history of inappropriate behavior, such as verbal or physical aggression, inappropriate sexual behavior, property destruction, or theft, we will not admit an applicant to the program.

Adapting and Teaching the Student Code of Conduct

Another preventive strategy comes during our orientation camp when we are giving final consideration to a group of applicants from whom we will select new students. At this time, we present and explain the university's *code of student conduct*.

We present this guide on acceptable and unacceptable campus behavior in clear terms, with an accompanying scaled-down manual, and with slides, so students begin to understand the dos and don'ts of on-campus living and the consequences that can occur if the code is violated. Discussions are held in small groups, with plenty of time for examples, questions, and discussions. Once we have officially admitted students, a printed copy and electronic version of the *code*, with relevant pictures and little jargon, is distributed to all new students with a request to review it over the summer with their family. As necessary, we will also discuss the *code* at monthly PCP meetings.

Although most colleges and universities will have similar student conduct manuals, the contents can be abstract for many students with ID. They include legal terms and different kinds of sanctions, and other terms that many college students with ID may not have encountered. We have found it helpful to provide our abridged and modified version and use it to explicitly teach it to our students.

Engaging Parents about Behavior

We also discuss the *code of conduct* with parents of applicants, and are clear in explaining that if there are violations that parents must work with our staff to resolve them. This means that parents must first agree with the requirements in the *code* and then collaborate with the UP staff to address any infractions. We explain that if there is an ongoing behavioral issue that we will implement a non-aversive *behavior intervention plan (BIP*, see below) in an effort to improve their son's or daughter's behavior, and we expect parents to cooperate with us on this plan. If the student does not learn to engage in more acceptable behavior, we may ask parents to temporarily remove their son or daughter from campus (usually for about a week) and the parents must agree to do so.

Ultimately if there are at least three violations to the *code*, the UP Program and university may elect to permanently dismiss their son or daughter from the program and the parents and the student must remove their personal belongings from campus within a 24-hour period. We point out to the parents that these conditions are included in the *memo of understanding* we have them sign when their son or daughter is admitted to the program (see Chapter 14 and Table 14.1).

In actuality, we have had only a few situations in which we have asked a student to leave the program even temporarily. But we have found that, by informing parents and students clearly of our position, they enter the program understanding that appropriate behavior is an expectation and that there are consequences if this does not occur.

Maintaining a Safe Environment Using a Tiered Approach

For the most part, college campuses are safe places, although many college students have found themselves in harm's way, sometimes by their own doing, sometimes by the doing of others. This is one of the main concerns of both parents and administrators, and it has been one of our concerns since initiating the UP Program. If a student in our program were to fall victim to an accidental injury or, worse, to intentional violence, we know that the student, the family, and likely the program, would all sustain a serious blow. And it should be understood that no university or college administration will allow a liability on campus that they can avoid.

As we have discussed elsewhere (Westling, Kelley, & Prohn, 2016), we view the maintenance of a safe environment for our students as occurring in three tiers, with each tier providing a more focused degree of security for our students. Figure 13.1 lists the three tiers.

Tier 1: Prevention and Intervention Strategies Directed Toward All Students

Tier 1 provides the most general degree of safety and is applicable to all students and other members of the campus community, including the students with ID in our PSE program. Most institutions support a variety of internal offices and departments for the specific purpose of providing

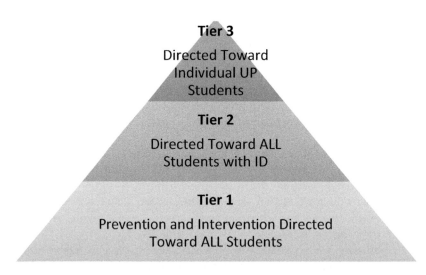

Figure 13.1 Three-Tiered Model to Promoting and Addressing Safety and Security (adapted from Westling, Kelley, & Prohn, 2016)

a safe and secure campus environment. At our university, we have several departments that provide Tier 1 safety services applicable to all students (see Table 13.1).

What may not be realized by some, is that federal law, *the Clery Act*, requires that colleges and universities make efforts to maintain safe environments. This includes making emergency notification and announcing evacuation procedures, issuing timely warnings about crimes, having missing person notification procedures, and reporting annually the breaches of safety that have occurred to the U.S. Department of Education. These data are made public (see: https://ope.ed.gov/campussafety/#/), which means that any potential student or student's family can investigate the overall safety of a specific campus. This would be relevant information for anyone looking at a particular PSE program.

Tier 2: Prevention and Intervention Strategies for all Students with ID

Whereas Tier 1 strategies apply to all students on campus, we consider those in Tier 2 as proactive strategies that provide an additional layer of safety specifically for students with ID. These program components are not meant to be rules or restrictions, but are simple efforts built into the program to ensure necessary supports that help students avoid undesirable consequences due to poor decisions. Table 13.2 provides a list of Tier 2 interventions.

Table 13.1 Tier 1 Campus Partners and Roles or Responsibilities

Department	Roles and Responsibilities
Department of Student Community Ethics	Educates students about their rights and responsibilities in the campus community
Residential Living Department	Educates and enforces the Community Code and Creed
University Police Department	Employs certified police officers to enforce laws for everyone on the college campus
University Health Services	Meets healthcare needs of the community related to physical, psychological, environmental, and health education needs
Department of Safety and Risk Management	Provides support for university activities and assures a safe and healthy environment
Emergency Services Department	Develops and promotes safety for all hazards or emergencies on campus
Campus Security Authority (CSA)	Persons at the university who help report Clery Crimes
University Office of Accessibility Resources	Ensures equal access for students with disabilities

Table 13.2 Tier 2 Interventions for Students with ID and the Purpose or Occurrence

Tier 2 Interventions	Purpose and Occurrence
Campus police safety talk	Educates students about how to remain safe and occurs during UP orientation camp
Discussion of modified code of conduct and community creed	Educates students about the rules they have to follow to live in the college community and occurs during UP orientation camp and as needed after this
Person-centered planning meetings	Meetings to discuss progress and goals, areas of improvement, and next steps. Occurs monthly
Cell phone use	Practiced and used to contact supports or emergency UP phone. Occurs daily
Use of natural supports	Undergraduate college students trained to help UP students while traveling or in campus activities as needed. Occurs daily
Suitemates in residence halls	Trained supports available at night in case of emergency situations. Occurs nightly

(continued)

182 Special Issues

Table 13.2 (continued)

About Life relationship courses, PEERS, and self-defense training	Training on sexuality, relationships, social communication, and protection. Occurs daily and weekly
Systematic approach to reducing support time	Prerequisite skills, behavior surveys, and monthly meetings to determine and adjust support needs. Occurs daily

Tier 3: Intervention Strategies Directed Toward Individual Students at Risk

Because of Tier 1 and 2 strategies, we estimate that 90% of our students experience the UP Program without any undue threat to their safety, and without threatening the safety of others. But we have had some situations that in our view have potentially infringed upon the safety of a small number of students, and when this has occurred we have implemented individualized, or Tier 3, strategies to address the issue.

Tier 3 occurs when UP students find themselves more at risk, whether it is due to their behavior, or another's behavior. This tier is only required for students who might demonstrate public behavior that raises concern among one or more of the members of the campus community, or if the behavior violates the student code of conduct or the law, or if it is apparent that danger may be possible because of the actions of another person.

Serious actions by others directed toward UP students that we believe would call for Tier 3 interventions could include teasing, taunting, bullying, threatening, stalking, or verbal or physical aggression. Actions by UP students themselves that would call for Tier 3 interventions could include under-age drinking, using illegal drugs, being abusive, showing aggression towards others, or putting themselves in places or situations that could be dangerous to themselves or others.

While Tier 3 interventions are by design individualized, they may take any of the following forms:

1) interacting with an appropriate university official if a UP student has been targeted
2) giving advice or suggestions to the UP student during PCP meetings
3) developing a behavior intervention plan to help the student with the problem behavior
4) enforcing and reviewing the code of conduct with other university officials
5) requiring temporary removal or suspension from the university
6) requiring permanent removal or suspension from the university.

Using this multi-tiered approach to safety, we feel we offer our students and their families a promise that their well-being is a central focus of our program. But we also know that living and learning comes with risks, and that a young adult with ID who is learning about life and how to make good choices sometimes will not. And sometimes this person will find themselves in a risky situation. So the challenge to a PSE program is to offer as much freedom as is possible, but to make sure an adequate safety structure is in place to prevent serious personal harm.

As part of all three tiers, we believe it is important to maintain close professional relations with key individuals and officials on campus and in the community. Looking at the offices and agencies in Table 13.1, we feel it is important that the leadership personnel in these offices know about our program and our students, and know how to contact us if relevant issues arise concerning our students. Likewise, we should be able to call them if we have concerns. As in all other aspects of our PSE program, we view collaboration related to safety as essential.

Addressing Individual Behavioral Issues

Much of what we have already discussed in this chapter pertains to addressing behavioral issues. As we have said, we try to admit only students who have a history of appropriate social behavior, we present the code of conduct and use other preventive strategies to head off inappropriate behavior, and we use one or more Tier 3 strategies if necessary to improve student behavior. Below we elaborate on two additional strategies that we feel are relevant to PSE programs.

Developing Behavior Plans Based on Positive Behavior Supports and Interventions

We view our program as being an educational program designed to lead to positive adult outcomes, not as a therapeutic or a behavioral health program. At times, however, as Tier 3 interventions suggest, we have had to make specific efforts to improve a student's behavior, attitude, or disposition. We make these efforts when we feel the student is being detrimental to themselves, the program, or the campus as a whole. So, when it has been necessary, we have created behavior intervention plans (BIPs) based on the tenets of Positive Behavior Interventions and Supports (PBIS, see www.pbis.org).

Developing and using BIPs requires more detail than we can provide here, so we direct you to other informative references, including Alberto and Troutman (2013), O'Neill et al. (2014), and Westling (2015).

A BIP occurs as a Tier 3 intervention at a point between talking to the student, and temporarily or permanently removing the student from the program and includes the following components:

- monitoring the frequency or duration of the behavior
- conducting functional assessments to determine factors and conditions related to the occurrence of the behavior
- if possible, identifying and eliminating conditions and antecedents that elicit the behavior in order to reduce the likelihood that the behavior will occur
- teaching a more socially appropriate behavior
- reinforcing appropriate behavior while avoiding reinforcing inappropriate behavior

A key to developing and using a BIP is to understand why the behavior is occurring (its function) and then to find solutions to address the cause of the behavior. This may mean avoiding certain situations, learning new and more appropriate ways to behave, and eliminating sources of reinforcement for the behavior.

Teaching Peers to Appropriately Respond

One of the key aspects of PBIS is finding a way to reinforce appropriate behavior and *not* reinforce inappropriate behavior. While this sounds logical, it usually is difficult to implement. From what we know about human behavior, in most cases, it is how a person reacts that can reinforce behavior.

Some students with ID are still learning how to be mature individuals and therefore may resort to immature behavior when attempting to interact with others, especially peers. This occurs often to gain social attention. As social attention is then given, immature behavior is reinforced – with comments, facial expressions, or reprimands – and is therefore likely to continue. When this happens, it is important to teach peers who serve as natural supports to respond consistently and naturally in an age-appropriate manner.

Immature behavior can include social deficits or excesses. Examples include: (a) saying or doing something inappropriate for a particular situation; (b) calling someone on the phone too often or with inappropriate messages; (c) texting someone too often with irrelevant or inappropriate messages; (d) invading someone's privacy when not invited; (e) not leaving someone's private space when someone wants to be alone; (f) sharing personal information with someone that is embarrassing or confidential; (g) spreading false information or rumors; (h) posting inappropriate or false information on social media; (i) lying; (j) being late to a planned event; (k) making excuses about why something did or didn't happen; and (l) engaging in any type of atypical behavior likely to draw attention to itself.

Behaviors such as these often result in a person being socially avoided or isolated and therefore warrant attention. If the person happens to be a student with ID, such behaviors are even worse because the person is

Table 13.3 How Peers Should Respond to Socially Inappropriate Behavior

1) Clearly and specifically express your dislike for the behavior. Don't hedge on your disapproval. Tell the person you don't like it and you are not going to hang out with them if it happens again.
2) If the behavior persists either in the present or in a subsequent meeting, reduce your contact with the UP student. See the person less often, and let them know why you don't wish to be around them. Do not respond to phone calls, texts, social media posts, etc. You *do not* have an obligation to be with anyone you don't like. If you are a support, contact the UP co-director and ask to be placed with another UP student.
3) If the behavior continues at those times when you do see the person, completely terminate your contact with the person and tell them why you are doing so. Again, do not respond to phone calls, texts, social media posts, etc. Maintain your distance from the person for at least one or two weeks.
4) After one or two weeks, you may try to reconcile with the person. If you do, let them know the *kind of behavior you like*. Then reinforce it when it occurs. *There is no point in lecturing the person about what happened in the past.*
5) If appropriate behavior is maintained, continue to enjoy your relationship with the UP student. If inappropriate behavior recurs, re-cycle through steps 1–4.
6) If you ever decide to completely terminate your involvement with a UP student because of their behavior, it is your right to do so. If you do decide to terminate your relationship with a particular UP student, you should tell them in the clearest way possible: (1) why you are doing so, and (2) that you do not want to have any further contact with them.
7) If you have terminated your involvement with a UP student as described above, and the student continues to attempt to contact you, you should (1) never respond to the student's attempts, and (2) if you so choose, take the action you have the right to pursue under the university's student code of conduct.

likely to have a more difficult time knowing how the behavior affects others. Consequently, the person may ultimately have a hard time living, working, and socializing in the community.

Our experience has taught us that lecturing, threatening, or cajoling the person rarely has any impact. The best form of intervention is probably that which can only come from peers (i.e., natural supports and other college students). If the peers reinforce the behavior, it is likely to continue. But if they take action to show their disapproval, there is a better chance that the person will learn that the behavior is not appropriate. Therefore, we ask that our natural supports and other college-age peers take certain steps. These steps are presented in Table 13.3 in an order going from least intensive to most intensive.

Final Thoughts

The college campus presents a positive living and learning environment to help students with ID navigate and achieve true community inclusion.

Since we started our program in 2007, as of this writing, none of our students have experienced harm while living on campus, to which we attribute the tiered, proactive approaches to safety described in this chapter. Furthermore, no students have been detained or arrested. Additionally, although inappropriate behavior has been rare, we have usually been able to address it effectively, and have never resorted to permanently dismissing a student from the program because of their behavior. Although addressing inappropriate behavior may be difficult, we maintain that we are not doing any favors if we ignore or reinforce it. If young adults with ID are going to be fully included in their communities, they have to learn what to do and what not to do in order to be successful and accepted.

References

Alberto, P. A. & Troutman, A. C. (2013). *Applied behavior analysis for teachers* (9th ed.). Columbus, OH: Merrill/Prentice-Hall.

O'Neill, R. E., Albin, R. W., Storey, K., Horner, R. H., & Sprague, J. R. (2014). *Functional assessment and program development for problem behavior: A practical handbook* (3rd ed.). Boston, MA: Cengage Learning.

Westling, D. L. (2015). *Evidence-based practices for improving challenging behaviors of students with severe disabilities* (Document No. IC - 14). Retrieved from University of Florida, Collaboration for Effective Educator, Development, Accountability, and Reform Center website: http://ceedar.education.ufl.edu/tools/innovation-configurations/

Westling, D. L., Kelley, K. R., & Prohn, S. M. (2016). A tiered approach to promote safety and security in an inclusive postsecondary education program for college students with intellectual disability. *DADD Online Journal, 3*(1), 160–171.

14 Working Effectively with Parents and Families

As discussed in Chapter 12, working with influential stakeholders such as parents can have a significant impact on post-program success. It is important to share the same goals and perspectives of the PSE program to achieve the success before, during, and after the program. Therefore, we felt it was important to devote a special issues chapter to working with families. In this chapter, we will specifically discuss the shared goals and perspectives, trusting the process, and how families have shown us what helps them most in empowering and achieving post-program success. We conclude this chapter by talking to PSE program personnel and highlighting key concepts to keep in mind related to working with families or preparing for college. The chapter concludes with a copy of our current parent memorandum of understanding (MOU), which can be referenced and adapted based on your unique PSE program characteristics or needs.

Shared Goals and Perspectives

As we stated in Chapters 3 and 12, the overall vision and post-program outcomes truly have to align from the very beginning of the partnerships among students, families, and PSE programs. Everyone can move forward when there are shared goals and perspectives with everyone connecting on the same page. In order to know and understand the perspectives and goals there has to be frequent opportunities for shared dialogue among the support team. While PSE personnel cannot "pretend" to walk in the shoes of parents or family members, they can facilitate the networks for parent-to-parent mentoring to better understand the shared perspectives and goals. In our program, we do not attempt or pretend to be in these important roles and do our best to honor and meet families where they are at the time we embark on the college life journey together. While families are valued, it is also important that everyone at the planning table remember that shared goals and perspectives should predominately come from the PSE student. The student truly should be in the driver's seat of their lives and in determining their next steps. It is up to the PSE program and families to work together to support the vision and goals expressed by the student. Therefore, self-determination and advocacy should be fostered and honored along with supported decision-making techniques to work towards common goals. Sometimes this collaborative model takes more time to allow for choice and voice of students, but we have found it is worth the investment if the student shows greater interest and ownership in their future.

Family partnerships are very important and add so much value to the team. Sharing resources regularly among families and students often leads to better opportunities. However, we also want to encourage PSE personnel to limit stereotypical assumptions when a family might not be able to participate or show up to every scheduled event or activity. It could be for many reasons, but one should not assume the family member or even professionals that are invited to the table do not care or want to be a part of the student's life. To avoid this assumption, it is important to reflect deeply and conscientiously on practices and attitudes that might encourage or hinder the shared goals and perspectives among the support team members. It is important to ALWAYS set high expectations among students, families, and PSE personnel. Give them the same opportunities as other college students until there is evidence to require additional support. Also, be sure as PSE personnel that you remember when a family may be more assertive with some things, it may be because they have had to fight for so many years to have inclusive experiences for their sons and daughters. Remember their advocacy efforts can be overwhelming at times and PSE personnel should not be the biggest roadblocks to their future victories if it is in the best interest and outcome of the student. It is important for everyone at the table to be sensitive and aware of these stereotypical assumptions while focusing on the shared goals and perspectives with the PSE student.

Trusting the Process

Many families are told this statement over and over throughout their educational experiences. Trust the process... In some cases, though, we have seen firsthand why families may remain skeptical with this statement that they truly have not always been able to trust the process. However, based on our observations and experiences with families, many have very good intentions, but tend to quickly want to step in and fix the problems because they simply do not like to see their child struggle. Rightly so, but sometimes this is not the best way to let students learn true independence. It is important to work with the families early on and encourage them to step back while letting the PSE student face the consequences and learn from experiences that might be coming their direction based on the choices they made. This may sound harsh, but if you think about your own experiences, you probably learned more and had greater "teachable moments" when you truly experienced the consequences rather than being protected. It is second nature sometimes for families and even PSE personnel to want to protect students with ID. Unfortunately, coddling and consoling does not always substantiate or foster more genuine growth towards adulthood.

Along with trusting the process with consequences, it is important to trust the process with peers. Peers can be more powerful influences or change agents sometimes than parents or PSE personnel. It is important to guide peers, but step back and let the process of positive peer influence make its impact. Peers tend to offer helpful feedback as they serve as role models to the students with ID, sharing in the same college experiences and struggles. They tend to look to their peers for guidance and affirmation as young adults. Peers have been powerful for us in their daily presence and also from their encouraging words spoken directly to UP students in our monthly person-centered planning meetings.

Special Considerations to the Parents and Family Members

As a lot of our parents have shared in initial orientation meetings, the first person-centered planning meeting (PCP) experience will be nothing like the public school meetings (e.g., IEPs) previously encountered. There is a significant difference in how the laws and paperwork are governed between school districts and PSE programs. There is more freedom that can be used in PSE programs, so it is important to be open to this format change and know more will be shared by your son or daughter leading their PCP meetings than the PSE personnel or peers. Students with ID should be leading their meetings and calling on you as an attendee in these meetings supporting their life goals and dreams. As a parent, it is important to take the time to celebrate the successes together, reflect on the areas of improvement without defense and more for future growth, and work as a true team member to implement strategies together that will consistently work and improve outcomes before quickly trying to step in to be the authoritative figure you might have been a few years ago in these meetings.

Even though there may be some uncomfortable times within these meetings, the PSE program is there for your son or daughter and you as the parent. As a family member, take time to work with PSE personnel to offer previous history or strategies that have worked in the past or you think might work in the future. Remember that you (as the parent) remain the true expert of your son or daughter as they transition into adulthood. PSE personnel are there to honor your son's or daughter's goals, interact with you as needed, but are not required to give daily updates. As parents, please research and respect the boundaries between colleges and families as responsibilities shift more to the PSE student advocating for their needs. While PSE personnel are there for you, it is important that you understand your role as the parent and keeping boundaries between you and the natural supports (peers). It is not the role of the natural supports that work with your son or daughter to update or communicate with you directly. Interacting with peers or bypassing the PSE program staff can sometimes cause more unintended miscommunications and simply make everyone more uncomfortable.

Again, as mentioned earlier, there will be news and updates delivered to you as your son or daughter engages in self-discovery and being away from home. Be open minded to what is being shared while setting higher expectations and new opportunities. College is the place and incubator for learning and taking some risks for students to truly be away from home, exploring who they really are or want to be. In addition, your talk and tone should change from the child talk you might have once used to having more adult conversations and interactions. Changes will come and sometimes all at once. These changes may not be most convenient for you, but they may make a lot of sense to your son or daughter. As the changes and conversations come, be willing to *actively listen* to your son or daughter and their future goals or plans, rather than quickly reacting or saying no. For example, if their future career goals seem very different from what you have in mind, remember it is their choice and life that they need to be happy about when they get up and go to that job every morning. While you can offer suggestions along the way, ultimately, the decisions at this point in their lives should be more in their hands when most possible.

As you see more self-advocacy, communication skills, and maturity quickly flourish in most PSE students during their first semester of college, take the time to embrace and appreciate it. In the same vein, take the time to ask constantly as you see this happening, "How can this be created within the community and beyond college in order to keep the skills being generalized and mastered among peers and being away from home?" As you ask this question while they are away at college, focus more on what's next and use the time to do your research on resources and networking for future goals. Parents should truly be as busy and know the expectations and roles they have while their sons and daughters are in college in order to be productive and contributing members of the support team during and after college.

Fear of the unknown and what is to come can immobilize all of us at times and be scary, but as parents it is important to monitor actions and reactions to new ideas so there are fewer intentions of being an obstacle or limiting your emerging young adult's outcomes or success. For example, strongly consider the overall pros and cons of seeking guardianship for your son or daughter and what consequences that could bring. Are you limiting their future in exchange for your own comfort and protection? Always expect the unexpected, and sometimes that will mean supporting some of the unknowns or biggest fears you face initially to let go of the comfort you want in order to achieve the unexpected.

Special Considerations to the PSE Personnel

Now that parents have had some suggestions about trusting the process and setting high expectations, it is now time for PSE personnel to consider these recommendations.

First, be there for families. Show them you care by going the extra mile sometimes to do the research that may not be easiest to understand. Help simplify the language or jargon causing confusion and bridge the gaps to navigating adult services. As stated to parents, partner with them and others when at all possible to hold PSE students accountable for their actions as adults. Parents may get defensive when the news of the actions are delivered, but remain professional and try your best not to take it personally. You are the messenger, and sometimes the closest messengers get the initial or rawest reactions.

Second, be aware and respectful of the family's time to avoid extra trips to campus or fees along the way. This builds trust and respect. Overall, the families and students will see the investments you make towards their best interests and making reasonable accommodations.

Third, anticipate the unexpected and be one step ahead when possible to provide a safety net. This is always hard to gauge, as you want the PSE student to learn the consequences of their actions, but you juggle the risk of liability and safety as well to your university. Find the balance between letting go and not being so close to the student that they cannot do the task effectively or be in the driver's seat in most situations.

Fourth, along with parents, strongly weigh the pros and cons of soliciting guardianship. Do your homework and research about this along with families and students to further consider alternate and less restrictive possibilities. Fifth, be willing to accept responsibility for your role and when you might need to be more transparent and direct to families and students. This could involve taking extra time to make some phone calls or respond to emails in a timely manner to eager or anxious families so they know you hear them. Open doors lead to greater outcomes.

Finally, keep in touch even after PSE students complete programs. Families get connected with more support networks, and that should continue more after college than before. This allows families and students to feel more supported in the rapidly changing transition years for everyone as roommates and jobs change. Brainstorming temporary solutions with families and students after graduation while having them trust the process can eventually lead to more stable outcomes. If families feel supported along the way and have some connections made with community resources, they are typically more willing to take the risks with some temporary supports than having none at all. Sometimes the roads that await them right after graduation can lead to achievement of more long-term goals and opportunities. Be willing to think outside the box along with families and students during the detours and keep in touch with the families, as you never know where those time investments may lead in the near future for everyone involved.

We want to leave you with a few highlights to consider further as both families and PSE personnel work together to prepare for college and beyond. This comes from a blog excerpt we submitted to Kelle Hampton (*Enjoying the Small Things*) and several conference presentations we have shared with families over the years:

Preparing Your Son or Daughter for College

Within the UP Program, we are often asked by parents: "What can we do to increase the chance our child will be admitted?" Often when this is asked, it can be too late. Many of the activities should start at birth and continue throughout adulthood. Here are our top ten suggestions to families as you think about preparing your son or daughter for college (Kelley, 2014; Westling & Kelley, 2015).

1) **Know the family's role.** You are a key factor to what your son or daughter can accomplish based on the expectations and opportunities you lay in their path. Potential leads to greater success, so make sure it occurs very early in your child's life.
2) **Know the roles change as the child grows up.** Nurturing and protecting is good, but changes and trying new things lead to greater independence.
3) **Focus on the future.** Life goes by quickly and school doesn't last forever. Be sure to focus on the future throughout every life opportunity that is experienced. The individuals that have had many of these responsibilities focused on their future are the ones that will be most successful in college and beyond.
4) **Expectations matter.** Good or bad, expectations set everyone's future path. Having realistic expectations, but setting the bar high, is what colleges look for in their applicants.
5) **Mistakes and taking chances are growth spurts.** There will always be risks, mistakes, and chances that need to be taken for true learning and independence to occur. Having a life that is too sheltered leads to an overwhelming college experience.
6) **Allow for choice and voice.** Decisions and choicemaking are two areas that can start early in a child's life and also empower them into their adult life. Parents are not always going to be around, so practicing more choice and voice is paramount to success in the adult world.
7) **Inclusion is a key ingredient.** Parents play a large role in the educational placement of their sons and daughters. Know your rights and advocate for the extra effort that might be needed towards inclusion in schools.
8) **Paid jobs serve as a true predictor of future employment success.** While the first few jobs may not be the dream jobs, the experiences within them can lead to long-term employment success. Learning the soft skills, decision-making, and responsibility goes a long way for their future and post-college success.
9) **Natural supports play a crucial part in maturity and development.** While paid professionals all play important roles in child development, maturity comes from enlisting informal supports such as friends, neighbors, relatives, church members, or extracurricular opportunities that will help in overall maturity and development into adulthood.
10) **Success should be shared.** When your son or daughter achieves success, if you can, get it publicized and share it with other families on the path behind or ahead of you. This lets the world know that your son or daughter is a capable person, and maybe more important, lets everyone learn that individuals with ID can be successful.

Table 14.1 Parent Memorandum of Understanding (MOU)

MEMORANDUM OF UNDERSTANDING BETWEEN THE WESTERN CAROLINA UNIVERSITY (WCU) UNIVERSITY PARTICIPANT (UP) PROGRAM
AND
THE PARENT OR GUARDIAN OF THE UP STUDENT

Western Carolina University's University Participant (UP) Program serves students with intellectual disability (ID) on the WCU campus. During this two-year transition experience, each UP student is expected to live on campus, audit classes, participate in campus activities, and gain employment experience.

The purpose of the UP Program is to facilitate transition by UP students into the adult community. This means that UP graduates are prepared to live and work as independently as possible and are expected to do so upon graduation. Specifically, the UP staff has an expectation that after the UP Program, the UP graduate will live in their own house or apartment with necessary support (i.e., not with parents or in a congregate living facility such as a group home), and will work in a community-based, career choice job with necessary supports (i.e., not in a sheltered workshop or in a day activity center). Only individuals with ID, who, along with their parents or guardians, agree with this expectation, should pursue the UP Program as a transition option.

This memo of understanding (MOU) is established to better assure success in the UP Program and to promote greater independence in the student's post-UP community. The agreement is intended to clearly convey that the UP Program requires a partnership between parents or guardians and the UP staff, and that both must make a commitment and take specific actions to achieve the desired outcomes of the UP Program. **Continuation in the UP Program by UP students requires that parents or guardians also fulfill their responsibilities as specified in this document to achieve these outcomes,** just as the UP staff will focus on preparing graduates to achieve the desired outcomes.

During the time the student is in the UP Program, parents or guardians agree to the following:

○ Provide materials necessary for successful college living in a timely manner *(within one week when requested by UP staff or student supports)* including but not limited to paper, pens, pencils, flash drive, printer, computer, ink, cell phone, binders, book bag, personal care items, Cat Cash, and cleaning supplies in dorms.
○ Pay a *non-refundable UP Program activity and support fee of $2,500* at the beginning of each semester posted in the student tuition and fee system. This is in addition to the university tuition and fee requirements.
○ Check student's accounts *each month* in the online billing system and provide payment for any outstanding charges that exist to avoid having holds or blocks placed on accounts. Meal plan balances should be checked and monitored on a *weekly* basis online.
○ Check student's schedule *each week* using the online UP scheduling system (whentowork.com) to know what activities or support needs can be provided to the UP staff by family members (e.g., community work schedules, transportation needs, leave time for breaks, weekend plans); *extra fees will apply if schedules are not followed or arrival to campus is earlier than planned.*

(continued)

Table 14.1 (continued)

- Provide necessary medical care and updates to UP staff *as needed and within 24 hours of being notified of a medical issue* (e.g., medications being filled and supplied while at school, setting up medical appointments, transporting to and from appointments, keeping cell phones on during night-time hours for emergencies, and paying for all related medical expenses).
- Talk to your son/daughter *at least once a month* about their college experiences and post-UP life goals (e.g., what has been learned on campus, supporting homework during breaks and weekend visits, researching and networking community resources with UP staff).
- Collaborate *at least once a month* with UP Program staff and supports to implement strategies, and interventions designed to facilitate the development of appropriate adult behaviors or social skills needed for success (e.g., behavior intervention plans, schedules at home).
- Support all behavioral requirements listed in the WCU code of conduct as interpreted for UP students. If behavioral issues occur, parents or guardians agree to collaborate *at least weekly if not daily* with the UP staff and support the behavior intervention plan (BIP) designed to improve their son's or daughter's behavior.
- If after implementation of the BIP serious infractions of the code of conduct continue to occur, parents or guardians agree to pick up their son or daughter and remove them from the WCU campus *on the same day they are contacted* when requested by UP staff.
- After three violations of the code of conduct, parents and guardians understand that the UP staff may elect to dismiss their son or daughter from the UP Program and agree to comply with this decision by removing their son or daughter and their personal belongings from the WCU campus *within 24 hours after notification*.
- Notwithstanding emergencies, at least one parent/guardian must attend (either face to face or virtually) **ALL** monthly person-centered planning meetings for their son/daughter.

In preparation for post-UP Program success, parents or guardians agree to the following:

- Notwithstanding emergencies, attend ALL parent meetings on housing, employment, finances, and community mapping related to post-UP planning. *(When possible, these will be held on weekends and/or virtual to accommodate work schedules.)*
- With UP staff, develop community-based work options that align with your son's or daughter's career choices (**not sheltered workshops or day activity centers**) and inclusive living options (houses or apartments, **not parents' or relatives' homes**) for post-UP life in the community where students will reside after leaving the UP Program. The timeline for the development of potential living and working options are as follows:
  - At the end of the first semester of the UP Program, parents or guardians will identify in writing eight seriously considered career option sites and eight seriously considered living arrangements in the community in which the student will reside after the UP Program.
  - At the end of the second semester, in collaboration with the UP staff, the original list must be pared to an intermittent list of four high-probability career option sites and four high-probability living arrangements.

- At the end of the third semester, the intermittent list must be pared to two very seriously considered career option sites and two very seriously considered living arrangements.
- *At the mid-point of the fourth semester, in collaboration with the UP staff, a specific career site and a specific living arrangement will be identified that the UP student can transition into no more than one year following graduation from the UP Program.*

○ In addition to the above, parents or guardians must work with the UP staff to identify employment opportunities during holiday breaks and the summer between the first and second year of the program, and to also identify other meaningful daily activities for the student during these times to engage in an activity level similar to that which was maintained while on the WCU campus. *As UP staff inquire or follow up, parents or guardians should give responses within a 72-hour period after request is made.*

○ At the beginning of the UP Program, parents or guardians must provide the UP staff a contact list of service providers, key community members, and agencies in their community that could provide support to the student during and after the UP Program. *If services or service providers change during the program, it is the responsibility of the parent/guardian and student to notify UP staff within a period of one week.*

○ Parents or guardians must work with the UP staff to identify local public transportation options for use by their son or daughter that allow them to travel independently, to the extent possible, to employment or recreational sites in their community. **It is the primary responsibility of the family to coordinate transportation to and from campus.** During longer breaks, carpools can be coordinated among WCU students (i.e., gas money welcome).

○ Parents or guardians must provide information to UP staff about their son's or daughter's post-UP status for at least two years after program completion by promptly responding to follow-up surveys, phone calls, and emails.

○ **It is understood that continuation of the UP Program will be determined each semester based on the student's and family's progress; appropriately following the code of conduct; and completion of the requirement** *by parents or guardians* **for identifying community career options and living arrangements as specified above.** *Parents or guardians understand that without adequate progress in any of these areas, including completion of requirements by parents or guardians,* **the UP staff may elect to dismiss their son or daughter from the UP Program and they will comply with this decision by removing their son or daughter and their personal belongings from the WCU campus.**

The WCU UP staff agrees to the following:

○ Provide an initial orientation period (camp experience) for the first-year students to allow for campus familiarity and a sample of on-campus college living experiences before full admission.
○ Collaborate with university faculty and staff to provide students with access to college courses attended by students without disabilities.
○ Provide academic advising that includes courses related to career and personal interests.
○ Allow students to audit courses that align with their career goals and assist with coursework.

(continued)

Table 14.1 (continued)

- Prepare students for competitive employment by facilitating meaningful on-campus unpaid internships or paid part-time jobs each semester.
- Provide additional organized activities as needed (e.g., health/wellness, visual supports, personal relationships).
- Schedule WCU student supports and monitor throughout the college experience and fading supports as independence is demonstrated (e.g., proper cell phone use, navigating campus, being safe and responsible).
- Collaborate and assist with families, university faculty and staff, university students, and community service providers to provide full access to campus life.
- Provide resources and community mapping options to students and families (e.g., job and housing policies).
- Provide a UP Certificate of Accomplishment to students who meet the 1,800-hour requirement and successfully achieve 80% of their goals in the Individual Plan for College Participation.

By your signature below, you indicate that you understand and agree to the provisions in this MOU:

Parent's Signature: _____ Date: _____

Parent's Name (Please print): _____

UP Student's Name (Please print): _____

UP Co-Director's Signature: _____ Date: _____

UP Co-Director's Signature: _____ Date: _____

Final Thoughts

We wish you the very best as a PSE program or family member in preparing for your future. It is a wonderful experience to be a part of the college journey that can emerge after this effective intervention occurs between school and the adult world. The sky is the limit on what you can do with determination and perseverance in the variety of roles you play in the transition process. We hope you have found this resource helpful no matter what role you play, from being a parent, PSE personnel, community service provider, administrator, alumni, or soon-to-be PSE student. For more information about the UP Program, please visit up.wcu.edu. And for more information about all college programs for students with ID, be sure to check out the great information at thinkcollege.net as we are all on this life journey together.

References

Kelley, K. R. (2014, November). *College and intellectual disabilities: YES! Strategies and tips for applying to college.* Paper presented at the Exceptional Children Division's 64th Conference on Exceptional Children, Greensboro, NC.

Westling, D. L., & Kelley, K. R. (2015). *Preparing your son or daughter for college: Suggestions for parents of children with intellectual disability.* Retrieved from http://kellehampton.com/?s=Westling

Bibliography

Alberto, P. A., & Troutman, A. C. (2013). *Applied behavior analysis for teachers* (9th ed.). Columbus, OH: Merrill/Prentice-Hall.

Association on Higher Education and Disability (2018). *Access and accommodations*. Retrieved from https://www.ahead.org/professional-resources/accommodations

Barron, T., Kelley, K. R., & Westling, D. L. (2017, December). *Effects of interacting with college students with intellectual disability on natural supports.* Paper presented at the 2017 TASH Conference, Atlanta, GA.

Brown, L., Shiraga, B., & Kessler, K. (2006). The quest for ordinary lives: The integrated post-school vocational functioning of 50 workers with significant disabilities. *Research and Practice for Persons with Severe Disabilities, 31*, 93–121.

Carter, E. W., Austin, D., & Trainor, A. A. (2012). Predictors of postschool employment outcomes for young adults with severe disabilities. *Journal of Disability Policy Studies, 23*, 50–63. doi: 10.1177/1044207311414680.

Casale-Giannola, D., & Kamens, M. W. (2006). Inclusion at a university: Experiences of a young woman with Down syndrome. *Mental Retardation, 44*(5), 344–352. doi:10.1352/0047-6765.

Causton-Theoharis, J., Ashby, C., & DeClouette, N. (2009). Relentless optimism: Inclusive postsecondary opportunities for students with significant disabilities. *Journal of Postsecondary Education and Disability, 22*(2), 88–105.

Claes, C., Van Hove, G., Vandevelde, S., Van Loon, J., & Schalock, R. L. (2010). Person-centered planning: Analysis of research and effectiveness. *Intellectual and Developmental Disabilities, 48*, 432–453. doi:10.1352/1934-9556-48.6.432.

Colorado Department of Education (2014). *Domain skills inventory and skill tracker.* Retrieved from https://www.cde.state.co.us/cdesped/tk_tab07_teachertransitionteam

Culnane, M., Eisenman, L. T., & Murphy, A. (2016). College peer mentoring and students with intellectual disability: Mentors' perspectives on relationship dynamics. *Inclusion, (4)*4, 257–269.

Curriculum Associates (2010). *Brigance transition skills inventory.* North Billerica, MA: Author.

Fiske, E. (2018). *Fiske guide to colleges.* Naperville, IL: Sourcebooks.

Gibbons, M. M., Cihak, D. F., Mynatt, B., & Wilhoit, B. E. (2015). Faculty and student attitudes toward postsecondary education for students with intellectual disabilities and autism. *Journal of Postsecondary Education and Disability, 28*, 149–162.

Griffin, M. M., Mello, M. P., Glover, C. A., Carter, E. W., & Hodapp, R. M. (2016). Supporting students with intellectual and developmental disabilities in postsecondary education: The motivations and experiences of peer mentors. *Inclusion, 4*(2), 75–88.

Grigal, M., Hart, D., Papay, C., Domin, D., & Smith, F. (2017). *Year one program data summary (2015–2016) from the TPSID model demonstration projects.* Boston, MA: University of Massachusetts Boston, Institute for Community Inclusion.

Grigal, M., Hart, D., Smith, F. A., Domin, D., Sulewski, J., & Weir, C. (2015). *Think College National Coordinating Center: Annual report on the transition and postsecondary programs for students with intellectual disabilities (2013–2014).* Boston, MA: University of Massachusetts Boston, Institute for Community Inclusion.

Grigal, M., Hart, D., Smith, F. A., Domin, D., & Weir, C. (2017). *Think College National Coordinating Center: Annual report on the transition and postsecondary programs for students with intellectual disabilities (2014–2015).* Boston, MA: University of Massachusetts Boston, Institute for Community Inclusion.

Grigal, M., Hart, D., & Weir, C. (2012). *Think College standards, quality indicators, and benchmarks for inclusive higher education.* Boston, MA: University of Massachusetts Boston, Institute for Community Inclusion.

Grigal, M., Hart, D., & Weir, C. (2013). Postsecondary education for people with intellectual disability: Current issues and critical challenges. *Inclusion, 1*, 50–63. doi: 10.1352/2326-6988-1.1.050.

Grigal, M., Hart, D., & Weir, C. (2014). Postsecondary education for students with intellectual disabilities. In M. Agran, F. Brown, C. Hughes, C. Quirk, & D. Ryndak (Eds.), *Equity and full inclusion for individuals with severe disabilities: A vision for the future* (pp. 275–298). Baltimore, MD: Brookes.

Hafner, D. (2008). *Inclusion in postsecondary education: Phenomenological study on identifying and addressing barriers to inclusion of individuals with significant disabilities at a four-year liberal arts college.* ProQuest Dissertations & Theses Global. Retrieved from http://ezproxy.lib.umb.edu/login?url=http://search.proquest.com/docview/288108493?accountid=28932

Jones, M. M., Harrison, B., Harp, B., & Sheppard-Jones, K. (2016). Teaching college students with intellectual disability: What faculty members say about the experience. *Inclusion, 4*(2), 89–108.

Kelley, K. R. (2014, November). *College and intellectual disabilities: YES! Strategies and tips for applying to college.* Paper presented at the Exceptional Children Division's 64th Conference on Exceptional Children, Greensboro, NC.

Kelley, K. R., & Prohn, S. M. (2018). Postsecondary and employment expectations of families and students with intellectual disability. *Journal of Inclusive Postsecondary Education.* Advanced Online Publication at https://kihd.gmu.edu/jipe/jipe-articles

Kelley, K. R., Prohn, S. M., & Westling, D. L. (2016). Inclusive study abroad course for college students with and without intellectual disabilities. *Journal of Postsecondary Education and Disability, 29*(1), 91–101.

Kelley, K. R., & Westling, D. L. (2013). A focus on natural supports in postsecondary education for students with intellectual disabilities at Western Carolina University. *Journal of Vocational Rehabilitation, 38*(1), 67–76. doi: 10.3233/JVR-120621.

Kelley, K. R., Westling, D. L., & Prohn, S. M. (2017, November). *Benefits, challenges, and reflections of study abroad experiences.* Paper presented at the 2017 State of the Art Conference on Postsecondary Education and Individuals with Intellectual Disabilities, Syracuse, NY.

Kelty, K., & Prohn, S. (2014). Belonging on campus. *Think College stories* (10). Retrieved from https://thinkcollege.net/sites/default/files/files/resources/kenneth_kelty_story_0.pdf

Laugeson, E. A. (2017). *PEERS® for young adults: Social skills training for adults with autism spectrum disorder and other social challenges.* New York: Routledge.

Lobosco, K. (2017). Tuition-free college is getting bigger. Here's where it's offered. *CNN Money.* Retrieved from http://money.cnn.com/2017/05/16/pf/college/states-tuition-free-college/index.html

Luecking, R. G., & Fabian, E. S. (2000). Paid internships and employment success for youth in transition. *Career Development for Exceptional Individuals, 23,* 205–221. doi:10.1177/088572880002300207.

MacMillan, D. L. (1977). *Mental retardation in school and society.* Boston: Little, Brown and Company.

Mamun, A. A., Carter, E. W., Fraker, T. M., & Timmins, L. L. (2017). Impact of early work experiences on subsequent paid employment for young adults with disabilities. *Career Development and Transition for Exceptional Individuals,* Advanced Online Publication. https://doi. org/10.1177/2165143417726302.

Martinez, D. C., & Queener, J. (2010). *Postsecondary education for students with intellectual disabilities.* George Washington University HEATH Resource Center. Retrieved from https://heath.gwu.edu/files/downloads/pse_id_final_edition.pdf

May, C. (2012). An investigation of attitude change in inclusive college classes including young adults with an intellectual disability. *Journal of Policy and Practice in Intellectual Disabilities, 9,* 240–246.

Merisotis, J. (2016). Want to be happier and healthier? Then go to college. *Huffpost.* Retrieved from https://www.huffingtonpost.com/jamie-merisotis/want-to-be-happier-and-he_b_8288354.html

Migliore, A., & Butterworth, J., (2008). Postsecondary education and employment outcomes for youth with intellectual disabilities. *DataNote Series, Data Note XXI.* Boston, MA: Institute for Community Inclusion.

Moore, E. J., & Schelling, A. (2015). Postsecondary inclusion for individuals with an intellectual disability and its effects on employment. *Journal of Intellectual Disabilities, 19,* 130–148. doi: 10.1177/1744629514564448.

Morgan, R. L., Ellerd, D. A., Gerity, B. P., & Tullis, M. D. (2000). *Your employment selections. YES!* Utah State University. Logan, UT: Technology, Research, and Innovation in Special Education (TRI-SPED).

National Center for Educational Statistics (2017). *Fast facts: back to school statistics.* Retrieved from https://nces.ed.gov/fastfacts/display.asp?id=372

National Core Indicators (2015). *Chart generator 2014–15.* National Association of State Directors of Developmental Disabilities Services and Human Services Research Institute. Retrieved from www.nationalcoreindicators.org/charts/

National Survey of Student Engagement (2011). *Fostering student engagement campus wide – annual results 2011.* Bloomington, IN: Indiana University Center for Postsecondary Research.

Newman, L., Wagner, M., Knokey, A. M., Marder, C., Nagle, K., Shaver, D., Wei, X., with Cameto, R., Contreras, E., Ferguson, K., Greene, S., & Schwarting, M. (2011). *The post-high school outcomes of young adults with disabilities up to 8 years after high school. A report from the National Longitudinal Transition Study-2 (NLTS2)* (NCSER 2011-3005). Menlo Park, CA: SRI International. Available at www.nlts2.org/reports/

Nisbet, J., & Hagner, D. (1988). Natural supports in the workplace: A reexamination of supported employment. *Journal of the Association of the Severely Handicapped, 13*, 260–267.

Nord, D., & Nye-Lengerman, K. (2015). The negative effects of public benefits on individual employment: A multilevel analysis of work hours. *Intellectual and Developmental Disabilities, 53*, 308–318. doi: 10.1352/1934-9556-53.4.308.

North Carolina Council on Developmental Disabilities (2016). *Disability benefits counseling first!* Retrieved from https://www.nccdd.org/disability-benefits-counseling.html

O'Neill, R. E., Albin, R. W., Storey, K., Horner, R. H., & Sprague, J. R. (2014). *Functional assessment and program development for problem behavior: A practical handbook* (3rd ed.). Boston, MA: Cengage Learning.

Papay, C. K., & Bambara, L. M. (2011). Postsecondary education for transition-age students with intellectual and other developmental disabilities: A national survey. *Education and Training in Autism and Developmental Disabilities, 46*, 78–93.

Papay, C. K., & Bambara, L. M. (2016). Best practices in transition to adult life for youth with intellectual disabilities. *Career Development and Transition for Exceptional Individuals, 37*, 136–148. doi: 10.1177/2165143413486693.

Pearpoint, J., O'Brien, J., & Forest, M. (1993). *PATH: A workbook for planning positive possible futures*. Toronto, Ontario, Canada: Inclusion Press.

Plotner, A. J., & Marshall, K. J. (2015). Postsecondary education programs for students with an intellectual disability: Facilitators and barriers to implementation. *Intellectual and Developmental Disabilities, 53*, 58–69.

Princeton Review (2018). *the best 384 colleges, 2019 edition: in-depth profiles & ranking lists to help find the right college for you* (College Admissions Guides).

Prohn, S. M., Kelley, K. R., & Westling, D. L. (2016). Studying abroad inclusively: Reflections by college students with and without intellectual disability. *Journal of Intellectual Disabilities, 20*(4), 341–353. doi: 10.1177/1744629515617050.

Prohn, S. M., Kelley, K. R., & Westling, D. L. (2018). Students with intellectual disability going to college: What are the outcomes? A pilot study. *Journal of Vocational Rehabilitation, 48*, 127–132. doi: 10.3233/JVR-170920.

Rimmerman, A., Hozmi, B., & Duvdevany, I. (2000). Contact and attitudes toward individuals with disabilities among students tutoring children with developmental disabilities. *Journal of Intellectual and Developmental Disability, 25*(1), 13–18. doi: 10.1080/132697800112758.

Ross, J., Marcell, J., Williams, P., & Carlson, D. (2013). Postsecondary education employment and independent living outcomes of persons with autism and intellectual disability. *Journal of Postsecondary Education and Disability, 26*, 337–351.

Rusch, F. R., & Braddock, D. (2004). Adult day programs versus supported employment (1988–2002): Spending and service practices of mental retardation and developmental disabilities state agencies. *Research and Practice for Persons with Severe Disabilities, 29*, 237–242.

Sanford, C., Newman, L., Wagner, M., Cameto, R., Knokey, A.-M., & Shaver, D. (2011). *The post-high school outcomes of young adults with disabilities up to 6 years after high school. Key findings from the National Longitudinal Transition Study-2 (NLTS2)* (NCSER 2011-3004). Menlo Park, CA: SRI International.

Shogren, K. A., Wehmeyer, M. L., Lassmann, H., & Forber-Pratt, A. J. (2017). Supported decision making: A synthesis of the literature across intellectual disability, mental health, and aging. *Education and Training in Autism and Developmental Disabilities, 52,* 144–157.

Sitlington, P., & Clark, G. (2007). The transition assessment process and IDEIA 2004. *Assessment for Effective Intervention, 32,* 133–142.

Smith, F., Grigal, M., & Papay, C. (2018). *Year one employment and career development experiences of college students attending Cohort 2-TPSID model demonstration programs.* Boston, MA: University of Massachusetts Boston, Institute for Community Inclusion.

Smith, F., Grigal, M., & Shepard, J. (2018). Postsecondary education and employment outcomes for youth with intellectual disability served by vocational rehabilitation. *Think College Fast Facts,* Issue No. 18. Boston, MA: University of Massachusetts Boston, Institute for Community Inclusion.

Sowell, R., & Maddox, B. (2015). Added value: Perspectives of student mentors working within a university level inclusive education program. *Online Journal of Education Research, 3*(1), 1–10.

Test, D. W., Fowler, C. H., Richter, S. M., Mazzotti, V., White, J., Walker, A. R., . . . & Kortering, L. (2009). Evidence-based practices in secondary transition. *Career Development for Exceptional Individuals, 32,* 115–128. doi: 10.1177/0885728809336859.

Test, D. W., Mazzotti, V. L., Mustian, A. L., Fowler, C. H., Kortering, L. J., & Kohler, P. H. (2009). Evidence-based secondary transition predictors for improving post-school outcomes for students with disabilities. *Career Development for Exceptional Individuals, 32,* 160–181.

Think College (2018). *College options for people with intellectual disabilities.* Retrieved from http://www.thinkcollege.net

Think College (2018). *Requirements of comprehensive transition programs.* Retrieved from https://thinkcollege.net/think-college-learn/comprehensive-transition-programs/requirements-comprehensive-transition-programs

Thoma, C. A., Lakin, K. C., Carlson, D., Domzal, C., Austin, K., & Boyd, K. (2011). Participation in postsecondary education for students with intellectual disabilities: A review of the literature 2001–2010. *Journal of Postsecondary Education and Disability 24,* 175–191.

United States Census Bureau (2015). *American community survey.* Retrieved from https://www.census.gov/programs-surveys/acs/

Wagner, M., Newman, L., Cameto, R., Garza, N., & Levine, P. (2005). *After high school: A first look at the postschool experiences of youth with disabilities.* Menlo Park, CA: SRI International.

Walker-Hirsch, L., & Champagne, M. (1991). The circles concept: Social competence in special education. *Educational Leadership, 49,* 65–67.

Wehman, P. (2013). Transition from school to work: Where are we and where do we need to go? *Career Development and Transition for Exceptional Individuals, 36,* 58–66. doi: 10.1177/2165143413482137

Wehman, P., Sima, A. P., Ketchum, J., West, M. D., Chan, F., & Luecking, R. (2015). Predictors of successful transition from school to employment for youth with disabilities. *Journal of Occupational Rehabilitation, 25,* 323–334. doi: 10.1007/s10926-014-9541-6.

Wehmeyer, M. L. (1992). Self-determination and the education of students with mental retardation. *Education and Training in Mental Retardation, 27,* 302–314.

Wehmeyer, M. L. (1996). Self-determination as an educational outcome: Why is it important to children, youth, and adults with disabilities. In D. J. Sands & M. L. Wehmeyer (Eds.). *Self-determination across the life span: Independence and choice for people with disabilities* (pp. 17–36). Baltimore, MD: Paul H. Brookes.

Wehmeyer, M. L., & Abery, B. H. (2013). Self-determination and choice. *Intellectual and Developmental Disabilities, 51,* 399–411.

Weir, C. (2004). Person-centered and collaborative supports for college success. *Education and Training in Developmental Disabilities, 39*(1), 67–73.

Westling, D. L. (1986). *Introduction to mental retardation.* Englewood Cliffs, NJ: Prentice-Hall, Inc.

Westling, D. L. (2015). *Evidence-based practices for improving challenging behaviors of students with severe disabilities* (Document No. IC-14). Retrieved from University of Florida, Collaboration for Effective Educator, Development, Accountability, and Reform Center website: http://ceedar.education.ufl.edu/tools/innovation-configurations/

Westling, D. L., Fox, L., & Carter, E. W. (2014). *Teaching students with severe disabilities* (5th ed.). Columbus, OH: Pearson.

Westling, D. L., & Kelley, K. R. (2015). *Preparing your son or daughter for college: Suggestions for parents of children with intellectual disability.* Retrieved from http://kellehampton.com/?s=Westling

Westling, D. L., & Kelley, K. R. (2018). Full inclusion of college students with intellectual disability: Western Carolina University's University Participant (UP) program. In W. Plaute, S. Harter-Reiter, & R. Schneider (Eds.), *Inklusive Pädagogische Hochschule – Potenziale der Diversität für die Zukunft der LehrerInnenbildung.* Studienverlag.

Westling, D. L., Kelley, K. R., Cain, B., & Prohn, S. (2013). College students' attitudes about an inclusive postsecondary education program for individuals with an intellectual disability. *Education and Training in Autism and Developmental Disabilities, 48,* 306–319.

Westling, D. L., Kelley, K. R., & Prohn, S. M. (2016). A tiered approach to promote safety and security in an inclusive postsecondary education program for college students with intellectual disability. *DADD Online Journal, 3*(1), 160–171.

Wilson, N. J., Jaques, H., Johnson, A., & Brotherton, M. L. (2017). From social exclusion to supported inclusion: Adults with intellectual disability discuss their lived experiences of a structured social group. *Journal of Applied Research in Intellectual Disabilities, 30,* 847–858.

Winsor, J., Timmons, J., Butterworth, J., Shepard, J., Landa, C., Smith, F., Domin, D., . . . & Landim, L. (2017). *StateData: The national report on employment services and outcomes.* Boston, MA: University of Massachusetts Boston, Institute for Community Inclusion.

Zafft, C. (2006). A case study of accommodations for transition-age students with intellectual disabilities. *Journal of Postsecondary Education and Disability, 18*(2), 167–180.

Index

About Life program 92, 128–129, 153, 154, 182
academic performance 21
academic roadmaps 76, 98, 135, 160, 162, 164
academic standards 15
accessibility resources 35–36, 100, 181
accommodations 36, 100–101, 103, 109, 113, 114, 191
accountability: natural supports 154, 155; students 102, 103, 191
ADA *see* Americans with Disabilities Act
administrators 14, 33, 34, 36–37, 46; budgets 51–52; challenges to course participation 96; champions 60; open house events 68; safety concerns 179
admissions 15–16, 20, 22, 30–31, 65–79, 135; accepting new students 77; admissions committees 65, 71–73; behavioral assessment 178; director of 34–35; final evaluation and selection 65, 74–76; outreach and recruitment 65, 66–70; parent meetings 76–77; supporting unaccepted applicants 77–78; systematic review 65, 70–74
advocacy organizations 45
agencies 13, 33, 40, 42–45, 137, 153, 165, 183
aggression 182
alcohol 83, 126, 182
Americans with Disabilities Act (ADA) 35–36
AmeriCorps 151
application materials 65, 70–71, 73
apps 123, 139
artifacts 163–164
ASD *see* autism spectrum disorders

aspirations 30, 76
assessment: behavior intervention plans 184; employment-related 107–108; psychological 70
assistive technology: communication skills 24; course accommodations 100; employment 113; person-centered planning 135; program agreements 70; technology assessments 76; training of natural supports 154; Vocational Rehabilitation 58
audited courses 91, 100, 102, 195
autism spectrum disorders (ASD) 20
autonomy 26

Bambara, L. M. 105
behavior intervention plans (BIPs) 11, 179, 182, 183–184, 194
behavioral issues 24–25, 82, 177–179, 182, 183–186, 194
benefits counselors 43, 116
Blackboard 101, 140, 154, 155
boundaries 114, 127, 128–129
braided funding 49, 55, 152–153
budgets 50–52, 60–61; *see also* funding
businesses 40, 42, 109–110
buy-in 14, 17, 83

Cain, B. 95
calendars 126, 141, 143, 155
campus living 21, 80–89
campus membership 118–129, 146
campus partners 40, 41, 83
career choices 8
Carlson, D. 106
Carter, E. W. 106
Casale-Giannola, D. 95–96
celebration 46, 158

Index 205

cell phones 144, 145, 181, 196
Center for Service Learning (CSL) 41, 122, 151
champions 14, 60, 61
chancellors 34
choice-making 9, 26, 141–143, 145, 192
CIRCLES program 128
Clery Act 180
clubs 8, 10, 81, 119, 121, 146
co-workers 114–115
codes of conduct 11, 15, 24, 76, 77; adapting and teaching 178; engaging parents 178–179; memorandum of understanding 194; peer responses to inappropriate behavior 185; tiered interventions 181, 182
collaboration 14, 33–47; building successful partnerships 45–46; community outreach 67; course participation 98; key partners in the community 40–45; key partners inside the institution 34–40, 41; living on campus 89; memorandum of understanding 194; safety issues 183
communication skills 8, 24, 133, 190
community connections 165–166
community living 20, 28; *see also* living arrangements
community outreach 65, 67
community participation 6, 9, 12
community partners 40–45
comprehensive transition and postsecondary programs (CTPs) 36, 55–56
conferences 66–67, 119, 158, 172
confidentiality 72, 140–141, 150, 156
contracts and grants offices 56–57
costs 50, 57, 74, 121; *see also* fees; funding
course accommodations 100–101, 103
course participation 6, 8, 91–103
credit-bearing courses 91
crime 180, 181
CSL *see* Center for Service Learning
CTPs *see* comprehensive transition and postsecondary programs
Culnane, M. 95–96
curricula 21

daily living skills 11–12, 24, 81, 154
deans 14, 36–37

decision-making 5, 6, 126–127, 192; future success 192, 196; living on campus 81; person-centered planning 134, 146; self-determination 9, 26; shared goals and perspectives 188
department heads/chairs 37–38
dependability 45, 156
development offices 56
director of admissions 34–35
director of disability support services 35–36
director of financial aid 36, 72
director of residential programs 14, 35
disability benefits 43
disability support services 35–36
discussion boards 101, 140, 143, 155
dismissal/removal from university 179, 182, 194, 195
drug use 82–83, 182
dual enrollment 21
Duvdevany, I. 95

e-learning 101, 140, 154, 155
efficiency 46
Eisenman, L. T. 95–96
emergencies 87, 88, 180
emotional reactions 82
employment 5, 6, 20, 105–116; artifacts 163–164; benefits of 105–106; expectations 28; family workshops 165; follow-along survey 167–169; future success 192, 196; knowledge application 94–95; memorandum of understanding 193–196; orientation camp 75; partnerships with businesses 42; post-program planning 12, 13, 161, 162–163, 194–195; rating of applicants 73; support staff 39; vocational and career preparation 21; Vocational Rehabilitation 13, 42–43, 50, 58, 61n1, 77, 116, 137, 165; vocational success 6, 9; *see also* internships; part-time jobs
employment support specialists 107, 110, 112, 113
empowerment 26
ethnicity 20
evaluation 6, 7, 10–11
expectations 13, 22–23, 188, 192; employment 111, 113, 115; parents 27–29, 106; person-centered planning 134; post-program planning 161; self-determination 26

expenses 51, 52
extracurricular activities 75, 76, 81, 118–129, 141, 146, 192

faculty liaison/researchers 52, 54–55, 57
faculty members 14, 38–39, 46; admissions committees 72; champions 60; course participation 96; identifying cooperative faculty 98, 99–100; natural supports 152; open house events 68; PCP meetings 103, 137
fading of support 29–30, 113, 114, 140, 145–146, 196
failure-avoiders 23, 29
family support networks 45, 67, 191
family workshops 165
feedback: accepting 46; employment 107, 113, 115; from peers 189; progress monitoring 10
fees 16, 19, 21, 48, 50, 121, 193; *see also* costs
financial aid 36
follow-along data 166–172
fraternities 81, 120, 121, 126, 129
friends 22, 82, 118, 127, 172; benefits of course participation 96; employment through 109; natural supports 11, 148, 149; post-program success 161; quality of life 29; time management 125
funding 19–20, 48–61, 172–173; braided 49, 55, 152–153; brief history of UP funding 49–50; budgets 50–52; CTPs 36, 55–56; departments 37–38; Home and Community Based Services 44; natural supports 152–153; partnerships 55–58; sustainability 58–61; Vocational Rehabilitation 42–43; *see also* fees

GAs *see* graduate assistants
gender 20
goals 3, 6, 190; campus membership 123; course participation 93; individualized 133, 137, 138; job-related 112–113; living on campus 81; memorandum of understanding 194; monitoring and evaluation 10–11; person-centered planning 8, 76, 134, 161; post-program planning 160; rating of applicants 73; self-determination 9, 26; support for unaccepted applicants 78; working with parents and families 187–188
Golden Leaf Scholars 151
graduate assistants (GAs) 49, 52, 54, 57, 151
graduation 119
grants 36, 56–57
Greek life 10, 119, 129, 146
Griffin, M. M. 96
Grigal, M. 6, 106
guardianship 190, 191

Hampton, Kelle 191
Harp, B. 96
Harrison, B. 96
Hart, D. 6
health maintenance organizations (HMOs) 57
Higher Education Opportunity Act (HEOA, 2008) 19, 20, 36, 55–56
Home and Community Based Services (HCBS) 44
homecoming events 119, 120
homework 11, 101, 124, 125–126, 154, 155
Honors College 122
Hozmi, B. 95

IEPs *see* Individualized Education Programs
IHEs *see* institutions of higher education
immature behavior 184
inclusion 6, 7–8, 185; behavioral issues 186; benefits of 96; campus membership 122; course participation 92–93; natural supports 149, 158; parental role 192; "reverse inclusion" 92; social justice 129
inclusive courses 91–92
independence 3, 7; barriers to 172–173; fading of support 29–30, 145, 192; living on campus 80, 82, 87, 89; memorandum of understanding 193; monitoring and evaluation 10; orientation camp 84; rating of applicants 73; staying overnight 74
independent living 5, 6; artifacts 164; expectations 28; orientation camp 84; rating of applicants 73; residential supports 86; transition to 116; *see also* living arrangements

individual plans for college participation (IPCPs) 8, 9–10, 123, 196; course goals 102; e-learning platform 155; job-related goals 112; weekly schedules 138–140, 143
individualization 98, 100–101, 133, 137, 138, 139, 166
Individualized Education Programs (IEPs) 70
institutions of higher education (IHEs) 4; HEOA funding 19–20; key partners 34–40; safety issues 177, 179–183; strategies for beginning a PSE program 13–17
instructional practices 7, 97, 98
integrity 45, 156
intellectual stimulation 94
interests 3; career 94–95, 108; person-centered planning 9, 76; rating of applicants 73; relevant courses 98–99
internships 13, 21, 77, 196; employment support specialists 107; natural supports 151; support staff 39; weekly schedules 143; *see also* work experience
IPCPs *see* individual plans for college participation

job applications 110–111, 114
job searches 109
job task lists 111–112, 113
Jones, M. M. 96

Kamens, M. W. 95–96
Kelley, K. R. 95
key players 14, 34–40, 41
knowledge acquisition 94
knowledge application 94–95

leadership 156, 158, 159
learning: extracurricular activities 118; living on campus 81; opportunities for 138; person-centered planning 8; stamina 94; UP Program goals 6
legal issues 17
letters of recommendation 70
liability concerns 17, 35, 59, 80, 89, 119, 179, 191
life experiences 22, 27, 30–31
living arrangements: community living 20, 28; daily living skills 24; director of residential programs 14, 35; follow-along survey 169–170; living on campus 21, 80–89; memorandum of understanding 193; post-program planning 13, 161, 162–163, 194–195; residential services 21, 35; safety interventions 181; *see also* independent living
local businesses 40, 42, 109–110
local management entities (LMEs) 44, 57, 165, 166
locus of control 23, 26

Maddox, B. 95
managed care organizations (MCOs) 44, 165, 166
Marcell, J. 106
Martinez, D. C. 50
maturity 82, 192
Medicaid waivers 44, 57–58, 77, 153, 165
medical issues 194
memorandum of understanding (MOU) 12, 29, 76, 111, 162–163, 179, 193–196
mentoring: informal 101; natural supports 11–12; parent-to-parent 54, 164, 165, 187; peers 7
Merisotis, Jamie 28
minorities 20, 46
mistakes 5, 192
moderation 127
monitoring 6, 7, 10–11, 113
motivation 25, 97
MOU *see* memorandum of understanding
Murphy, A. 95–96

National Center for Educational Statistics 19
natural supports 6, 7, 11–12, 39–40, 148–159; behavioral issues 185; benefits of 148–149; campus membership 120; conflicts 157–158; coordination of 153; course participation 95, 98, 102–103; crucial role of 192; decision-making 127; employment 112, 113, 114, 115; evaluation of 155–157; fading of support 146; funding 51–52, 53, 152–153; limitations of 149; open house events 68–70, 71; PCP meetings 137; PushUPs 122–123, 152; qualities of 150; recruitment of 150–152, 153; residential supports

51–52, 53, 85–86; roles of 149–150, 153; safety interventions 181; service learning 122; showing appreciation 158; training 103, 153, 154–155, 158–159; weekly schedules 138, 139–141, 144–145, 149, 154; working with parents and families 189–190

Obama, Barack 19
Office of Disability Services 15, 100, 181
open house events 27, 65, 67–70, 71, 134–135, 161
openness 45
orientation camp 65, 74–76, 77, 84, 135, 162, 195
outerdirectedness 23, 29
outreach 65, 66–70

Papay, C. K. 105, 106
parents: admissions committees 72; behavioral issues 178–179; costs of college 50, 74; expectations 27–29, 106; family workshops 165; living on campus 83, 86–87; meetings with 76–77; memorandum of understanding 193–196; open house events 68; parent mentors 54, 164, 165, 187; PCP meetings 137; perspective of 3–4; post-program planning 12–13, 162–163, 194–195; preparing child for college 192–196; rating of applicants 73; safety concerns 76, 177, 179; support from 12, 23, 27, 29–30, 31; working with 187–197
part-time jobs 28, 108–109, 115, 196; employment support specialists 107; life experiences 22; local businesses 42; orientation camp 75; vocational preparation 21; *see also* employment
partnerships 33–47; building successful 45–46; campus membership 121–122; employment 115–116; funding 55–58; key partners in the community 40–45; key partners inside the institution 34–40, 41; living on campus 83, 89; recruitment of natural supports 152
PATH plans 76, 160, 164
PBIS *see* positive behavior interventions and supports

PCP *see* person-centered planning
peer influence 189
peer supports 121, 126, 127, 185; *see also* natural supports
PEERS program 92, 128, 182
person-centered planning (PCP) 8–9, 13, 77, 133–137, 146; academic roadmaps 98; campus membership 123–124; codes of conduct 178; e-learning platform 155; employment 107, 113, 114, 115; future goals 161; initial meetings 76; memorandum of understanding 194; orientation camp 74; post-program planning 163; progress monitoring 10, 102, 103; safety interventions 181, 182; training of natural supports 154; UP Program conceptual framework 6, 7; working with parents and families 189
personal care 8, 11–12
personal development 6, 8, 21, 80
personal responsibility *see* responsibility
personal skills 10, 23–24, 70, 75, 81
pilot programs 14, 58
planning *see* person-centered planning
police 181
policies 15
positive behavior interventions and supports (PBIS) 11, 183
post-program planning 12–13, 160–173, 194–195
presidents 34
prioritization 124, 125, 126
proactiveness 46
problem-solving: employment 114; natural supports 153, 155, 156; self-determination 9, 26
program agreements 70
program coordinators 51, 52–53
program directors 51, 52–53
Prohn, S. M. 95
provosts 34, 59
PSE programs: admissions 22, 30–31, 35, 65–79; characteristics of 20–21; collaboration with university and agency partners 33–47; conceptual framework for 4–6; course participation 91–103; employment 105–116; expectations 28; funding and staffing 48–61; living on campus 80–89; person-centered planning 133–137; post-program planning

160–173; safety issues 177; strategies for beginning 13–17; weekly schedules 138–139; working with parents and families 187–197; *see also* University Participant Program
psychological assessment 70
psychological empowerment 26
public benefits 43
public transportation 9, 43, 123, 195
PushUPs 122–123, 152

quality of life (QOL) 5, 6, 7, 116; campus membership 118; decision-making 126; expectations 28–29; person-centered planning 133
Queener, J. 50

RAs *see* residential assistants
recognized student organizations (RSOs) 122, 152
recruitment 65, 66–70
reinforcement of behavior 184, 185
relationships 38, 59, 82, 128–129, 182; *see also* friends; partnerships
residences *see* living arrangements
residential assistants (RAs) 84–85
residential services 21, 35
residential supports 51–52, 53, 85–86
responsibility 26–27, 124, 126; future success 192, 196; living on campus 81, 87; post-program planning 161; rating of applicants 73
resumes: application materials 70, 73; job applications 110; updates 116; video 114, 115, 163
"reverse inclusion" 92
Rimmerman, A. 95
risks 82–83, 87–89, 183, 192
role models 11–12, 150, 159, 189
Ross, J. 106
RSOs *see* recognized student organizations

safety 127, 145, 177, 186, 191; minimizing risks 87–88; orientation camp 75–76; residential assistants 85; tiered approach 179–183
scheduling *see* weekly schedules
scholarship 60
scholarships 16, 50, 56, 172
selection of applicants 65, 73–74
self-confidence 7, 10, 94–95, 96, 145
self-determination 3, 5, 9–10, 23, 25–26, 146; decision-making 126; living on campus 81; personal development 8; post-program planning 161; quality of life 28; shared goals and perspectives 188; soft skills 7; UP Program conceptual framework 6, 7; weekly schedules 141
self-discovery 80, 146, 189
self-management 26–27
self-monitoring 11, 25
self-realization 26
self-regulation 26
self-reliance 25
service learning 122, 151, 152
sexuality 128, 182
shared goals and perspectives 187–188
Shepard, J. 106
Sheppard-Jones, K. 96
Smith, F. 106
social behavior 24–25, 120, 127, 128–129; *see also* behavioral issues
social development 6, 8, 10, 21, 75, 81; *see also* campus membership; extracurricular activities; social skills
social justice 129
social media 158, 172, 184; campus membership 120, 125; moderation 127; organized events 141; recruitment of natural supports 152; social skills and boundaries 128; staffing 52; weekly schedules 143
social skills 128–129; employment 21, 112, 114; individualization 133; living on campus 81; memorandum of understanding 194; orientation camp 75
soft skills 5, 7, 112, 113, 192
Sowell, R. 95
specialized courses 91, 92
sports 118, 119
staffing 48, 49–55
state benefits 43
States of the Art Conference 66–67
student champions 60
student organizations 8, 10, 81, 118, 119, 121–122, 152
students without disabilities 4–5, 7–8, 39–40, 91–92, 95–96; *see also* natural supports
study abroad 119
substance use 82–83, 182
success: expectations for 22–23, 27, 106; parental support 27, 29;

person-centered planning 135; post-program planning 160; sharing 16, 192; support for PSE outcomes 31
suitemates 51–52, 53, 57, 137, 153, 181
support: college support networks 166, 172; disability support services 35–36; employment 113–115; fading 29–30, 113, 114, 140, 145–146, 196; family support networks 45, 67, 191; homework assignments 126; institutional support for PSE programs 16; monitoring and evaluation 10; parents 12, 23, 27, 29–30, 31; residential 51–52, 53, 84–86; senior support survey 164; for unaccepted applicants 65, 77–78; *see also* natural supports
support staff 39; administrative support coordinators 51–52, 53; admissions committees 72; open house events 68
sustainability 58–61
"sweat equity" 51

technology assessments 76
Test, D. W. 106
Think College 5–6, 20, 31n1, 36, 66
thinking outside the box 46
time management 124–126, 143, 145
transition and postsecondary education programs for students with intellectual disabilities (TPSIDs) 19–20, 54, 58, 106
transitions 6, 7, 12–13, 40, 58, 116; *see also* post-program planning
transparency 45, 56, 61, 159, 191
transportation 9, 43, 107, 123, 165, 195
traumatic brain injury (TBI) 20
Truman, Harry S. 16
trust 45, 83, 191
trust in the process 188–189
"try ons" 74–76, 84
tuition fees 16, 19, 21, 48, 50, 121, 193

Universal Design for Learning (UDL) 54–55, 97, 100–101
University Centers for Excellence in Developmental Disabilities (UCEDDs) 67
University Participant (UP) Program 4–13, 197; admissions 15–16, 22, 30, 65–79, 135; behavioral issues 185; campus membership 121–123; career interests 108; collaborative partnerships 45; conceptual framework 6; course participation 91–93, 98, 102; employment 109–110; expectations 28; faculty members 38–39; funding 48–51, 58–59, 60–61; living on campus 80, 81; LMEs/MCOs 44; memorandum of understanding 193–196; natural supports 122–123, 149–159; number of students 31n2, 48; parental support 29; person-centered planning 133–134; post-program planning 160–173; safety issues 182; staffing 51–55; sustainability 58–61; weekly schedules 138–145

values 7, 17, 59, 126
vice-presidents 34
videos: applications 70, 72–73; open house interviews 68–69, 71, 134–135; practice job interviews 110; video resumes 114, 115, 163
visibility 59, 65, 66–67
vision 30, 187
Vocational Rehabilitation (VR) 13, 42–43, 50, 58, 61n1, 77, 116, 137, 165
vocational training 21, 105, 107–108, 109
volunteers 11, 51, 53–54, 120; *see also* natural supports
voting 119
VR *see* Vocational Rehabilitation

WCU *see* Western Carolina University
weekly schedules 133, 138–146, 149; extracurricular activities 120; memorandum of understanding 193; monitoring and evaluation 10; post-program planning 166; self-determination 9; training of natural supports 154
Wehmeyer, Michael 9, 26
Weir, C. 6, 133
Western Carolina University (WCU) 4, 58; admissions 22; campus membership 129; Code of Conduct 24, 76; collaborative partnerships 45; faculty members 38–39; funding 49–50; memorandum of

understanding 193–196; rating of applicants 73; senior support survey 164; *see also* University Participant Program
Westling, D. L. 95
WhenToWork 138–141, 143–145, 149, 154

Williams, P. 106
women 20, 46
work experience 42, 108–109, 163; *see also* employment; internships
Work Incentives Planning and Assistance Program (WIPA) 43
worldly sophistication 95

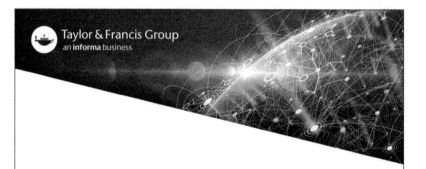